MAO TSE-TUNG

MAO TSE-TUNG
A CRITICAL BIOGRAPHY/STEPHEN UHALLEY, JR.

NEW VIEWPOINTS
A Division of Franklin Watts, Inc. New York, 1975

Design by Rafael Hernandez

Library of Congress Cataloging in Publication Data
Uhalley, Stephen.
  Mao Tse-tung, a critical biography.
  Bibliography: p.
  1. Mao, Tse-tung, 1893-   2. China—History—
1949-
DS778.M3U35   951.05′092′4 [B]   74-13441
ISBN 0-531-05363-6
ISBN 0-531-05571-X (pbk.)

For Kathryn and Stephen
and for Mark, Dawn and David
with gratitude for the joy they are

CONTENTS

PREFACE

During his talk with Edgar Snow in 1970, Chairman Mao Tse-tung spoke of what "a nuisance" the so-called Four Greats were to him. The Four Greats were the epithets being applied to Mao—"Great Teacher, Great Leader, Great Supreme Commander, Great Helmsman"—during the height of the Mao cult which attended the Cultural Revolution in the late 1960s. Such titles, he pointed out, were to be eliminated sooner or later, and only the designation "teacher" would be retained. Mao had been a teacher most of his life, beginning as a primary school teacher in Changsha before he ever became a Communist. He considers himself to be teaching still. Mao also indicated concern that others might be too dependent upon him. At the conclusion of their conversation, as Mao escorted Snow to the door, he remarked that "he was not a complicated man, but really very simple." Mao summed up his self-description saying that he was "only a lone monk walking the world with a leaky umbrella."

It is partly the insight that such occasional humble self-references afford us into the character and the personality of Mao Tse-tung as well as the general need for an updated interpretation of him that moves me to offer this brief critical biography. In doing so I have tried to build on the valuable insights and information provided by earlier biographies and in the mushrooming scholarship on modern and contemporary China. There is no pretense here of complete comprehensiveness, nor of having had the last say on this important subject. I frankly concede that it is too soon to seek definitiveness for such an important figure as Mao. He is, after all, still living, teaching and leading. Also, we must await additional evidence on all too many crucial points in the story. Nevertheless, I believe the present interpretation is needed.

Chairman Mao is one of the greatest political leaders in the history of mankind. Perhaps no one has had a greater impact and influence upon as many people in the course of his own life. How many others have confronted as many staggering obstacles and successfully surmounted so many? The milieu in which he has lived has been complex and exciting. The revolution which he largely formulated and led has had no historical peer in magnitude, duration, or effect. That revolution continues determinedly under his direction even today. His life has been extremely busy and complex, yet through it all, Mao Tse-tung has remained what he was at the beginning—a simple man of the earth. Many peasants share Mao's personal qualities and attitudes, including his profound sense of justice, his high intelligence, dogged determination, and common sense. What is unique is Chairman Mao's combining of all these characteristics with a desire to climb above the limitations of his original station in life to combat injustice and inequity. Mao proved to be unusually adept militarily. He had an instinct for marshaling and cultivating sparse resources, for cooperating with doubtful allies, and for the timing of engagements to gain maximum advantage. He developed a sound sense of his main constituency, China's immense agrarian population. The support he established and maintained with it, largely by encouraging its active and conscious participation in politics, translated into a power that overwhelmed his enemies.

Mao rose to leadership at a time in history when change was in the air and when doctrines sanctioning such change and promising guidance were available. He armed himself with Marxism-Leninism for the struggle. Mao would learn to adapt this imported ideology to China's circumstances; its organizational advantages and discipline were to be useful in China's revolution, and its apparent success in the Soviet Union would remain for years an inspiration to hard-pressed Chinese revolutionaries. Its rigidities, however, would complicate life for Chinese intellectuals, and exacerbate Mao's fundamental peasant distrust of them. The tension between Mao and the intellectuals did little for his popular image over the years in the cities of China or abroad, for it was an image fashioned by those who had little in common with this earthy rebel from the countryside.

Very early in the long hard experience Mao learned the value of struggle. He has shown a voracious appetite for struggle. He sees in it a reliable motor of progress, and has been wary of success and the relaxation and self-satisfaction it brings. He has devised techniques for countering unwanted behavior and for renewing revolutionary commitment and spirit. The viability of the Chinese revolution is testimony to the success of his efforts. Yet Mao has tempered the injunction to struggle with disarming moderation and human sensitivity. His intriguing poetry is a manifestation of a civil dimension. So are his humane treatment of political opponents and his emphasis on education and persuasion rather than fiat and coercion. These qualities have helped cement his authority and have won for him the genuine admiration of most of his countrymen and of many others around the world, irrespective of ideology. Mao believes that the revolution cannot aim only at a more desirable social order. The values that are part of such a utopia must be practiced now as much as practicable. If not, the revolution will be undermined. Conversely, the practice of more humane relationships will naturally lead to a society in which all men might live with pride and dignity. This may all be debatable, especially when the question of individual freedom is raised. But Mao has selected not to spend his life debating with pessimists and cynics, nor worrying about the civil liberties of the relatively few while China and its teeming masses languished. It is of interest that this great leader who has embraced Marxism as a way to end the alienation of man should stand at the head of a people with a long tradition of belief in man's perfectibility. Such a philosophical disposition among others from the cultural past, however much such displaced "class" ideologies may be foresworn, is probably a help to Mao's ambitious enterprise. Yet Mao has not seen the need, despite his own instinctive pride in his people's heritage, to mobilize suspect concepts of the past. Using his own adapted ideology, which he believes speaks to the present generation, he has, more than any leader in history, experimented in direct social engineering in order to achieve his idealistic purpose.

ACKNOWLEDGMENTS

This book is a modest effort, yet it owes a great deal to many. I am grateful to those teachers, colleagues and students whose ideas may be found here, admixed however curiously with my own. The notes will reveal more specific sources of inspiration as well as data. I am indebted to Jo Ann Yamashita for managing the typing of the manuscript, and particularly to Judy Horio and Myra Matsushima for the excellence of their typing services. As always, my wife Joan deserves full credit for having the patience and fortitude to enable me to write under circumstances that are sometimes trying.

I am grateful for the following permissions:

Chingkang Mountain translated from the Chinese by Michael Bullock and Jerome Ch'en and included in MAO AND THE CHINESE REVOLUTION by Jerome Ch'en, published by Oxford University Press. © Oxford University Press 1965.

About the peak . . . Stuart Schram POLITICAL LEADERS OF THE 20TH CENTURY: MAO TSE-TUNG. © Stuart Schram 1966. Reprinted by permission of Simon and Schuster, Inc. and Penguin Books, Ltd.

MAO TSE-TUNG

ONE
The Casting of a
Young Revolutionary

Mao Tse-tung was born on December 26, 1893, in Shaoshan, a village in Hsiang-t'an County, located almost in the dead center of Hunan Province.[1] Hunan itself is strategically placed in south-central China. Its main water course, the deep, blue Hsiang River bisects the province as it flows north to join the mighty Yangtze. Accordingly the province has been important in China's internal commerce, and its alert denizens were quickly acquainted with events and ideas in major centers such as Canton to the south and Wuhan, Nanking, and Shanghai to the north. Hunan had, in fact, a tradition of contributing to vital developments in China. The Hunanese are an energetic, handsome, and outgoing people who seem akin to the hot peppers of which they are so fond. Hunanese scholars and national political and military leaders molded a tradition that would influence Mao.

There was Wang Fu-chih (1619–92), a redoubtable anti-Manchu whose principled stand and iconoclasm were to be extolled by radicals more than two centuries after his death. Confucianism in Hunan traditionally emphasized interpretive and pragmatic thinking rather than textual and metaphysical. This found expression in the work of such nineteenth-century scholars as Ho Ch'ang-ling (1785–1848), who compiled an influential anthology of political and economic essays (1827), and Wei Yuan (1794–1857), whose *Hai-kuo t'u-chih* (1844), a treatise on world history and geography, had immense influence.[2] Tseng Kuo-fan (1811–72), the principal Chinese leader whose extraordinary measures helped the Manchus suppress the Taiping revolutionaries and at the same time destroyed effective central political authority, hailed from a county adjacent to Mao's. Closer to Mao were such famous Hunanese as T'an Ssu-t'ung, one of the martyrs of the 1898 Reform Movement, and Huang Hsing, one of the military leaders of the 1911 Revolution.

Much has been made of the relationship between Mao and his stern father, Mao Jen-shen. Mao himself has noted the bitterness of the conflict, and he clearly had a greater affection for his illiterate, devout Buddhist, and gentle mother, Wen Chi-mei. But such a familial relationship pattern could not have been so unusual in rural China when Mao was a youth. Certainly Mao gained much from his father, more than a repeated detailing of the harsh and ungenerous treatment he was often accorded would suggest. Mao learned from his father the value of hard, productive work. He himself would remain a lifelong advocate of such physical labor to a country which needed to pull itself up by its own bootstraps. Mao saw how his father by dint of such labor and by entrepreneurial shrewdness managed to better the family's circumstances. His father, who had had only two years of schooling, was once nearly destitute and was forced to join the army to earn enough to repurchase the land he had lost. By the time Mao reached his teens, his father had achieved the status of rich peasant and grain merchant.[3]

Mao's father can also be credited with at least inadvertently keeping Mao on his mettle and for constantly testing his resourcefulness. Humorously recalling the two "parties" in his family, Mao later said that his mother advocated indirect attack for the family "opposition" arrayed against the father. Nevertheless, Mao became adept at employing more direct confrontations, for example by learning choice Confucian phrases. This began during his five years of early schooling at the Shaoshan Primary School, and he used the classical quotations to best the old man on his own little understood ground of argumentation.[4] This was defiance, a sacrilegiously unfilial stance in a Chinese family. But Mao learned at an early age that such resistance paid dividends. His father would back down from such an encounter, paying tacit respect to the son's wit and knowledge, undoubtedly consoling himself with the thought that such talent would someday pay off in business transactions on behalf of the family. In like fashion Mao discovered that running away from home on one occasion to protest the thoughtless cruelty of his primary school teacher, far from resulting in punishment, actually improved his situation.[5] Impressed with the results of this initial "strike" Mao organized student protests against erring teachers at other schools he attended.

The Mao household was a comfortable one by the prevailing standards in China's countryside. The Mao family, which by 1905 also included two younger brothers and an adopted sister, occupied the better furnished half of a large two-family dwelling. The house (now a much-visited national museum) is ideally situated in a sequestered, sylvan spot, with no nearby dwellings, overlooking two large ponds and beyond, the richly verdant, exceedingly beautiful Shaoshan valley.[6] It was a wonderful place for a boy to grow up, especially a boy endowed with a sense of beauty and poetry and with a rich, romantic imagination that could profitably use the isolation of the immediately adjacent woods and hills for continued nourishment and expansion. Here his mind would be filled with the swashbuckling deeds of the heroes and villains of his favorite novels, especially the *San Kuo Chih* (*Romance of the Three Kingdoms*) and the *Shui Hu Chuan* (*The Water Margin* or, as translated by Pearl Buck, *All Men are Brothers*). These stories had a profound influence upon Mao, and much of his own later experience would approximate the Robin Hood-like exploits of the bandits of Liangshanpo who in the many chapters of the *Shui Hu Chuan* were in open rebellion against the tyranny and injustice of their day. However, it is said that he did wonder about the stories' glorification of men of arms who made peasants work the land for them.

Mao was compelled by his father to quit primary school when he was thirteen.[7] Although he had helped in the fields part-time since the age of six, he was now to work full-time. Mao's father unwisely sought to use the boy rather than hire an additional hand to help with the increasing acreage of the farm. Mao put up with this burden for a time, working extra hard to fulfill his daily quota in order to have time to continue his reading. Now he was getting into political writings and his interest in the wider world was excitedly awakened. One book, *Shing-shih Wei-yen (Words of Warning to an Affluent Age)*, written by the comprador Cheng Kuan-ying, called for modernization and for a constitutional monarchy.[8] The book also denounced foreigners' abuses in Shanghai. It also helped move Mao to continue his studies. He ran away from home temporarily and tried to study the classics with an old scholar of the village, but this did not work out. When he was sixteen, despite the continuing opposition of his father, Mao enrolled at the Tungshan Primary School in the nearby busy market town of Hsiang Hsiang.[9] Here for the first time Mao was exposed to a modern curriculum. Here his horizons began to enlarge.

Mao had not been oblivious of the outside world or of troubling social problems. Even in Shaoshan the turbulence of outside events and of systemic dysfunctions in China disturbed the idyllic valley. As Mao grew in awareness such events left their mark. In 1904 he was impressed by the reported escapade of Huang Hsing, who had attempted to assassinate some high Manchu officials at Changsha. He heard talk of other rebellious actions, which became increasingly numerous in the waning years of the Ch'ing dynasty. In Shaoshan itself there was a revolt by members of the Ko Lao Hui, a secret society, in the spring of 1910. The rebels protested an injustice of a local landlord, rioted, and were forced into the hills where they were eventually hunted down and killed. Mao and his friends sympathized with the rebels and regarded their leader as a hero. The Shaoshan incident had followed similar revolts and executions that spring in Hunan, the result of a widespread famine. Mao says that he "deeply resented the injustice of the treatment" given to the rebels, whom he regarded as ordinary people like the members of his own family.[10] His own father became a target on one occasion. The old man continued to export grain to the city for profit, despite the famine-bred shortage. Desperate villagers attacked and seized a shipment, which provoked an ambiguous response from Mao, who was still confused. "I did not sympathize with him," explained Mao. "At the same time I thought the villagers' method was wrong also." [11]

Mao's insatiable appetite for learning revealed itself at the new school. At sixteen Mao was six years older than most of his classmates and, thanks to his father's sense of economy, was poorly clothed. He was admitted only provisionally and endured for a time the taunts of the younger boys, scions of more affluent families. But Mao was serious and his scholarly concentration and intelligence soon transformed derision into respect.[12] He read the works of the most famous radical intellectuals of the time, K'ang Yu-wei and Liang Ch'i-ch'ao. These two men had led the abortive Reform Movement of 1898, during which they had succeeded in persuading the emperor to make needed reforms. But the period of reform lasted only some three months. In a sudden coup the emperor was removed from power by the Empress Dowager Tzu Hsi with traitorous help from Yuan Shih-k'ai, a developer of China's first modern army. K'ang and Liang escaped with their lives. Mao greatly admired these two national heroes, advocates of constitutional monarchy for China. Mao's conception of history was broadening too. He learned more of China's humiliation at the hands of foreigners, and he heard from a teacher who had been to Japan of that country's progress and of her smashing, historic victory over Russia in 1905.

Small wonder that the young man's imagination was fired by such a story of national salvation, and of men who could provide such momentous leadership. He read a book called *Great Heroes of the World,* which gave the biographies of such luminaries as Catherine and Peter the Great, the Duke of Wellington, Napoleon, Rousseau, Lincoln, and Washington. He was particularly impressed that George Washington's struggle to build his nation came only "after eight years of difficult war." [13] Mao found more heroes in his own heritage as well. He was fascinated by the legendary Emperors Yao and Shun. He read many accounts of the powerful early emperors, Ch'in Shih Huang-ti, the founder of the short-lived revolutionary dynasty, the Ch'in (221-207 B.C.), which first unified China, and Han Wu-ti (140-87 B.C.), the martial emperor, who greatly extended the empire during the following Han dynasty.

One year at the Tungshan Higher Primary School was enough for Mao. It was the summer of 1911, and he hoped to go on to Tungshan's middle school located in Changsha. Even with a letter of recommendation he feared that he would not be accepted in such "a great school." But Mao's apprehensions were unjustified. He was admitted without incident. However, his stay in Changsha this time would be short. One month following his arrival the Revolution of 1911 was to commence. The Ch'ing dynasty, founded in 1644, had only days to live.

Mao now read for the first time the revolutionary newspaper, *Min Li Pao.* This was the organ of the T'ung Meng Hui, a Chinese revolutionary society founded in Japan in 1905 by Sun Yat-sen. Sun was a fiery Cantonese who had lived much of his life abroad where he had considerable financial support from overseas Chinese. Sun had gained an international reputation in 1896 as a result of his kidnaping in London by the Chinese Embassy staff and his release due to public pressure. Since then he had been involved in nine attempts to overthrow the Manchus. The latest effort took place that April in Canton, and was led by Mao's fellow Hunanese, Huang Hsing. Seventy-two revolutionaries were killed. The event amazed Mao and led him to write his first political piece. He composed it in the format of a wall newspaper, a *ta tze pao,* which he posted on the school wall. Mao admitted later that the contents of the piece were "somewhat muddled." [14] He had synthesized his old and new heroes, calling for a republic with Sun Yat-sen as president, K'ang Yu-wei as premier, and Liang Ch'i-ch'ao as minister of foreign affairs.

Mao was not one to rest content with words. When the revolution broke out, accidentally, on October 10 in Wuhan, the triple city (Wuchang, Hankow, Hanyang) in Hupeh Province, Mao cut off his pigtail, the badge of subservience imposed on the Chinese by the ruling Manchus. He joined friends in cutting off the pigtails of several others, sometimes forcibly. He also decided to go to Wuhan and join the republican army. However, as he prepared to leave, fighting broke out in Changsha itself. Mao climbed a hill within the city from which vantage point he observed the spectacle. He saw, and did not forget, how the republican soldiers were admitted to the city with the help of working people who stormed the gates, wresting them from the Manchus.[15] Nor would Mao forget how a few days later, after the formation of the new revolutionary government in Changsha, it would turn upon the representatives of these same workers. It was Mao's first encounter with civil war in an urban setting, with the "for keeps" seriousness of class struggle. Mao had seen enough, and felt strongly enough about it to join the regular army, rather than the student contingents. In this way he could join the fight against the remaining Manchus and still identify with the common peasants and workers rather than with an elite maintained by militarists and landlords. Already, he had a hankering to "complete the revolution," and prevent usurpation by an exploitative elite.

Despite this brave effort to become part of the "masses," Mao found that he was in fact different. His one year of schooling and his ability to read and write set him apart and gave him pretensions he scarcely realized he possessed. Feeling it beneath his dignity to carry anything, he even used part of his wages to have others fetch his water.[16] This experience would trouble Mao over the years, and he would try to find ways to remove such psychological attitudes that prevented a genuine classless camaraderie. Eventually he would find that only a total revolutionary commitment and the actual living and sharing with commoners finally broke down the attitudes ingrained as a result of the training received by those of privileged status. It would not be an easy road.

During his six-month stint in the army Mao saw little action. But he read a great deal. One day, while reading a newspaper he found for the first time articles on socialism, which excited his interest. He discussed the topic with friends and even wrote "enthusiastically" to several classmates about it, "but only one of them responded in agreement." [17] Nothing more came of this new interest for the time being.

The 1911 Revolution stalled. Sun Yat-sen, who was in the United States when it began, had quickly returned to China where he was made president of the new Republic of China. However, the realities of the situation in the country were such that he was soon to relinquish the office to Yuan Shih-k'ai, whose double-dealing had given him control of a preponderance of the military power of the new government. Sun's deferral to Yuan in March of 1912 was an idealistic gesture, by means of which Sun hoped progress might still be made in bringing modern democratic government to his country. Thinking the revolution was over, Mao resigned from the army in March 1912, determined "to return to my books." [18]

For a time Mao remained indecisive as to what to study. Clearly there was no future to classical studies, which were for many centuries the only way to a respectable career in China. This path had been precluded by the abolition of the proud tradition of the government civil service examination in 1905. Mao must have been similar to many other young men in China in wondering which of the modern subjects might be most beneficial for one's own career and for China's national needs. He scanned the newspaper classifieds and registered successively at various schools—soapmaking, police, law, and commercial studies. Mao was puzzled, and would later look back upon this confusion jestfully.[19]

He studied a restrictive curriculum at the First Provincial Middle School in Changsha for six months, but then decided he would accomplish more by studying on his own. For the next six months he read from morning to night at the Hunan provincial library. This was an exceedingly productive period for Mao as he acquainted himself with such Western writers as Adam Smith, Montesquieu, Spencer, J. S. Mill, and Darwin, by means of the Chinese translations of Yen Fu. "I mixed poetry and romances, and the tales of ancient Greece, with serious study of history and geography of Russia, America, England, France and other countries." [20] For the first time, Mao saw and studied "with great interest" a map of the world. The rapture of this intellectual discovery was spiced with less pleasant experiences. At his boardinghouse, students and soldiers often quarreled. One night it erupted into physical violence. Mao recalled, "I escaped by fleeing to the toilet, where I hid until the fight was over." [21]

This interlude came to an end when Mao's parents refused any longer to support him unless he returned to a regular school. He decided finally on a career. He would be a teacher, the one role he would ever after identify with. Mao entered the First Hunan Normal School in 1913, remaining there until 1918. These were to be extremely important, formative years in Mao's career. The First Hunan Normal School is a large, attractive building with high ceiling halls, airy classrooms, and adorned by pillars and arches, all reminiscent of British colonial architecture.[22] It was a place conducive to study, a center of provincial intellectual activity, and, as such, conscious of academic standards.

Mao was deeply influenced by some of the teachers at the First Hunan Normal School, and some of his friends here would be very helpful to him later. One teacher, Yuan Li-chin, nicknamed "Yuan the Big Beard," ridiculed Mao's writing as being journalistic. Yuan despised Liang Ch'i-ch'ao, who had been a model for Mao, and regarded him as half-illiterate. Thus Mao studied the writings of Han Yü, mastered classical phraseology, and altered his own style.[23]

The teacher who made the strongest impression was Yang Chang-chi, a man of high character who taught ethics to the senior class and who had spent ten years abroad in Japan and England. Yang was an outspoken advocate of women's rights. Mao wrote an essay, "Energy of the Mind," for Yang which impressed the distinguished teacher so much that he awarded the earnest young thinker a perfect grade of 100. Mao developed a great affection for Yang who would one day become his father-in-law. Mao would later testify of Yang that he "tried to imbue his students with the desire to become just, moral, virtuous men, useful in society." [24] Clearly, this teacher influenced his student, and probably made Mao ponder deeply the importance of a teacher in imparting a sense of ethics to society. One teacher, Hsü Te-li, had coined the school motto, "Seek truth from facts." [25] Hsü, though eighteen years older than Mao, would become a devoted follower of his student, joining the Communist Party in 1927, participating in the heroic Long March, and living through the Cultural Revolution to 1968.

Two of Mao's closest friends at the First Hunan Normal School would later take sharply divergent paths. One, Tsai Ho-sen, was a quiet, brilliant young man from the county in which Mao had gone to upper primary school (Hsiang Hsiang). He would die for the revolution in 1931. The other, Hsiao Hsü-tung (also known as Siao-yu) shared an interesting adventure with Mao. Hearing of two students who had traveled to the edge of Tibet, Mao was inspired to follow their example. But lacking sufficient funds he settled, the next summer, on a trip through Hunan instead. Hsiao Hsü-tung accompanied Mao as they walked through five counties "without using a single copper." Mao recalled years later that "the peasants fed us and gave us a place to sleep; wherever we went we were kindly treated and welcomed." [26] Hsiao later became a Kuomintang official, and many years afterward, in 1950, wrote an interesting but prejudicial account of his acquaintance with Mao.[27] Mao told Edgar Snow in 1936 that two years earlier, in 1934, Hsiao, who had been appointed to the office of custodian of the Peking Palace Museum, "sold some of the most valuable treasures in the museum and absconded with the funds." [28]

As a student Mao was exceptional. He studied hard and for long hours, devouring book after book. He was also an outspoken activist. He argued against many regulations and red tape and on behalf of fellow students. He even tried on one occasion to have the school's principal fired, and was himself threatened with expulsion for his action. However, even some of those who had opposed him respected him and rallied to his defense. Fittingly, Mao was honored in 1917 by four hundred classmates who chose him as a model for ethical conduct, self-control, courage, and ability.[29]

Mao studied hard but did not neglect his health. In fact he became and has remained an ardent proponent of proper physical exercise. He saw examples of poor health all around him, and perceived this to be a manifestation of national weakness that must be corrected, regardless of the cultural tradition that inhibited his advocacy. Mao's earliest extant essay, published in 1916 in the exciting, leading intellectual magazine of the day, *New Youth,* was on the subject of physical education.[30] Mao believed that Chinese must want to be healthy, and could not be compelled to be. But physical education was a necessary complement to education in virtue and knowledge. And a physically fit people are militarily courageous. This was a political exhortation, for military strength was among China's desperate needs. His country was still smarting from the humiliation of Japan's infamous Twenty-One Demands of 1915, which had threatened to make China into a virtual colony. But China was in no condition to respond to the challenge.

China's domestic polical situation was deteriorating. Yuan Shih-k'ai, the strong-man militarist to whom Sun had deferred had hardly provided enlightened leadership. Yuan had murdered one of the leading democratic oppositionists in 1913, and on the day that the investigatory tribunal announced its report implicating him, Yuan himself captured public attention by announcing that a loan of 25 million pounds sterling had been made to the government by an international consortium. An analysis of this Reorganization Loan, as it was called, gives further insight into the country's deplorable state. It was secured by the Salt Gabelle, one of the leading sources of internal revenue. But of the 25 million pounds, almost 8 million were for liabilities due or shortly maturing, almost 3 million were to repay provincial loans, 2 million went to reorganize the Salt Gabelle, and 5½ million for current government expenses from April to September of 1913. The loan was used up within the year, but China was to be obliged to repay it over the next forty-seven years in the amount of almost 43 million pounds sterling.[31]

Yuan tried to revive the monarchy in 1915 and install himself as first emperor of a new dynasty. But clearly the time had passed for such an adventure. If China scarcely knew how to be democratic, it did not want to go backward either. The nation revolted, and Yuan died in 1916 settling the question of restoration. But the revolt did not resolve China's domestic political travail. Things would get worse. The era of the warlords had begun.

Mao was deeply aware of this national tragedy, but in these years he could have but small effect on the large forces involved. Under the circumstances no individual could. Sun Yat-sen had likened the Chinese people to "a sheet of loose sand." Organization and wide-scale mobilization and commitment were needed. In the meanwhile, each day, summer or winter, Mao prepared himself physically. He doused himself daily in the school's courtyard with a bucket of cold well-water, and with friends took swims, mountaineered, and walked shirtless in wind and sleet as he steeled himself for ever-widening social and political activism.[32]

Once, in an expansive mood, Mao placed a newspaper ad inviting those interested in patriotic work to get in touch with him. "I received three and one-half replies," Mao said of this abortive effort. One respondent later joined the Communist Party only to betray it. Two others became "ultra-reactionaries." The one-half response was from "a noncommittal youth named Li Li-san," who would be a thorn in Mao's side for many years. "Li listened to all I had to say, and then went away without making any definite proposals himself, and our friendship never developed." [33]

Yet Mao was not one to be easily discouraged. His life would be addressed to overcoming one obstacle after another. For now, the development of activist organizations and the expansion of awareness was China's urgent need, and Mao would keep trying. He became a natural leader of student groups. He served as secretary of the school's students' society and he formed an association for student self-government, which provided for collective resistance against the principal, but also engaged in political demonstrations against the warlords and against the Japanese. Mao's concerns were comprehensive. He organized student visits to factories to learn of conditions there and he immersed himself in military affairs.

Later, Mao would come to have an even greater awareness of the crucially important role of the military in Chinese politics. As a middle-school student, however, he was made mindful of martial considerations by World War I in Europe and the antics of warlords at home. He read inverately of campaigns on European battlefronts and wrote and lectured on strategy and tactics. In 1917 he was made leader of a school volunteer self-defense corps. With arms borrowed from policemen with whom he had become acquainted and by means of surprise and scare tactics Mao's charges compelled some warlord soldiers billeted at the school to surrender.[34] He taught his "troops" the use of sharp-edged bamboo sticks that would pierce the limbs and gouge the eyes of unwary assailants.[35] He proved a born leader; his commands were said to have been instantly obeyed, even by men many years his senior.[36]

Mao recognized the need to extend consciousness on the part of the population as a whole, of working people, and not just the educated classes of society. In 1917, with his teacher friend Hsü Te-li, he opened an evening class for workers. Today, a copy of one of Mao's posters advertising to workmen this free opportunity to learn hangs on the wall of the old classroom in Changsha.[37] It enjoins those interested to come and hear "some plain speech," given in the vernacular they could understand, rather than in the stuffy, stylized language then associated with formal schooling. Dress was optional, and along with free tuition, study materials were supplied gratis. Several dozen tired but curious workers responded. Mao, the instinctive educator, must have learned a great deal from the experience. He taught history and current affairs and in his classes prompted active discussion. He would always be insistent upon the need for student participation in the learning process as an effective means of assuring real comprehension.

These extracurricular activities and experimental methods culminated in the establishment in late 1917 of the *Hsin-min Hsueh-hui,* or the New People's Study Society.[38] Along with several friends Mao created this organization in order to discuss and debate the new ideas and schemes flooding into Chinese intellectual life. The new society represented another stage in Mao's development, for not only did it provide further leadership opportunities for him, but it stressed in its charter the need for action as well as study. There was a conviction in the society that study, discussion, and self-analysis could bring about a changed and improved personality. This was the beginning of the notion that man can be consciously remolded and that with this change in outlook the world itself can be transformed.

The men and women who joined the society were serious and highly motivated. Mao, twenty-five years old at the time, said that the members "had no time for love or romance and considered the times too critical and the need for knowledge too urgent to discuss women or personal matters. I was not interested in women." [39] Mao had in fact been married by his parents to a girl of twenty when he was fourteen, but the marriage was never consummated.[40] The society was extremely active, with incessant programs of study, debate, and social action. The experience garnered by the society over the next couple of years would make its members a natural and effective nucleus for Communist party organization in Hunan. As a matter of fact, all thirteen of the original members of the society would later join the Party.

In 1918 Mao also cooperated with the Hunan branch of the Society for Work and Study in France, an organization started in 1903 and which now had branches in several cities. Mao's friend Hsü Te-li started the Changsha branch, and with Mao's help soon many members of the New People's Study Society joined.[41] These included his best friend Tsai Ho-sen and his sister, the beautiful, brilliant early feminist, Tsai Chang. It was at Mao's insistence that women be allowed to participate and to go to France.[42] Mao also argued that aptitude for languages should not be the exclusive determinant for selection. Even at this early period he was insisting that criteria such as the candidate's conduct, ideals, and willingness to serve China be taken into account. Soon after graduation from the First Normal School in April 1918, Mao accompanied the group of thirty students from Hunan to Peking. There they would study the French language in preparation for the trip to France. Mao could have gone to France with the group, along with some of his best friends.

Mao had reached a definite new stage in his life. He had just finished middle school and had no set plan for the months ahead. His beloved mother had died early in the year, and he now had less reason than ever to stay close to home. Yet he chose not to undertake the foreign adventure with his friends. He did not feel comfortable learning foreign languages, and this may have been one reason for his decision, although it was not likely the determining one. Mao himself explained: "I felt I did not know enough about my own country." [43] This was no simplistic excuse. There was much to learn and much to do. Mao walked a good part of the way to Peking on this initial trip outside Hunan. He used the opportunity to observe socioeconomic conditions, immersing himself among the common people. During his stay in Peking he would make similar personal social investigations among the workers on the Peking-Hankow railway and among the poor of the city. All of this knowledge he was soon to place in a new conceptual framework. It would be a world view that would explain the inequities that troubled him so deeply, and it would point the way, for him, toward their abolition.

Peking was an exciting and beautiful city. Mao's six months there during this first visit were busy. Soon after arrival he called upon Yang Chang-chi, his teacher who had moved from Changsha in 1917 to take a post at Peking University. Yang was delighted to see his young friend. Since Mao was destitute, Yang introduced him to the university librarian who had him appointed to a librarian's assistantship. The position was a menial one that afforded only subsistence pay. "My own living conditions in Peking were quite miserable," Mao recalled. "I stayed in a little room which held seven other people. When we were all packed fast on the kang bed there was scarcely room enough for any of us to breathe. I used to have to warn people on each side of me when I wanted to turn over." [44] The job also had drawbacks in status-conscious Chinese intellectual society. "My office was so low that people avoided me . . . to most of them I did not exist as a human being." Mao recognized the names of many famous intellectuals who used the library. "I tried to begin conversations with them on political and cultural subjects, but they were very busy men. They had no time to listen to an assistant librarian speaking southern dialect." [45] The aloofness and arrogance of intellectuals who, preoccupied with their sophisticated abstractions, had little time for common folk was a problem Mao would later deal with.

But there were compensations. Mao walked about the city, exulting in its beauty. "In the parks and the old palace grounds I saw the early northern spring, I saw the white plum blossoms flower while the ice still held solid over the North Sea. I saw the willows over Pei Hai with the ice crystals hanging from them. . . . The innumerable trees of Peking aroused my wonder and admiration." [46] Mao also fell in love . . . with Yang K'ai-hui, the daughter of Yang Chang-chi, whose house he often visited. This romantic liaison and the exhilaration of Peking's splendor were further complemented by the new opportunities for intellectual growth and activism.

Of course, Mao took advantage of the library to read more deeply. He was not a regular student, but joining the philosophy and journalism societies he could audit courses. In this way he made many interesting contacts. Among others, he met Chen Kung-po, who became a Communist, then a supporter of Chiang K'ai-shek; Tan Ping-shan, also to become a Communist, then a member of a "third party"; Chang Kuo-t'ao, who would become a rival of Mao's in the mid-1930s and be expelled from the Party; and Kang Pei-chen, "who joined the Ku Klux Klan in California." (!) [47]

Mao also became acquainted with the prestigious intellectual leader Ch'en Tu-hsiu, dean of liberal arts at Peking University and editor of the important *New Youth* magazine, to which Mao had already contributed. Ch'en was a radical Westernizer who mercilessly condemned traditionalism and extolled to his excited audiences "Mr. Science" and "Mr. Democracy." Ch'en was to be disenchanted with Western liberalism and would become a founder and first chairman of China's Communist Party. This impressive thinker-activist influenced Mao "perhaps more than anyone else," as Mao himself later acknowledged. [48] However, Ch'en turned out to have an unhappy career in the Party.

Another important influence on Mao in this period was his employer, the university librarian, Li Ta-chao, who was five years older than Mao and a professor of history. Li, deeply nationalistic and profoundly moved by the Bolshevik Revolution in 1917, became the first major Chinese intellectual to show interest in Marxism. Li is thought to have interpreted Marxism loosely, or subjectively. He thought less of class divisions within China than he did of China being of "proletariat" status in the international community. By extension, the Chinese people as a whole possessed a latent proletarian consciousness. Li also was impatient with dependence upon the economic forces of history, expecting instead that man's will, and his "self-consciousness" would determine the course of history in China. Li's latitudinous, voluntaristic, and populistic interpretation of Marxism, and his adherence to it as a rational explanation of man's past and a scientific guide to national salvation would have an effect on Mao.[49] So too would Li's conviction that students and intellectuals should spend time in the countryside with laboring people. Mao read all of Li's writings, and joined his Marxist study group. "Under Li Ta-chao, I developed rapidly towards Marxism." [50]

In early 1919 after six months in Peking, Mao went to Shanghai to see his friends off for France. En route, he visited the grave of China's erstwhile most esteemed thinker, Confucius, and climbed traditionally sacred Mount T'ai Shan. In Shanghai he stood at the quay and bid his colleagues farewell as their ship slipped into the channel.

Mao returned to Hunan, his mind brimming with new ideas and as yet unsettled plans. He was primed for action. Fortuitously, the junction between this thoughtful man of action and a challenging set of historical events was at hand. Only days later a demonstration was to take place at Peking University. It was a protest that would quickly escalate to convulse all China. A readied Mao was on the scene to be swept along with the others. He was also a determined young leader who would try to discover the best mechanism for controlling and constructively using the mighty force unleashed.

TWO
Into the Cauldron

The May Fourth Movement was a vast and profound surge of liberated expression whose importance in modern Chinese history cannot be overemphasized.[1] It was China's first modern cultural revolution. The Movement, which began in 1915, reflected the growing national consciousness that was stimulated by Japan's high-handed interference in China's troubled domestic politics. After shaking the foundations of the country's thought and value system for several exciting years the Movement was to peter out in the 1920s. There would never again be such a period of free cultural questioning and creativity in China, so that this span of years still stands out. These were also the crucial, formative years in Mao's own intellectual growth.

The bold, thoroughgoing questioning of traditional values and practices, and the well-publicized advocacy of new ideas and the debates over them set the stage for the coming social and political upheavals. The language reform that was part of the Movement, with its promotion of the use of the spoken language of the people rather than the refined exclusive literary language of the educated, helped immeasurably to spread the new ideas and national awareness throughout the heretofore neglected and inarticulate populace. Mao, like his mentor Li Ta-chao, saw the importance of mobilizing the masses and bringing their energy into direct political action.

Intellectuals of the May Fourth period divided between those who, like Hu Shih, a leading proponent of literary reform educated in the United States under John Dewey, advocated gradual, educational reforms that would lead toward democracy in China, and activists like Ch'en Tu-hsiu who insisted upon the need for political change. From the beginning it was clear which side Mao was on.

The May Fourth Incident, from whence the name of the Movement derives, brought the issue to a head. The Incident must be understood against the background of the previous several decades as well as the events of the preceding three or four years. Ever since the Opium War of 1839–42 foreign powers, sensing the weakness of the ebbing Ch'ing Dynasty, had exploited China at every opportunity. The Treaty of Nanking and the supplemental agreements of 1842–45 exacted from China such concessions as the cession of Hong Kong and the granting of extraterritoriality and the most-favored-nation clause. Extraterritoriality relieved foreigners from the jurisdiction of Chinese law courts, while the most-favored-nation clause automatically conferred on each nation that possessed the clause in its treaty with China any new concession which some other nation might wrest from China. While some foreigners may have wished for a more equitable relationship with China, it was clear that such treaties took advantage of the weak and often venal Peking government. These treaties and their successors came to be known collectively as the Unequal Treaties.

Successive efforts to overthrow the Manchu government before 1911 failed, as did the attempts to reform it. The Taiping Revolution of 1850–64 was cruelly suppressed with foreign assistance. The Reform Movement of 1898 was betrayed and crushed. That effort had been a flash of hope after the bitterness and despair following China's defeat by Japan three years before in 1895. In one final desperate and irrational act the Boxer rebels struck out against foreigners in 1900. They were summarily crushed, and China was in deeper travail. As we have noted, even the 1911 Revolution soon aborted, and following Yuan Shih-k'ai's losing bid for a renewed monarchy, China was beset with warring military factions. With Europe embroiled in World War I Japan moved in for the kill.

However, by late 1918 and early 1919 there seemed to be cause for renewed hope in China. The country was developing a new spirit, as reflected in the May Fourth Movement's many-faceted activities. True, warlord politicking was still dominant, but there was encouraging word from abroad. World War I ended in November 1918. China was cheered. She had joined the side of the Allies and had sent 200,000 workers to shore up the depleted manpower situation in France. China looked forward therefore to consideration in the councils of the victors. Her hopes were buoyed by the establishment of the League of Nations and by the pronouncements of President Woodrow Wilson on the subject of self-determination. It was a good feeling, to be on the side of the democracies in this hour of triumph over tyranny.

It was a shock for Chinese, therefore, to learn during the Paris Peace Conference in early 1919 that there was no substance to such optimism. There would be no repudiation of the Unequal Treaties. Woodrow Wilson's brave talk was scornfully forgotten with the publication of the secret Lansing-Ishii agreement which had already given Japan a free hand in China in 1917. China got nothing from the peace settlement. On the contrary, it was learned on May 3 that concessions previously enjoyed by defeated Germany were given over to Japan.

On the following day, May 4, 1919, three thousand students in Peking representing thirteen academic institutions marched to the house of a pro-Japanese official to protest. The police and army, called to action, made arrests. Martial law was declared. Students immediately turned to rallying and organizing all who were sympathetic. Almost everyone in the indignant populace responded. A grand alliance of merchants, workers, small shopkeepers, and craftsmen was swiftly formed. This massive united front directed itself not only against the imperialists who had abused China, but against the warlords who had betrayed the country. Their campaign was well-publicized. It spread throughout the country in the days and weeks that followed. Strikes precipitated arrests which led to further support for the protesters. By June 28, 1919, when the Treaty of Versailles was signed, the organization and will of the protesters had succeeded to the point of preventing Peking's delegate from signing the document.

In Changsha, Mao embodied the excitement of the times, and during the weeks and months following the May Fourth Incident he was deeply involved. He gave a lecture on "Marxism and the Revolution," and although he was not yet a Marxist himself, he enjoined others to study the new philosophy.[2] Toward this end he formed Changsha's first Marxist Study Group. Other established groups, including his own New People's Study Society, similarly studied Marxism. Under Mao's direct influence the ground was being prepared for a substantial Communist Party branch in Hunan. In the meantime, in June 1919, he established the United Students' Association of Hunan, which he linked with contacts he had made in Peking with the All-China Federation of Students. The Students' Association inspired the creation of the Hunan United Association of All Circles which provided for participation by both merchants and workers. That two such social groups could get together for political purposes testifies to the strength of national outrage currently being experienced in Hunan, as well as elsewhere in China.

In July Mao began editing the new weekly magazine of the United Students' Association, the *Hsiang River Review.* Here he published an interesting three-part article entitled "The Great Union of the Popular Masses," obviously inspired by the coalition of forces forming throughout the country, and so tangibly before his eyes in Changsha itself.[3] This was not a particularly Marxist article, but it typifies much of his later thinking and practice. He urged a union of the oppressed in society, a union that included peasants, women, workers, and students. It was a union that anticipated the later "united front" concept rather than the orthodox Marxist class-distinction formulation. The importance of will was stressed, as was individual consciousness and awareness. The aroused union of oppressed masses constitutes the greatest force, declared Mao. It is a force that cannot be stopped. The traitors and the wicked will flee before it. Mao wrote with passion, and with nationalistic prideful-ness. "Our Chinese people possess great inherent capacities!

. . . one day, the reform of the Chinese people will be more profound than that of any other people, and the society of the Chinese people will be more radiant than that of any other people. The great union of the Chinese people will be achieved earlier than that of any other place or people.''

However lofty such sentiments were, the immediate target of much of this organization and writing was the local Hunan warlord, Chang Ching-yao. He had been installed by the pro-Japanese clique that ruled in Peking and was generally considered a brutal man. Mao called him a "vicious character." Predictably, Chang struck back at his critics. He closed down the *Hsiang River Review* after its fifth issue and outlawed its sponsor, the United Students' Association. Mao then became editor of another weekly, the *New Hunan*. Chang soon banned this newspaper too. Mao then wrote articles for the leading Changsha daily, the *Ta Kung Pao*. Among the pieces he wrote were an interesting series of nine articles, composed in a period of thirteen days and inspired by the suicide of a young girl whose parents had forced to marry against her will.[4]

By November of 1919 Mao took the dangerous step of reorganizing the United Students' Association. Only weeks earlier Chang had warned a meeting of student representatives that if they did not stop meddling in politics he would cut off their heads. On hearing this threat one of the girl students began to cry. Mao, seated nearby, advised her to pay no more attention to Chang than to a dog barking.[5] Following his own advice, Mao organized a student strike in December that was partially successful. However, it became clear to Mao that Chang was not to be removed from power in Hunan without help from outside. Accordingly, representatives were sent to various major centers to solicit such help. Mao went to Peking.

This brief visit to Peking was an important milestone in Mao's career. He was saddened by the death of his good friend and former teacher Yang Chang-chi. But in addition to soliciting help against Chang Ching-yao and consoling his beloved Yang K'ai-hui, Mao did some reading and discussing that was to be decisive for him. He read about events in Russia, and "eagerly sought out" the little available Communist literature then translated into Chinese. "Three books especially deeply carved my mind, and built up in me a faith in

Marxism, from which, once I had accepted it as the correct interpretation of history, I did not afterwards waver." These books were *The Communist Manifesto,* Kautsky's *Class Struggle,* which was the first Marxist book translated into Chinese, and Kirkupp's *History of Socialism.* "By the summer of 1920 I had become, in theory and to some extent in action, a Marxist, and from this time on I considered myself a Marxist." [6]

There were important talks too with Li Ta-chao, who now received Mao with new respect, earned through Mao's writings and exploits in Changsha in recent months. The two men undoubtedly discussed the road they were coming to believe that China must follow. They discussed the need to go beyond Marxist study groups, to the formulation of a political organization. Only in this way could they move forward with their political objectives for China.

Mao went to Shanghai where he supported himself for several weeks as a laundryman. Here he met again with Ch'en Tu-hsiu, who had been jailed for six months as a consequence of his support of the May Fourth demonstrations. This experience had moved Ch'en further in the direction of Marxism. The conversation helped firm up Mao's own decision. He would recall: "Ch'en's own assertions of belief deeply impressed me at what was probably a critical period in my life." [7] Mao discussed with Ch'en plans for achieving provincial autonomy for Hunan. He also called on Hu Shih to try to get his support for the struggle in Hunan.[8] It is uncertain how much support or encouragement he actually received.

It was a changeful political situation that Mao returned to in Changsha in the summer of 1920. Warlord T'an Yen-k'ai displaced Chang Ching-yao but was himself soon driven out by a new militarist, Chao Heng-t'i. Mao's personal circumstances improved, however, as he was appointed principal of the primary school attached to his alma mater, the First Normal School. He used his new prominence to increase the effectiveness of his political work. He established the Cultural Book Society in July, in order to make available radical literature.

Chao Heng-t'i, who had utilized the autonomy movement in his own struggle against T'an, now turned upon and vigorously suppressed the democratic aspirations of its supporters. Mao's New

People's Study Society tried to celebrate the third anniversary of the Russian October Revolution, but their demonstration was suppressed. The members argued with the police who prevented them from hoisting a red flag. They claimed that the Constitution permitted them the right to assembly, to organize, and to speak. The unimpressed police replied that they were not there to be taught the Constitution, but to carry out orders. "From this time on," Mao said "I became more and more convinced that only mass political power, secured through mass action, could guarantee the realization of dynamic reforms." [9]

Word came to Changsha that Communist party nuclei had been established in Peking and Shanghai. Mao immediately formed one in Changsha in October 1920. He also formed a branch of the Socialist Youth Corps, following the establishment of one in Shanghai that August. He now turned in the winter of 1920–21 to the organizing of workers and was guided in this "by the influence of Marxist theory and the history of the Russian Revolution." [10] The die was cast.

The First Congress of the Chinese Communist Party was held, beginning July 1, 1921, in Shanghai. Attending were thirteen persons representing a total membership of fifty-seven Marxists. There were two representatives from each of the six groups then in existence in China—Shanghai, Peking, Changsha, Wuhan, Canton, and Tsinan—and one representative from the Chinese group in Japan. Similar groups in Paris, Berlin, and Moscow had been established but had no representatives at the First Party Congress. Mao was one of the two Hunan delegates representing the largest single group in China—sixteen members. Also present were two foreigners representing the Comintern. One was a Russian named Voitinsky, the other a Dutchman named Sneevliet, also known as Maring.[11]

The first four days of the congress were held in the Po-Ai girls' school, then in summer recess. On the fourth day, however, the delegates were compelled to move elsewhere. Their suspicions were aroused by a stranger in the next room, and they barely escaped the premises before the police arrived. The meetings were concluded aboard a holiday boat on South Lake, some eighty miles from Shanghai, near the famous wine town of Chia Hsing.

Mao spoke with authority at these meetings, in the absence of Li Ta-chao and Ch'en Tu-hsiu, but his conciliatory and moderate views were not upheld. For several years in the early history of the Party Mao would have to live with the frustration of being overruled by arguments he could not agree with and with policies he believed to be improper. Yet he seemed to recognize the need for Party discipline. He continued to exert considerable effort in trying to make reasonable policies work and in any case never wavered in his revolutionary commitment. The First Congress adopted an exclusivist policy that eschewed working with other political forces in China. This ran counter to Mao's already expressed convictions. Mao was not amused when the successful advocate of the exclusivist policy, Ch'en Kung-po, later turned renegade and became a virulent anti-Communist. The congress also elected Ch'en Tu-hsiu as secretary-general of the central committee. Headquarters were established in Shanghai.

Mao returned to Hunan by the end of July 1921 to engage in organizing and teaching until he was compelled to leave less than two years later. Most of his work in this period was with workers. Within weeks of his arrival he set up the first Communist trade union. In recognition of his signal efforts, which curiously have been somewhat obscured until as late as 1967, the Al' China Labor Federation in 1922 named him chairman of its new Hunan branch.[12]

One of Mao's most important successes was in establishing secure Party links among workers at the Anyuan coal mines in southern Hunan. To do this, Mao spent time among the miners learning at firsthand of the wretchedness of their lives. He presented himself as a new kind of scholar indeed, for it was unheard of for an educated man to crawl with illiterate "expendables" into the earth. His purpose was not to learn more profitable engineering techniques, but to build bases upon which something could be done to improve the lot of more workers. He spoke to them man to man on their level and his credibility ran high. His approach brought glimmers of hope where only hopelessness had been known. By January 1922 he had established the first Anyuan Party cell. His brother Mao Tse-min joined him and put together a workers' cooperative. To round out this ministry to the hard-working miners, Mao formed an Anyuan branch of the Changsha Bookstore, a day school for the miners' children, and a workers' club where the miners could attend lectures and read radical literature.[13]

Mao carried on similar tasks elsewhere in Hunan. He organized a Party cell at a middle school in Hengyang in January 1922 and formed such cells among railway workers on the Canton-Hankow line. One of the most typical of his enterprises was the establishment of the Self-Education College in Changsha in August 1922.[14] Students were sought who lacked resources and who opposed the regulations of other schools. The school was extraordinary. There were no formal classes. Seminars encouraged discussion and debate. The objective was to stimulate political consciousness and the identification and training of potential Party members. Mao's wife helped at the school, and Mao Tse-min was one of the students. The school soon added a preparatory class for junior middle school students, and by the time Mao left Hunan in April 1923, it began to publish a Marxist monthly. It was closed by Hunan governor Chao Heng-ti in November 1923, but later reopened under a different name.

Mao missed the Second Party Congress in 1922 because he had forgotten the address of the secret meeting and could not make contact.[15] That meeting had decided to continue the Party's exclusivist policy with regard to cooperating with other political forces. By the spring of 1923, however, views were changing in this regard. The February 4 brutal massacre by northern warlord Wu P'ei-fu of the railway workers at Chengchow in Honan Province and Chao Heng-ti's subsequent suppression of the Anyuan strike convinced many that the diminutive Party could not afford to remain isolated. There was also pressure from outside the Party to adopt a conciliatory stance toward others. As early as July 1920 the Comintern in Moscow had decided that it should collaborate with national-revolutionary movements in Asia, i.e., as Lenin himself interpreted the decision, with bourgeois-democratic elements who invariably constituted such a movement in that part of the world.[16] Chinese representatives to the First Congress of the Toilers of the Far East in Moscow and Petrograd in January 1922 were urged to make common cause with the bourgeois nationalists.

The Third Party Congress was held in Canton in July 1923. Mao successfully argued for a united front with the Kuomintang, Sun Yat-sen's party, probably as much because he saw the necessity for such an alliance as because it accorded with Comintern policy. Mao was elected to the Central Committee of the Party, which now numbered 342 members throughout all of China, and he soon became the head of the Party's Organization Department.

For his part, Sun Yat-sen had become increasingly receptive to overtures of Soviet aid. Over the years Sun's fortunes had ebbed and flowed, but mostly ebbed. He had become disenchanted with the West. His repeated entreaties for succor had gone unheeded. Conversely, he had been impressed with the success of Russia's October Revolution, especially with Lenin's offer to return to China concessions made under the Unequal Treaties. Sun finally agreed to receive Soviet assistance, including help in reorganizing the Kuomintang Party and in establishing and training a new revolutionary army, in return for active collaboration with the Chinese Communist Party. The form of alliance ultimately agreed upon was the unusual device of permitting Communists to become members of the Kuomintang, a form of collaboration known as the bloc-within technique.

The alliance, called the period of the First United Front, was a busy one replete with many opportunities for the heretofore relatively isolated Communists. But it was also an exceedingly dangerous adventure for them because they would, as identified members, become vulnerable to suppression. In the end, after some four years of active cooperation with the Kuomintang they would in fact be brutally suppressed. It remains a moot question whether the policy was worth it. But at the time, given the immensity of the problems and strength of the warlords backed by powerful foreign interests, it must have seemed worth the risk. Had the Chinese not been additionally hassled by Soviet interference, they might have gained more from it than they did.

In the next four years Mao himself remained active and gained a great deal more organizational experience. He also learned things that a revolutionary party should not do, particularly not to depend too heavily on outside support and advice. He learned the limits of cooperative possibilities with well-intentioned and not so well-intentioned members of the bourgeois-nationalist classes. He would also discover in the midst of this period the proper locus of revolutionary support in his own country, in contrast to what had been the case in the Soviet Union.

In January 1924 Mao attended the First Congress of the KMT.[17] At the congress he was one of three Communist participants on the nineteen-member committee chosen to deal with the new KMT constitution. He was named an alternate member of the new KMT Central Executive Committee (CEC). Soon afterward he picked up further crucial assignments, including alternate membership on the KMT's Shanghai executive committee, and then as secretary of this organ's organization department. This was of special importance in that the chairman of both of these organizations was a high-ranking member of the KMT, Hu Han-min. Mao was also known as an admirer of Sun Yat-sen. He supported Sun's Three Principles—the principles of people's nationalism, people's democracy, and people's livelihood, the last of which became increasingly socialistic to Sun himself. Mao became one of the most important liaison men between the two party organizations. But given irreconcilable differences between the two parties it proved to be an impossible task. It also made him vulnerable to criticism within his own Party for being too compromising. Nevertheless, Mao worked hard at his assignments. He spent much of the year 1924 in Shanghai, with one visit to the coal miners of Anyuan and another in August to Canton. Here he gave a talk at the Peasant Movement Training Institute, an institution that grew out of his insistence for a peasant committee at the First KMT Congress earlier in the year. Communists dominated the work of this committee and its institute. Hence, even though he remained for the time being immersed in urban work, Mao still managed to give attention to needed work among the peasants. But a fuller awareness of the basic role that was to be played by China's teeming countryside masses would begin to dawn on him only in the following two years.

Illness brought on by overwork and exhaustion compelled Mao to return to his family home in Shaoshan in January 1925.[18] On recovering, he spent time observing conditions in the countryside, and then began quietly organizing peasant associations and peasant Party cells. While he was engaged in this labor an event occurred in Shanghai that rocked all of China.

On May 15, 1925, a Chinese worker was killed by a Japanese textile mill foreman in Shanghai.[19] Two weeks later, on May 30, students demonstrated in the International Settlement where British police opened fire, killing twelve. National outrage was instantaneous. Less than a month later another incident added fuel to the flames. On June 23, workers, students, and military cadets from Whampoa demonstrated in front of the Shameen concession area at Canton. They were fired upon by British soldiers. Fifty-six demonstrators were killed. The protest movement now raged throughout the country, with wide-ranging strikes bringing production and transportation to a halt in many places. Participation far exceeded the impressive numbers recorded in the famous Hong Kong seamen's strike of 1922. Now 150,000 workers visited Canton from Hong Kong, completely tying up the latter city. This national venting of anger against the callousness of foreign imperialism was extremely beneficial to Communist recruiting and to the expansion of the trade union movement in the cities. The Party which had 995 members at the beginning of the year could count 10,000 by November 1925, and another 9,000 in youth organizations.

Mao, who was among the peasants of Hunan while this was going on, could see the radicalizing effect such news had upon them as well. "Formerly, I had not fully realized the degree of class struggle among the peasantry." Thanks to this newly elicited militancy "more than twenty peasant unions were formed" within a few months of the May 30 Incident.[20]

Mao's activities came again to the attention of Chao Heng-t'i. When he was spotted in Changsha that August orders went out for his arrest, and he was forced to flee the province. He went to Canton, where he became secretary to Wang Ching-wei in the KMT's Propaganda Department. Wang, who early won fame as a patriot in an unsuccessful assassination attempt before the 1911 Revolution was an active contender for Sun Yat-sen's mantle. Since Sun had died in Peking that March, Wang's preoccupation with the struggle for leadership gave Mao opportunities. Mao edited the official journal and served for a time as deputy director of this important department. He helped work out demands through this channel for radical agrarian reforms in Kwangtung. His report on propaganda to the Second KMT Party Congress in January 1926 stressed peasant organizing activity. At this time Mao was reelected an alternate member of the KMT's CEC. In addition to continuing as acting director of the Propaganda Department he was soon appointed as well to the KMT's peasant committee.[21]

Mao's propaganda work was useful in promoting the programs of P'eng P'ai, the Communist organizer since 1922 of peasant associations in Hai-lu-feng in Eastern Kwangtung province.[22] The success of these radical agrarian programs in turn spelled success for the first eastern expedition into this area in 1925, for it undermined landlord power in territory occupied by warlord armies. Unfortunately, the same radical programs and supporting propaganda could not be carried forward in areas controlled by the KMT. This was because the officer corps of the KMT revolutionary army itself derived from the landlord class. This contradiction eventually destroyed the KMT-CCP alliance. In the meantime it led to a rift within the CCP. The Central Committee under Ch'en Tu-hsiu remained desirous of placating the KMT to preserve the alliance. The CCP was joined in this policy of restraining the peasants by the Soviet advisers. They promoted the Moscow line of maintaining the alliance, seemingly at all costs. Mao was for a more radical line of peasant action that would lead to reduced rent and interest charges.

The heavy influence of Communists in Canton's KMT organs came abruptly to a halt with Chiang K'ai-shek's coup of March 20, 1926. Chiang d been Sun Yat-sen's favorite military subordinate, and was now moving toward control over the KMT. He managed to curtail Communist influence at the Second Plenum of the KMT CEC in May 1926. Mao was stripped of his propaganda department post. He undoubtedly sensed the approaching doom of the alliance but chose to remain affiliated with the KMT for some time, for good reason.

Clearly by now, Mao saw the central role of the peasantry in the Chinese Revolution. His activities for several months already showed his preoccupation. He now seized the best opportunity available for continuing work in this direction. It was a good opportunity. Mao became head of the KMT's Peasant Movement Training Institute from May through early fall of 1926. He undoubtedly believed this to be an important job, for the students here were potential contacts selected from several provinces. Mao changed the curriculum much more along Marxist lines. He himself lectured, and he called upon other prominent Communists to give classes. Mao guided one entire class, the sixth, through to completion.[23]

In July 1926, while Mao's class was still in progress, the National

Revolutionary Army began its march to the north to fight the warlords and to unify the country. Soviet advisers had opposed this northern expedition at the time, because the Soviet Union, serving its own national interest, was currently exploring relationships with some of the warlords. Chiang K'ai-shek had been commandant of the Whampoa Academy, where this new army's officer corps was trained with the assistance of Soviet advisers. The Communists played a role in this training too. Chou En-lai, who had been a member of the original Communist nucleus in France, was the academy's political adviser. There was an expectation that Chiang K'ai-shek would heed Communist advice, at least in order to assure continued Soviet support. But the Communists had misjudged their man. Chiang ignored the opposition and launched the northern expedition.

The army moved north on two fronts, one toward the tri-city complex on the Yangtze River in Hupeh province known as Wuhan, the other toward the major commercial center on the east coast, Shanghai. This campaign was a successful one, due both to the courage and astute maneuvering and fighting of the officers and men, and to the timely help afforded it by propagandists and activists along the way who stirred up support from peasants and workers. During the campaign the Chinese Communists remained sharply divided on the peasant issue. The Central Committee continued to go along with the Soviet advisers, who now perforce went along with Chiang. The Central Committee was against making the peasant issue one that would split the KMT-CCP alliance. Mao remained opposed. Ch'en Tu-hsiu, perhaps invoking Party discipline, dispatched Mao to Hunan to investigate the peasant movement there, expecting him to restrain radical activity. Instead, Mao delivered an explicitly contrary speech on December 20, 1926, to a conference of peasant delegates in Changsha.[24] He said simply and forthrightly that the peasant problem was the central issue. Only with its resolution could the revolution succeed. Spurred on by this speech, and in fact under Mao's direction, the peasants began to seize and redistribute land.

Three months later, in March 1927, Mao wrote one of his most famous pieces, the "Report on an Investigation of the Peasant Movement in Hunan." [25] His findings were unequivocal. "The present upsurge of the peasant movement is a colossal event." "In a very short time, in China's central, southern and northern provinces, several hundred million peasants will rise like a mighty storm, like a hurricane, a force so swift and violent that no power, however great, will be able to hold it back. They will smash all the trammels that bind them and rush forward along the road to liberation. They will sweep all the imperialists, warlords, corrupt officials, local tyrants and evil gentry into their graves." [26]

Mao estimated that membership in peasant associations had jumped to two million, and that this implied a mass following of ten million since "peasants generally enter only one name for the whole family on joining." He credited the strength of extensive organization for bringing about "within four months . . . a great revolution in the countryside, a revolution without parallel in history." [27] Mao may have been exaggerating somewhat, although there can be little doubt that Hunan's peasants were in the forefront of such developments at this time.

Mao used the report to argue against his critics who chose to ignore the implications of peasant power and who deplored peasant excesses as they sought to preserve a political alliance rapidly turning sour. He painstakingly demonstrated that the so-called riff-raff, whose actions were "terrible" and who were "going too far," were actually the poor peasants, who comprised 70 percent of the Changsha County population. They were the real "vanguards of the revolution," the most dependable class element of social upheaval. "Without the poor peasants there would be no revolution. To deny their role is to deny the revolution. To attack them is to attack the revolution. They have never been wrong on the general direction of the revolution." [28]

Mao listed the fourteen "great achievements" of the peasant associations, which confirmed their power and ability to rectify injustices and bring about tangible social benefits to their communities.

Mao posed the question. "Every revolutionary party and every revolutionary comrade will be put to the test, to be accepted or rejected as they decide. There are three alternatives. To march at their head and lead them? To trail behind them, gesticulating and criticizing? Or to stand in their way and oppose them? Every Chinese is free to choose, but events will force you to make the choice quickly." [29]

Events did move swiftly. Chiang K'ai-shek was in rough agreement with Mao, but he believed that such revolutionary impulses ought to be snuffed out rather than accommodated. In February 1927 Chiang had already announced that the time had come to expel Communists. He did so in Kiangsi while his headquarters were temporarily at Nanchang. On his approach to Shanghai his army was halted while an insurrection timed to coincide with his entry into the city was suppressed by the warlord army. One month later, on March 22, 1927, there was another general strike in Shanghai, again in the expectation that the Kuomintang army would coordinate its advance with the strike. Again the army awaited the pacification of the workers. But this time the workers succeeded in disarming the warlord troops and opened the gates to the waiting KMT army.

Chiang K'ai-shek immediately set about negotiating with bankers, foreign interests, and a local crime syndicate for support. Once this was secured he struck without warning. On the morning of April 12, 1927, his troops, along with hired thugs, attacked the workers. The latter had been ordered to hide their arms so as not to give offense and endanger the KMT-CCP alliance. The orders had come from Stalin in Moscow. Thousands of Communists and suspects were executed. The Party organization in Shanghai was destroyed.[30]

This tragic setback for the Communists was compounded again by the decision to continue the KMT-CCP alliance with the Left KMT in Wuhan. Mao himself was never able to fall into step on this sure path to destruction. Instead, he continued to oppose the official line of the Party and to implement programs that were decidedly to the left of that line. Mao reaffirmed the substance of his March report at the founding Congress of the All-China Peasant Association in April 1927. The congress adopted his proposal, but it was rejected by the CCP Politburo. Mao was made chairman of the new All-China Peasant Association, but was expected to suppress rather than promote the movement he represented. Of course, he did not carry out such orders. Mao submitted his report to the Fifth Party Congress which was held in late April and early May 1927, but it was excluded from the agenda of the meetings.[31] Mao only attended the initial sessions of this congress, and left town before the final decisions were made. The Party decision on the peasant problem held that the radical policy of land confiscation and redistribution was to apply only to enemies of the revolution.

Back in Changsha Mao joined in the call of the Hunan Provincial Peasant Association for the confiscation of all land belonging to big landlords, not just of the "enemies of the revolution." He also helped plan an uprising against the Hunan warlord, T'ang Sheng-chih, who was supporting the Wuhan government, and therefore was supposed to be off-limits. This uprising had to be postponed. But the response of the peasants to the call for land confiscation was so enthusiastic that it led to a summons for Mao's arrest.

While Mao was still in hiding, on May 21, 1927, the Changsha garrison commander attacked the headquarters of the peasant associations. A bloodbath ensued. Hapless victims were marched outside Changsha's west gate and killed in batches. Women and girls were made sport of. They were reportedly killed with bullets fired upward through the vagina. Men were tortured cruelly.[32] The peasants began to mobilize for armed struggle but were restrained from carrying on the fight because of pleas from Wuhan that such a conflict might persuade T'ang to turn on the Wuhan government. This request was acceded to, but as the last of the armed peasants turned to leave Changsha, they were treacherously attacked from behind and butchered by troops of the Changsha garrison.[33]

Despite such Communist concessions to keep the KMT-CCP alliance alive, the period of collaboration was soon to end. Wang Ching-wei was shown a copy of a telegram from Stalin to Borodin, proposing a revolutionary court be set up "to try reactionary generals." The alarmed Wang immediately turned against the Communists and, despite their continued conciliatory proposals to continue the alliance, had them expelled from the Left KMT on July 15, 1927. Even then Stalin persisted in the belief that the alliance could be reconstituted, once Wang Ching-wei was gotten rid of. The Communists unilaterally maintained the fiction of an alliance until September 1927. The record of the CCP had been a sorry one. In order to obey Moscow's line they had to cooperate with Chiang K'ai-shek while he attacked workers in Shanghai, with T'ang Sheng-chih while his troops attacked peasants, and with the Left KMT as it expelled them from office. For a man who had already come to a realization of the road to successful revolution in China, Mao, one can imagine, could only have shaken his head at this point.

THREE
To the Hills

The Communists who survived the disastrous finale to the First United
Front in the summer of 1927 were a disheartened lot. They were desperate men. They embarked on a program that led to further disaster.
On August 1, 1927, Communist military units took control of the city of
Nanchang in Kiangsi province. Four days later they were driven out,
and the remnants of this force fled south, where they suffered further
defeats. The August 1 Nanchang Uprising, even though it failed, would
come to be commemorated as the founding day of the Red Army.
More than ever would Mao be persuaded that "political power grows
out of the barrel of a gun."

On August 7, 1927, as the Nanchang rebels were in flight, Mao participated in an "emergency conference" in Kiukiang. The meeting
deposed Ch'en Tu-hsiu and formed a provisional politburo under the
direction of Ch'u Ch'iu-pai. Mao was made an alternate member. The
conferees planned a series of rural uprisings along the Yangtze River
and its tributaries with the objective of surrounding and eventually
capturing the major urban centers of this important region. This line
would soon be regarded as "putschist," and was predicated on the as-
sumption that the tide of the bourgeois revolution was still on the rise,

and that a KMT properly reorganized by the Communists was still the best means of proceeding. Mao was censured for his alleged opportunism among the peasants in the preceding weeks. He was now given the assignment of staging a rising of the peasantry in Hunan and Kiangsi, a part of the widespread campaign known as the Autumn Harvest Uprising.[1]

Mao threw himself into this task with energy and for a time in early September he saw several victories. However, it was soon clear that there was a shortage both of adequate military experience on his part and of popular support from workers and peasants who were becoming understandably apprehensive of the immediate prospects. By October the Uprising had failed. Mao too was in flight. He headed for the remote mountainous terrain between Hunan and Kiangsi provinces. The Politburo met in Shanghai in November and declared that the 1927 revolution had not been a failure. It criticized Mao for military adventurism and removed him as an alternate member of the Politburo and from his position in the Hunan Provincial Party Committee. The next month this revolution that had not failed saw one final crushing defeat for the year when the Canton Commune, which had been staged as much as anything to provide Stalin with a China victory in time for the Fifteenth Soviet Party Congress, was suppressed.[2]

The fortunes of the CCP had reached a very low point. But for Mao and his ragtail band of followers there was the hope of a new beginning. He recognized the unique political situation in China that allowed for the phenomenon of a territorial Red base, i.e., the continued in-fighting among the "white" armies, and the advantage of being strategically located between two provinces at a time when these were ruled by warlords. From the mountain fastness of Chingkangshan he could begin to fashion a more pragmatic and independent course. He even allied for a time with known bandits with secret society connections. He would continue to be hassled by directives from the outside and would not always have adequate power over the next several years of work in the "wilderness." But he would have ample opportunity to begin to experiment and to put together his own distinctive formula and policies for revolution.

Mao's contingent was reinforced by the arrival on Chingkangshan of troops under Chu Teh in the spring of 1928. The merged Chu-Mao force numbered about 10,000, and was designated the Fourth Army. Chu was military commander, Mao the political representative (later "political commissar"). This new Red Army soon proved itself in battle by scattering two KMT divisions deployed against them in May 1928. The victory was occasion for jubilation. Mao must have seen more than ever the similarity between himself and his boyhood heroes, the just bandits of Liangshanpo mountain. He was moved to express his sentiments in a poem that has since gained wide currency:

> At the foot of the mountain
>   waved our banners.
> Upon its peak
>   sounded our bugles and drums.
> A myriad foes
>   were all around us.
> But we stood fast
>   and gave no ground.
>
> Our defense was strong
>   as a mighty wall.
> Our wills united
>   to form a fortress.
> From Huangyangchieh
>   came the thunder of guns.
> And the army of our foes
>   had fled into the night! [3]

Representatives of the Party held the first congress of the border area on May 20 and elected Mao the secretary of its First Special Committee. Differences soon appeared between this body and the Hunan Provincial Committee, its hierarchical superior. The latter advocated what Mao considered to be "ultra-left" policies. He refused outright to implement the policy "of burning and killing." The Hunan Committee also changed its military policy frequently, leaving Mao puzzled and disobedient. He was finally replaced by Yang K'ai-ming as secretary of the special committee. Yang now ordered the best of Chu Teh's troops to attack Chenchow. This elicited another KMT attack on Chingkangshan which also failed, but so too did the Communist assault on Chenchow in August 1928. The second congress of the border area reinstated Mao as leader.[4]

By November of 1928 Mao had learned from experience some of the main ingredients for maintaining an independent regime of "workers and peasants." What was necessary, he wrote, was "(1) a sound mass base, (2) a sound Party organization, (3) a fairly strong Red Army, (4) terrain favourable to military operations, and (5) economic resources sufficient for sustenance." [5] All of this was predicated on a continued split among the white armies, for when real pressure was brought to bear it was difficult to make the formula work. This proved to be the case when P'eng Teh-huai joined the Fourth Army in late 1928. P'eng brought with him soldiers who had deserted the KMT during the previous year. His arrival was soon followed by renewed KMT assaults on Chingkangshan. These attacks eventually led to the abandonment of this first mountain base. Moving eastward into Kiangsi, the Fourth Army fought a series of battles against KMT armies for the next half year. These ranged from south Kiangsi, to west Fukien to north Kwangtung. The Communists were unable to increase their numbers appreciably under these battle conditions. But they were able to consolidate a viable new base area around the town of Juichin in southeast Kiangsi. Juichin became their new headquarters, and later the capital of the Chinese Soviet Republic.

Much of the year 1929 was given to consolidation of the new southeast Kiangsi base. Mao went into west Fukien three times and established a smaller soviet area there. In September 1929 he contracted malaria and was fortunate to have survived for there was no quinine available.[6]

In December 1929 at Ku-t'ien, Kiangsi Mao wrote a resolution for the Ninth Party Congress of the Fourth Red Army. Entitled "On Correcting Mistaken Ideas in the Party," the resolution has become famous for it would often be referred to in subsequent political campaigns, particularly in the military.[7] Basically the resolution summarizes Mao's view of the experience of the Red Army to date with regard to mistakes. He cautioned that the military must be subordinate to politics and must be used "as only one means of accomplishing political tasks." A purely military viewpoint was wrong, for the military was subordinate to politics and is to be used "as only one means of accomplishing political tasks." He deplored becoming conceited in victory and dispirited in defeat, or being afflicted with limited vision, or giving way to the "malady of revolutionary impetuosity." The sources of these mistakes, he said, are a low political level, a prevailing mentality of mercenaries on the part of some, an overconfidence in military strength, a lack of confidence in the masses of the people, and a failure to discuss military work. Mao also discussed such errors as "ultra-democracy," the disregard of organizational discipline, absolute equalitarianism, subjectivism, individualism, the ideology of "roving rebel bands," and the remnants of putschism. For each of these categories of mistaken notions and behavior he advocated methods for correction. Basically, the methods boiled down to intensified programs of education, the recruitment into the army of workers and peasants experienced in struggle so as to change its composition and purify its ideology, the encouragement of criticism, active discussion of military work, and the drawing up of clear rules and regulations.[8]

Just as basic for the military were Mao's famous Three Rules of Discipline and Eight Points for Attention, which had been worked out and articulated in 1928. The three rules enjoined prompt obedience to orders, no confiscation of peasant property, and prompt delivery directly to authorities of all items confiscated from landlords. The eight points (the last two of which were added by Lin Piao) were:

1 | *Replace all doors when you leave a house;*
2 | *Return and roll up the straw matting on which you sleep;*
3 | *Be courteous and polite to the people and help them when you can;*
4 | *Return all borrowed articles;*
5 | *Replace all damaged articles;*
6 | *Be honest in all transactions with the peasants;*
7 | *Pay for all articles purchased;*
8 | *Be sanitary, and especially establish latrines a safe distance from people's houses.*[9]

These injunctions, usually complied with, came to make of the Red Army a distinctive type of army in China and an exceptionally popular one.

On January 5, 1930, Mao followed up his "mistaken ideas" talk with a letter written (to Lin Piao, it would be revealed later) to criticize "certain pessimistic views" currently extant in the Party. This piece, "A Single Spark Can Start a Prairie Fire," was, along with the Ku-t'ien resolution, aimed in part at a particular individual within the Party, and the policy he represented.[10] This was Li Li-san, the man who years earlier had responded to Mao's advertisement in Changsha but with whom a friendship did not grow. At the Sixth Party Congress, which was held in July 1928 in Moscow rather than in China, and which Mao did not attend, both Mao and Li Li-san were elected to the Central Committee. Li Li-san returned from the Soviet Union to Shanghai with Soviet support and he soon dominated the new Central Committee. Li and Mao clearly had little use for each other to begin with, but now their respective positions and outlooks compounded the problem. Li presided over Party affairs in Shanghai, but the real locus of power was out in the countryside, mostly in the base area controlled by Mao.

Li Li-san tried to persuade Mao to break up his large military units into smaller, mobile guerrilla bands that would incite revolutionary readiness among the country population. Mao attacked this notion of "roving rebel bands" as being inadequate. Only through the building of strong base areas, could power be built, the revolution deepened, and the confidence of the people won. Li's view was that only by the workers in the cities could the revolution be initiated, led, and won; that the peasant population was ancillary to this. Li evolved a grand scheme, the Li Li-san line, to attack and capture several major cities of central China. Mao was strictly opposed to this policy, yet found that almost everyone else from other base areas was in favor. Since the Fourth Red Army was the largest single Communist military unit his agreement was essential for the plan. Reluctantly, Mao eventually decided to go along. In June 1930 the Fourth Army was reorganized as the First Army Corps with Chu as commander and Mao, political commissar. P'eng Teh-huai's troops were reconstituted into the Third Army Corps.[11]

Implementation of the scheme began on July 28, 1930, with P'eng Teh-huai's entry into Changsha. This successful occupation was surprisingly good news to Mao and Chu Teh who were about to attack Nanchang, their assigned target city, and to Chang Kuo-t'ao and Ho

Lung aiming toward Wuhan. But the August 1 attack on Nanchang, which had been delayed, apparently to commemorate the third anniversary of the Nanchang Uprising, was fruitless. The enemy was too well-entrenched and too well-armed. The remnants of the assault now headed toward Wuhan to assist the action there. On their way they met with P'eng Teh-huai's unit which had now been driven out of Changsha after its ten-day occupation of the city. P'eng had orders from Li Li-san for a renewed attack on Changsha. The combined force of the First and Third Corps numbered about twenty thousand men, which for the Communists was a record-size military force. The second assault on Changsha lasted from September 1 to 13. It was a brave effort, but impossible in the face of the overwhelming firepower of the defenders. Sensing that continued attack would be disastrous, Mao and Chu took the serious step of calling off the operation and retired into south Kiangsi.[12] The Li Li-san line had proven itself erroneous, even though Li Li-san continued to find support for it for several more months.

What this effort did do, despite its failure, was to make clear to Chiang K'ai-shek and many of his political opponents the seriousness of the red menace. This led to an earlier settlement of their differences, by September 1930, so that requisite attention could be given to the Communists. Hence a concerted search for Communists was launched in the major cities of China, and preparations were made for a final military resolution. The fiasco touched Mao personally, for his beloved wife Yang K'ai-hui and his younger adopted sister were both arrested and then executed by the KMT after the departure of P'eng Teh-huai's troops from Changsha.

On the eve of the KMT's anxiously awaited attack on the south Kiangsi base in December 1930, Mao was suddenly faced with a severe challenge to his leadership. The details of this chapter of history are not entirely clear, but it is clear that under the circumstances Mao had no choice but to act swiftly and with resolution. He did so. The soviet base area in southwestern Kiangsi had remained toward the end of 1930 heavily influenced by men loyal to Li Li-san. These men continued to believe that they represented the legitimate policy of the Central Committee in Shanghai, not having heard until this incident was over that Li Li-san was now discredited. The differences between Mao and these vestigial adherents of Li Li-san came to a head over the implementation of agrarian policy. Mao held that the Li line was favorable to the local gentry despite its claim of being more radical than his own. Complicating the entire issue was the known presence of a vast KMT spy network in the area known as the A-B Corps. Mao probably, in his frustration at his opponents, and because of the oncoming threat of the KMT invasion, did not make distinctions as carefully as he might have done had circumstances been different. There was the priority need to dispose of the KMT spies before the imminent attack. Thus, on the basis of the reports of his own intelligence people, he placed under arrest several thousand officers and men of the Red Army. Suddenly, on December 7 or 8, 1930, there was a mutiny elsewhere in the ranks. The mutineers went to Fu-t'ien where they freed the arrested leaders. They also overthrew the provincial soviet government, arrested many of its members and killed more than a hundred of Mao's supporters. However, the majority of the army and its principal leaders remained loyal to Mao. The mutineers were isolated. While many lives were lost in this distasteful episode, it would be unfair to allege, as some have, that Mao was particularly ruthless in this entire affair. An agreement was finally reached with some of the misled dissidents, and while many disloyal rebels and spies were shot, most of those arrested were eventually set free following investigation and a short period of reeducation.[13]

Now there was the formidable external threat with which to deal. In the same month of December, indeed before the Fu-t'ien incident had been concluded, the KMT launched the first of its five encirclement campaigns against the Communists. The first proved unsuccessful and was terminated by the end of January 1931. As a result of this engagement the Communists came by their first radio sets, a war prize that improved their communications system.[14] The fighting also revealed Mao's military genius. Despite the numerical superiority of the enemy, some 100,000 men to 40,000, and despite the remaining tensions within his own ranks engendered by the Fu-t'ien incident, Mao employed effective, yet simple guerrilla tactics that soon dismembered the opposing force. The military principles used are concisely expressed in a slogan of the Red Army:

The enemy advances, we retreat;
The enemy encamps, we harass;

The enemy tires, we attack;
The enemy retreats, we pursue.[15]

The KMT's second encirclement campaign in the spring of 1931 was more ominous. Their offensive now had double the number of men, 200,000, against the weakened Communist force of 30,000. Yet once again, Mao and Chu outmaneuvered the superior army, cutting it to ribbons and defeating it in a series of five battles separated by great distances. Twenty thousand enemy soldiers were captured along with their rifles.[16] Following this even more convincing victory, Mao once again expressed his relief and joy with boastfully taunting verse:

About the peak of White Cloud Mountain clouds are pressing upward,
Beneath White Cloud Mountain the cries grow more desperate,
Dry wood and hollow trees gather together for the struggle.
A forest of rifles press forward,
The flying generals sweep down from the void into battle.

In 15 days we have driven 700 li,
Green and majestic are the waters of Kiangsi,
And the mountains of Fukien like jade.
We have swept through armies thousands strong like rolling up a mat.
Someone is weeping,
How bitterly he regrets the strategy of step-by-step advance! [17]

The third encirclement campaign in the summer of 1931 was even more serious. Now Chiang K'ai-shek was fully aroused. He took personal command of 100,000 of his best-trained troops, and overall enjoyed a numerical superiority of ten to one. Mao continued using his tactic of luring the enemy deep and striking at his weakest point. Chiang's disciplined crack troops might have proven a much more respectable foe than the earlier contenders. However, the sudden Japanese occupation of Manchuria at this moment of truth, compelled Chiang to call off the third campaign.

While Mao and Chu Teh were accomplishing these military successes by means of masterfully conceived and implemented practical soldiering, a whole new political situation was evolving back in

Shanghai, somewhat out of the line of fire. Amidst intense and bitter politicking in the fall of 1930 Li Li-san was finally deposed and had left for Moscow where he would remain for the next decade and a half. In his place there now emerged an entirely new leadership, often referred to as the Twenty-eight Bolsheviks. All of the members of this group had been trained in Moscow, and now under the patronage of Pavel Mif, the new Comintern representative, enjoyed Stalin's support. Their leader was Ch'en Shao-yu, more commonly called Wang Ming. Closely allied with this group was Chou En-lai, now an energetic member of the new Politburo. This new leadership considered themselves to be well-versed in Marxism as well as in the latest developments in the Soviet Union and world communism. This knowledge and their experience abroad gave them considerable prestige in China. They would prove to be a real thorn in Mao's side over the next few years. The pain began in 1931 when they decided to move from Shanghai to the Kiangsi base area. No longer would Mao be able to ignore or implement directives from Shanghai at his convenience.

In November 1931 the First All-China Congress of Soviets was held in Juichin, Kiangsi. It established the Chinese Soviet Republic, and gave Mao two of the highest posts in the new regime. He was now chairman of the Central Executive Committee, or head of state, and chairman of the Council of People's Commissars, essentially the cabinet. He was also one of fifteen members of the Central Revolutionary Military Council, which was headed by Chu Teh.[18] Within the Party, however, his position was much less impressive. Even within the government machinery Mao's authority was limited, for the two deputy heads of state, Chang Kuo-t'ao and Hsiang Ying, were not his own men. It is evident that the Twenty-eight Bolsheviks' leadership had to give some grudging acknowledgement of Mao's achievements in the past few months and also needed him and his associates, at least until they themselves became more familiar with their new nonurban environment.

But attacks on the circumscribed Mao and his policies began immediately and he would lose even more power in the months and years immediately ahead. His military strategy was opposed as outdated. At the Ningtu conference in August 1932 Chou En-lai had Mao ousted from the Military Council, and in May 1933 succeeded him as political commissar of the Red Army.[19] The two men were, in fact, sharply opposed to each other throughout the Kiangsi period. Fortunately for their cause the differences would eventually be resolved, and they would comprise an effective combination in later years. The immediate issue in June 1932 was the launching by the KMT of the fourth encirclement campaign. Mao insisted on continuing the winning tactics previously employed, since the overall situation of sympathetic peasants and superior enemy units was the same. Chou wanted to fight positional warfare, using larger, centralized units to defend a fixed base. The argument was clinched in favor of Chou En-lai, for the time being at least, when his policy prevailed and did succeed in repulsing the fourth encirclement campaign. Mao's position was weakened in part through illness during this period.[20]

Underlying the difference on military policy were different perceptions of the overall national and international situation. In April 1932 Mao and Chu Teh had declared war on Japan in the name of the Chinese Soviet Republic. Mao believed that Japanese aggression was the cardinal consideration and that imperialism and feudalism were more pressing issues than capitalism of which there was very little in China. Mao therefore advocated a new alliance or united front with the KMT in order to deal with the more urgent crisis. Chou En-lai and the Central Committee strongly disagreed. They intended to confront the KMT rather than collaborate.

Freed from military and important Party responsibilities, Mao spent much time in the next few months working on economic and social problems.[21] In June 1933 he launched a large-scale land verification movement in order to determine if the land reform law of November 1931 had been properly implemented. The 1931 law was a moderate one that had provided even cooperative rich peasants with land, albeit of inferior quality, and allowed middle peasants to retain their own land. Middle peasants could also remain outside the land-reform process unless they chose to participate. Moderation was deemed necessary to secure support from the peasants as a whole in these beleaguered times. The object of the verification movement was to promote class struggle where necessary, because Mao knew by now that even in a moderate land-reform program the more well-to-do peasants would seek to take advantage of the poor and landless. Mao knew the latter needed encouragement and help in order to raise their consciousness to the point necessary for them to have the courage and knowledge to speak up for their rights. Mao believed that a very important three-stage process was involved in the agrarian program. The first stage of land reform had to be followed by second stage verification in order to bring about the desired third stage of increased agricultural production. Only a meaningful change in social relationships in the countryside could lead to such increased production. And higher production was becoming necessary in the landlocked republic that was increasingly feeling the pinch of the KMT economic blockade. The Central Committee also wished to raise additional funds to support an ambitious new policy of expansion, but Mao disagreed with such a line.

Wang Ming had gone to Moscow in 1931, but the new "Bolshevik forward and offensive line" was pursued with vigor by his successor Po Ku and Comintern military adviser, Li Teh, a Chinese alias for Otto Braun. The line was strikingly similar to the erstwhile Li Li-san line. It called for expansion of the Red Army to one million men, the incorporation of all local militia into the regular army, and a general mobilization of economic resources. This was all in preparation for an impending all-out offensive against major cities. The difference with the Li Li-san line was that this time there would be no need to rely upon a co-ordinated uprising of workers inside the target cities.

Opponents of this Wang Ming line were to be accused in 1933 of being adherents of the erroneous Lo Ming line, an indirect attack on the dissident policies of Mao himself.[22] Lo Ming was an old-line commander in the Fukien base who continued to follow guerrilla strategy even as late as mid-1933 because such a course of action seemed to them to make more sense in their areas. Such dissidents were systematically identified in the months ahead, isolated and increasingly removed from office and positions of power and influence. Mao played little if any part in the CCP Fifth Plenum held in January 1934. Later the same month, at the Second All-China Congress of Soviets, Mao was reelected to the chairmanship of the Central Executive Committee, but was replaced by one of the returned students as chairman of the Council of People's Commissars. His position was largely figurehead, for his supporters were now outnumbered on the Central Executive Committee.[23]

This was an intolerable situation for Mao, who by now could sense the impending disaster. Yet his struggle to correct the situation was unavailing. The resulting intraparty dispute became increasingly bitter and divisive. Mao would complain later of the tactics used by his persecutors: "Instead of regarding the veteran cadres as valuable assets to the party, the sectarians persecuted, punished, and deposed large numbers of these veterans in the central and local organizations." He noted that "large numbers of good comrades were wrongly indicted and unjustly punished; this led to the most lamentable losses inside the party." [24] The "Bolshevik reconstruction" of the Party which the Twenty-eight Bolsheviks had set about to accomplish was succeeding in replicating in the Chinese revolution the terror techniques and the dispiriting atmosphere of Stalinist Russia. By the summer of 1934 things had deteriorated to the point that Mao was expelled from the Central Committee and placed under house arrest, perhaps even imprisoned, to silence his dissident voice.[25] He became ill once again with malaria in September and October.

As for the brave "Bolshevik forward and offensive line," this withered in the face of the mighty juggernaut now arrayed against the Communists. The fifth encirclement campaign had begun the preceding August (1933), again under the personal command of Chiang K'ai-shek. This time preparations for the campaign were even more thorough. Chiang had almost a million men under arms, a huge arsenal, and four hundred planes. His two German military advisers had devised a seemingly inescapable campaign of ever-tightening pressure. An economic blockade deprived the entrapped population of essentials such as salt, cloth, kerosene, and medical supplies. Narrowing circles of concrete blockhouses with overlapping fields of fire and connected together by barbed wire made guerrilla tactics extremely difficult if not impossible, even if the Communists had elected to fight such a campaign, which they did not.[26]

The KMT campaign proceeded as planned except for a brief interlude known as the Fukien Revolt which began in October 1933. The KMT Nineteenth Route Army which distinguished itself in fighting the Japanese near Shanghai in 1932 had been sent to Fukien to comprise the eastern flank of the fifth encirclement campaign. The soldiers, restive at the notion of fighting Chinese rather than Japanese, revolted and set up a government in Fukien that claimed to have socialist objectives. The rebels sought an alliance with the Communists, but this obvious opportunity for both parties was not consummated. The reasons for this remain obscure, and Mao is sometimes accused of having opposed the alliance. This accusation is not credible for Mao had an instinct for such alliances, and when was the need greater? He later made quite clear that he thought that cooperation would have been possible if it had not been for the advice of Li Teh and others.[27] Unfortunately for the Communists, the rebels were suppressed in January 1934, and the encirclement campaign resumed in earnest.

It was evident by April 1934 that the military plan of defensive, positional war was disastrous. The Communists were badly defeated at Kuangchang, on the Fukien-Kiangsi border, sustaining casualities of four thousand killed and twenty thousand wounded. The road to Juichin was now unprotected. Desertions became as big a problem as the enemy.[28] By summer the conclusion was reached that there was no chance of saving the Chinese Soviet Republic. Only breakouts could prevent a total holocaust.

The first unit broke through the blockade in June 1934. It was called the Anti-Japanese Advance Detachment, to put the best face on the situation. The appellation also suggests Mao's fine hand. It succeeded in reaching the Yangtze at Wuhu and preoccupied KMT troops for a time before being driven back into Kiangsi. One of its leaders was caught, caged, displayed, then beheaded.[29] In August another large group of ten thousand broke out, this time going into northeastern Kweichow province. This group merged with Ho Tung's Third Army into a new Second Front Army and controlled a Hunan-Hupei-Szechuan-Kweichow soviet base. This diverted KMT forces in Hunan to the northern part of the province, thus opening space through which Chu Teh's main retreat would later pass. A third breakthrough was Cheng Tse-hua's Twenty-fifth Army which made it all the way to Shensi, marching through central China.[30]

On October 15, 1934 about 100,000 men, with only about 35 women, left their base in Kiangsi and began a relatively orderly march to the west.[31] Curiously, this vast throng with all its baggage was underway for several days before the overcautious KMT army detected the movement. Left behind were 20,000 wounded, most of the women and children and a rear guard of 6,000 regulars and more militia. Many of

Mao's supporters were among these, their fate indicative of Mao's powerlessness at this exceedingly low point in the history of the Chinese revolution. But Mao was no stranger to adversity. He joined in the march, and "with giant strides" set off on what would prove to be one of the most incredible feats ever achieved in the history of armed struggle on this planet. The adventure ahead would be decisive for Mao's own career of leadership and would have incalculable impact on succeeding events of the Chinese Revolution, for its participants would be endowed with a legendary aura and a mystique that no political opponents could seriously challenge.

Indeed, it is difficult to conceive of the Long March without risking an overuse of superlatives. A brief review of the fundamental facts of the epic performance bears this out. The heroic, exhausting trek lasted 370 days, beginning on October 15, 1934, in Kiangsi and ending October 20, 1935, in Shensi in China's northwest. The Long Marchers traversed a total of more than six thousand miles, all of it afoot. Only 100 days were given to rest, and during many of these breaks, fighting continued unabated. The Red Army maintained an average pace of about twenty-four miles a day. A forced march of such duration is remarkable. What makes it incredible is that it took place over some of the toughest terrain in the world. The Communists crossed eighteen mountain ranges, five of which are perpetually blanketed by snow. They forded twenty-four rivers, some exceedingly hazardous, and often under highly dangerous conditions. They passed through six different aboriginal areas, which was no small accomplishment in itself, since these peoples have traditionally been hostile to Han Chinese. The marchers took as many as sixty-two cities while passing through twelve provinces. Almost the entire time they were harried by pursuing warlord or KMT armies and aircraft. Yet they managed to defeat or elude all of them. Such an unbelievable accomplishment required an inspiring and remarkable leader. The leader of the now legendary Long March soon after its dispirited beginning was Mao Tse-tung.

Mao's leadership of the Long March and for the first time of the Chinese Communist movement was confirmed in early January 1935 at a special meeting during a twelve-day pause at the town of Tsunyi in northern Kweichow province. Most of the Long March to this point can only be described as an aimless rout that had absorbed terrifying losses. The stiff inflexibility of Li Teh's military deployment laid open the long elephantine columns, overladen with unnecessary baggage, to incessant, murderous air bombardment by German fliers. Li Teh's insistence upon a juncture with Ho Lung's northwest Hunan soviet base resulted in set battles with overwhelmingly superior forces with predictably crushing defeats. In one major battle alone, at the Hsiang River it is estimated that as much as half of the Red Army, perhaps fifty thousand, were lost.[32] Such maladroit military leadership dramatically vindicated Mao's position. Even before reaching Tsunyi his advice was again being heeded. Following a meeting at Li Ping in Kweichow, where his suggestions were acted upon, the Long March began to take on a purposive demeanor.[33]

The Tsunyi Resolutions criticized systematically, if not comprehensively, the erroneous military line that had been followed for some time and that had led to defeat in the fifth encirclement and extermination campaign, to the loss of the Chinese Soviet Republic, and to the terrible casualities and destruction of morale during the first two and a half months of the Long March.[34] Political and ideological issues were avoided. This was an indictment of the towering stupidity of inept military policy alone. Mao condemned positional warfare, the objective of never yielding an inch of ground, and purely passive defense. All such notions were singularly inappropriate to the circumstances at hand. The resolutions reveal rather well the main principles of war that Mao would go on to articulate more fully during the period from 1936 to 1940. This was the strategy of protracted revolutionary war, the appropriate strategy when there is no supporting urban proletarian uprising, no White Army mutinies, no airplanes, no artillery, and when the Red Army is constrained to fight on interior lines only. The Red Army must concentrate superior forces, Mao argued, select enemy weaknesses, and using mobile warfare destroy the enemy piecemeal. The enemy is to be lured to penetrate deeply . . . there is to be no hesitation to surrender some parts of territory . . . so that the initiative can be held. There is compelling need to preserve the personnel of the Red Army, to avoid the needless waste of human lives. Mao had won his argument overwhelmingly.

Mao was elected chairman of the new Revolutionary Military Council and political commissar of the First Front Army. He may yet have had a nominally subordinate position in the Party hierarchy itself, but there seems to be little doubt that he was in charge in Party matters as well. Deeper political and ideological differences were shelved for the time being. These would be hashed out later, with most of the essential ones resolved during the early 1940s. Chou En-lai, however, one of Mao's erstwhile more formidable opponents, chose this moment to acknowledge his own mistakes of the past and to ally himself firmly with Mao Tse-tung. Unity was called for throughout the ranks. With new resolve the Long March recommenced its journey with an objective now clearly articulated "to march to the northwest in order to fight Japan."

The initial destination may have been a junction with Chang Kuo-t'ao's forces in northern Szechuan province by means of a more direct route through that rich and naturally well-protected inland province. However, the approaches were too well guarded by warlord armies, united through fear of the common threat and assisted by Chiang K'ai-shek. After what may have been only a northward feint, the Red Army suddenly wheeled and for the next fifteen weeks crisscrossed in "sinuous lines of motion" vast stretches of northern Kweichow. During this period Mao's forces captured a well-fortified pass that drew from Mao another expression of poetic determination:

Cold blows the west wind.
Far off in the frosty air the wild geese call
  in the morning moonlight
In the morning moonlight
Horses' hoofs ring out sharply
And the bugle's note is muted.

Do not say that the pass is defended with iron.
This very day at one step we shall cross over it.
We shall cross over it.
The hills are blue like the sea,
And the dying sun is like blood.[35]

In the course of this action, the Red Army went on to take Tsunyi once again and destroyed twenty pursuing enemy regiments in the process. This was the first major victory of the Long March.

Chiang K'ai-shek might well have expected the Red Army to try again to breach Szechuan's southern defenses after such a success. However, Mao was not to be so easily figured. The rested and replenished Red Army now moved to the west toward the Yangtze River, but just as suddenly reversed itself making a feint toward the Kweichow provincial capital of Kweiyang. Chiang K'ai-shek quickly moved to protect Kweiyang, but the Communists now turned southwest into Yunnan province, boldly making a similar feint at Kunming. These highly successful feints enabled the bulk of the Red Army to cross the upper Yangtze River, where it is called the Chin Sha or Golden Sands River, much further to the west than the KMT seems to have expected. In fact, Chiang considered the river impassable in that area. He once again underestimated his adversary. The strategy gave the Communists about a week's head start over the pursuing KMT forces. The Communist force under Lin Piao which had made the feint toward Kunming now undertook a spectacular forced march of fifty-three miles in one day to make the crossing of the Golden Sands River itself. The Red Army was now in southwestern Szechuan province, in the land of the fierce, warlike Lolo minority people.[36]

The Red Army's next urgent objective was to cross this hostile territory in order to reach and ford the awesome Tatu River. Many an earlier legendary hero had perished in the raging waters of this tempestuous stream, including warriors of Three Kingdoms renown, and the popular Taiping prince, Shih Ta-k'ai. Chiang K'ai-shek felt he could afford to be confident of a similar outcome this time, but he flew on ahead to make the defenses foolproof. He had time on his side, he believed, because the Red Army's advance would be necessarily slowed as the Communists struggled with the intractable Lolos, a people who had never been assimilated by the Chinese.

However, the Communists had already traversed aboriginal territory, that of the Miao and the Shan in both Kweichow and Yunnan, and had learned how to win the support of these minorities. Fortuitously too, they also had the opportunity to free a number of imprisoned Lolo chieftains in Chinese towns near the Lolo district. The Communists also negotiated an agreement with the Lolos acknowledging their independence and even surprised the tribesmen by honoring their request for arms and ammunition. Thus the grateful Lolos did not slow, but instead facilitated a safe and speedy passage through Lolo territory. As a result, the Communists came upon and surprised the napping KMT soldiers once again. But even with their best efforts it was impossible for the main units of the Red Army to cross the Tatu at the river town of An Jen Ch'ang for there were only three boats and time was insufficient. Hence, the crossing had to be supplemented by another at Luting Chiao, a famous iron-chain suspension bridge, some 135 miles west of An Jen Ch'ang. It was the last crossing point over the Tatu east of Tibet. The Communists literally raced for their lives toward this bridge. When they arrived at the bridge, somewhat ahead of a main force of enemy support troops on the other side of the river, the Communists saw the frightening obstacle in front of them, and their hearts must have missed a beat. The bridge consisted of sixteen iron chains, spanning by about a hundred yards an awesome chasm. Many of the wooden floor planks had been removed, displaying the roaring cataract below. A machine-gun commanded the opposite side of the bridge. But there was no time to worry or to bemoan their fate. Volunteers were called for. Repeated, heroic, suicidal dashes soon secured the bridge. As the Red Army crossed this tiny, now repaired lifeline, Chiang's planes circled helplessly above. History was not repeated. Mao and his courageous comrades pressed onward.

The crossing of Luting Bridge may have been the most dramatic and symbolic episode of the entire Long March epic, but there was still some two thousand miles left to go before the northwest destination of Shensi province would be reached. Yet to conquer were truly formidable natural barriers. Immediately ahead were seven towering mountain ranges. It was June by now and very hot in the lowlands, but as the inadequately clad men ascended the sixteen-thousand-foot Great Snowy Mountain, many perished from exposure. On Paotung Kang Mountain, one army corps lost two thirds of its transport animals. Each of the succeeding ranges exacted their terrible tolls. The physical torture of this endurance test was translated by Mao into more verses:

Mountains!
Faster I spur my coursing horse, never leaving the saddle.

I start as I raise my head,
For the sky is three foot three above me!

Mountains!
Like surging, heaving seas with rolling billows,
Like a thousand stallions, rearing and plunging
In the thick of battle.

Mountains!
Piercing the blue of the sky, their peaks unblunted!
The heavens would fall
If their strength did not support them.[37]

Poetically expressed sentiment aside, it was a profound relief when on July 20, 1935, the bedraggled marchers finally met their comrades of the Fourth Front Army from the Oyuwan Soviet in the much healthier Mou Kun area of Szechuan. At Maoerhkai the weary army from the south rested, and the Communist leaders held important meetings that highlighted new differences as well as old enmity. Chang Kuo-t'ao proposed that the Communists retire to the west where a new soviet republic might be established in relative safety. Mao opposed this as flightism and warlordism, for the Red Army would be going in the wrong direction from the necessary struggle ahead to promote the revolution, and it would have to live off the land in such a remote and underpopulated area in the same way that warlords sustained themselves. Instead, Mao insisted on continuing the northward trek to northern Shensi where the Communists could be in a position to lend credibility to their anti-Japanese policy.

There was more than simple policy difference at issue. At bottom a raw power struggle was brewing. Chang Kuo-t'ao was desirous of wresting the leadership of the Communist movement from Mao. He would never be in a better position to accomplish this end. His soldiers were more numerous and in much better physical shape than were Mao's. Also his men were basically at home in the Szechuan region and his suggestion for them to remain in the area was naturally well-received. The dispute ended in a seeming compromise, for the Communist forces split into two parts. The First Front Army under Mao, Chou En-lai, and Lin Piao proceeded toward the north, while

Chang Kuo-t'ao and Chu Teh remained in the Szechuan-Sikang region for another year. In fact, Mao may have averted disaster at this moment by suddenly moving out before Chang had an opportunity to strike.[38] The reason why Chu Teh remained behind is still not clear. As a Szechuanese himself he may have been honestly confused and divided on the proper course to take. In the end his staying behind probably was beneficial in that it gave Mao a solid supporter in Chang's camp, and may have prevented the latter from moves that would have been more divisive. As matters stood, however, when Mao's First Front Army renewed its northward march the prospects ahead remained grim, and they were not improved by Chang's uncooperative, even threatening, posture.

Mao's forces, numbering thirty thousand at the most, now faced a most rigorous test. They wended their way through the Great Grasslands, an inhospitable land of perpetual precipitation, swamps, and confusing trails. For the first time in their experience, the Communists were unable to communicate with the minority peoples of the area. The Mantzu tribesmen and the Hsifan nomads remained implacably hostile to them. The crossing was a nightmare. Money and guns offered by the Communists were refused. They could not buy food. They could not even find their tormentors in order to attempt to communicate. Everything edible was removed from their path of march. Malnutrition appeared. Those who searched farther afield for food were cut down in ambush. Many marchers roasted and ate the cowhide of their shoes. But the lack of shoes resulted in ruined feet, illness, and disease. Little wood was available for fire, so that what food was found often had to be eaten raw. This sometimes led to food poisoning. When the Red Army emerged from this ordeal, the only comforting thought afterward was that the pursuing KMT army did not.

There were yet many more dangers ahead, both man-made and natural. Perhaps the most intimidating was Latsekou Pass in southwestern Kansu province. This natural narrow bottleneck was flanked by overhanging cliffs. The only approach was a wooden bridge that spanned another swift-flowing river that raged forth out of the pass. On the other end of the bridge were two battalions of the enemy. Another life-or-death situation. But once again the Red Army proved equal to the task. Flying squads of hastily composed "dare-to-die" vanguards courted the withering enemy fire, and in the end wore down the amazed and frightened defenders.

Among the remaining armies that the Communists were compelled to face and to dispatch were hardy Muslim cavalrymen in Kansu. These fierce warriors were expected to administer to the ragged and undernourished survivors of the March the *coup de grace.* But the climactic encounter merely resulted in the addition to the relentlessly advancing Communist columns of a huge number of fine horses.

On surmounting the Liup'an Mountains, their last major natural obstacle before reaching their destination Mao, without pausing, looked ahead with determination and proclaimed:

The sky is high, the clouds are pale,
We watch the wild geese flying south till they vanish;
If we reach not the Great Wall, we are no true men!
Already we have come two thousand leagues.

High on the crest of Liup'an Mountain
Our banners idly wave in the west wind.
Today we hold the long cord in our hands;
When shall we bind fast the grey dragon? [39]

The grey dragon, the name of a constellation in the sky, here refers to the Japanese invaders. Mao's poetic challenge affirmed the larger conception of his thoughts.

On October 20, 1935, a full year after the outset of the withdrawal from South China, a tired Red Army of six thousand men arrived at Paoan in northern Shensi province. Mao's assessment of the Long March saw its larger significance:

. . . the Long March is the first of its kind in the annals of history, that it is a manifesto. . . . It has proclaimed to the world that the Red Army is an army of heroes, while the imperialists and their running dogs, Chiang Kai-shek and his like, are impotent. It has proclaimed their utter failure to encircle, pursue, obstruct and intercept us. The Long March is also a propaganda force. It has announced to some 200 million people in eleven provinces that the road of the Red Army is their only road to liberation. Without the Long March, how could

the broad masses have learned so quickly about the existence of the great truth which the Red Army embodies? The Long March is also a seeding-machine. In the eleven provinces it has sown many seeds which will sprout, leaf, blossom, and bear fruit, and will yield a harvest in the future. In a word, the Long March has ended with victory for us and defeat for the enemy.[40]

FOUR
Forging the Yenan Way

It is difficult to overestimate the seminal importance of the next several years for the development of the Chinese Communist Party. The rich experience in northern Shensi, known as the Yenan Period (for the Communists moved their headquarters to Yenan in 1936), is characterized by great creativity and massive expansion. Mao was able to fashion programs and techniques that would deal successfully with immediately pressing problems. He would also come to believe these solutions to have a timeless utility in later forwarding the revolution. As Mao found time to refine and more fully articulate his ideas, and the opportunity to consolidate his own leadership, so the Communist movement would broaden and deepen its roots among the Chinese people. In the next decade, from 1935 to 1945, the Communist Party would increase its membership from perhaps 20,000 in 1936 to 1,200,000 in 1945.[1] Its control would be extended from the sparse population of northern Shensi to as many as 95 million people in sizable areas of north China.[2] As important for the future, it would have won the reputation of having remained uncorrupted by the war and of having led the nation in the struggle against the Japanese.[3]

The reputation was deserved. Mao had early sensed the need to unify China against the Japanese, and he consistently promoted this end. The Comintern, in July-August 1935 reflecting the Soviet Union's fear of being flanked by fascism, also called for united front tactics. Therefore, Mao was supported on this issue by the Russian student group who still had a great deal of influence in the Party. While still on the Long March, at Maoerhkai in early August 1935, the Communists initiated the first uncertain step toward a united front in China, by appealing to all classes to join them in fighting Japan under a "united national defense government" of all patriotic forces.[4] However, Chiang K'ai-shek and the KMT were still sharply attacked. In December 1935 at the important Politburo meeting at Wayaopao, held only two months after Mao's arrival in Shensi, it was resolved that a new united front with the KMT had replaced agrarian revolution as the fundamental tactical line.[5] Teeth had already been put into this by the moderation of the agrarian revolution on December 15, ten days before the Wayaopao Manifesto was issued. This was a resolute course to take because the agrarian revolution had been proving successful in winning support for the Communists in Shensi. It was difficult to explain the sudden leniency toward rich peasants and landlords who joined the patriotic anti-Japanese struggle. But Mao had insight into the larger issue at stake, and dissenting "Chinese Trotskyites" were opposed. However, even the toned-down agrarian revolution was beneficial to poor peasants and their support continued.

The Communist appeal to the nation to unify in the face of Japanese aggression struck a responsive chord among Chinese everywhere. On December 9, 1935, students in Peking had demonstrated to the same end, only to be cruelly repressed by KMT police.[6] But the sentiment could not so easily be crushed. Patriotic groups proliferated. Many of these coalesced in 1936 to form a National Student Union and a National Salvation Association. The former was said to number some 200,000 students. The latter included many prominent professional luminaries. Mao undertook further measures to provide a national focus for this rapidly growing national consciousness. The workers and peasants soviet government in Shensi changed its name to Soviet People's Republic and declared its desire to have the "broad petit-bourgeois class" participate. In July, Mao appealed to the Elder Brothers Society, an important secret society, and to Muslims to join in the alliance against the Japanese.[7] Mao's appeal spoke to the sense of social justice of the secret society reflected in its principle "strike at the rich and aid the poor," and to the patriotism of its members "to come to the aid of our country in its need." Mao's reference to the glory of the Hans in this appeal, as well as other such references to his country's proud past is sometimes interpreted as evidence of an exaggerated nationalism on his part. This seems unfair, for, one could ask, what national leader would not make such pride-provoking remarks when his nation has been so long abused by foreigners and is in grave danger of losing its sovereignty altogether?

In late 1935 and early 1936 the Central Soviet Republic in Shensi was again under siege. Mao now made a sudden and dramatic move to capture national attention to his Party's leading role in the campaign to resist Japan. On February 20, 1936, thirty-four thousand Red Army men struck across the frozen Yellow River into Shansi province. They appealed to Yen Hsi-shan, the local warlord, to join in the fight against Japan. They also conducted a program of agrarian revolution among the Shansi peasantry. By April, Yen received heavy KMT reinforcement, and the Red Army was compelled to retire back into Shensi. There was no actual attack on the Japanese, but Mao had scored a heavy propaganda point. His forces had also broken the back of the blockade and had recruited eight thousand fresh troops in Shansi.[8] Shortly after their return to Shensi real fighting ceased between the Communists and the blockading forces. There was no formal agreement, but the Manchurian soldiers under Chang Hsueh-liang who were supposed to be fighting the Communists were homesick and highly responsive to Communist appeals for national unity. The Communist military posture improved even more by late 1936 when the Second and Fourth Front armies finally arrived in northern Shensi. By the end of the year the position of the Communists was no longer desperate, and there was much sentiment in the land for a unified Chinese effort against the Japanese. But Chiang K'ai-shek stubbornly refused such a course of action. To his mind, before he could address the Japanese menace, he must first exterminate the Communists.

Then, in December 1936 there occurred the celebrated Sian Incident which was to force Chiang K'ai-shek to change his mind, however unhappily. In December Chiang flew to Sian in order to exhort his reluctant generals to launch a new suppression campaign. Instead, generals Chang Hsueh-liang and Yang Hu-ch'eng kidnaped Chiang and held him for two weeks during which time negotiations were conducted with the Communists acting as mediators. The upshot was Chiang's orientation to a Second United Front with the Communists. He was safely returned to Nanking, and was now regarded as a national hero. The details of the impending collaboration were left to be worked out over the next few months.

The principal elements of the Second United Front were spelled out in a telegram of February 10, 1937, from the Communist Central Committee to the Third Plenary Session of the KMT's Central Executive Committee.[9] The Communists made four concessions: (1) the abandonment of armed insurrection to overthrow the national government; (2) the Soviet Republic would be reorganized as the government of a "special region" of the Republic of China, while the Red Army would be redesignated as a unit of the national army; (3) a democratic system based on universal suffrage would be established in the special region; and (4) the confiscation of the land of landlords would cease.

In return, the KMT would be obliged to accept the following five points: (1) end the civil war; (2) provide democratic freedoms and release all political prisoners; (3) hold a conference of representatives from all parties to concentrate on saving the country; (4) make speedy preparations to resist Japan; and (5) make improvements in the people's livelihood. These terms were finally agreed to on September 22, 1937, two months after the Marco Polo Bridge incident of July 7, which signaled the all-out Japanese invasion of China.

Mao had achieved his objective of securing the new united front. For this he agreed to make concessions for the time being and to curtail the social revolution. This was justified and necessary because the invader constituted the greater enemy; unless China's sovereignty were maintained the social revolution itself would be even more difficult and further delayed. The new alliance would prove to work for a couple of years only, even though the Communists were to maintain the pretense for the duration of the war against Japan. While it did work, however, national unity was brought about in timely fashion, and the Communists were given respite to consolidate and expand their political program. Mao achieved these important objectives without having to concede either territory or effective control over his military capability. Taking advantage of the new situation, Mao characteristically made the most of his opportunities.

This is most intriguingly seen in Mao's taking time from his busy schedule to reflect upon Marxism-Leninism perhaps more deeply than previously. As a result of his effort, Mao gave talks and wrote his two most famous philosophical essays, "On Practice" and "On Contradiction." These writings have been criticized as lacking philosophical originality and profundity, but it is absurd to compare Mao's efforts with those of a professional philosopher. He didn't have such pretensions. "On Practice" is a relatively simple exercise in Marxist epistemology which stresses a proper relationship between theory and practice.[10] It was written specifically to expose the subjectivist errors of dogmatism and empiricism. Mao had in mind particularly his "dogmatic" opponents during the period 1931-34, and by implication those still of such a mind "who rejected the experience of the Chinese revolution." It was also critical of the "empiricists" "who could not see the revolution as a whole and who worked blindly even if industriously." The title was chosen because it stressed the exposure of dogmatism that belittled practice. Mao had long been, and would long remain, concerned that practical realities be taken fully into account, even if viewed from a theoretical perspective. Theory, in short, must be combined with practice.

"On Contradiction" is more abstruse; but it succeeds for the most part in expressing Mao's way of looking at the world and of analyzing it.[11] Contradictions inhere in all things both subjective (in the mind) and objective (in the real world). Of special importance to Mao was the need to make certain distinctions in the behavior of the omnipresent, ever-dynamic contradictions, particularly in their various manifestations of struggle. Twenty years later Mao would carry this distinction-making even further, defining the difference between antagonistic and nonantagonistic contradictions in society, and this would be credited as a creative theoretical contribution. In 1937, however, there were more immediate concerns. The two essays were published in July 1937, the month of Japan's invasion of North China. The fundamental notions of distinguishing between major and minor contradictions and of properly combining theory with practice required that Mao give attention to military considerations.

Mao dispatched the Eighth Route Army, the new designation of the Red Army under the united front, into Shansi province again, but this time at Yen Hsi-shan's invitation, and in the face of the mighty Japanese advance. Suddenly, Lin Piao inflicted a surprising, stinging defeat on a superior Japanese column at Pingshangkuan in northeastern Shansi in the fall of 1937, giving Chinese everywhere a timely morale boost. But such head-on major battles were mostly avoided afterward. Instead, Mao's forces concentrated upon expanding their reach and developing bases behind the Japanese lines. In this they were dramatically successful over the next few years. By the end of 1944, the Communists had established more than sixteen revolutionary base areas throughout north, central, and south China, controlling all or part of some 635 counties with an army of about one million men.[12] This expansion took place especially rapidly in 1937-38 in the vacuums left in the wake of Japanese offensives and KMT retreats.

Such a strategy was in accord with Mao's May 1938 essays "Problems of Strategy in Guerrilla War Against Japan" and "On Protracted War." In the first essay, Mao explained that in the circumstances of a war in which a large, weak country is attacked by a small, strong one, the enemy will have insufficient men to occupy the large country.[13] The many gaps left will invite the use of guerrillas who will fight along exterior lines independently of main forces, rather than along interior lines in support of them as under most other circumstances. China also had regular forces and mass support so that the total military picture required both an overall strategic view of the use of guerrillas and their use in special, unusual tasks. Such strategy must follow the primary principle of "preserving oneself and destroying the enemy." The specific strategic principles of the present war are: "1) the use of initiative, flexibility and planning in conducting offensives within the defensive, battles of quick decision within protracted war, and exterior-line operations within interior-line operations; 2) co-ordination with regular warfare; 3) establishment of base areas; 4) the strategic defensive and the strategic offensive; 5) the development of guerrilla warfare into mobile warfare; and 6) correct relationship of command."

In his "On Protracted War" Mao predicted the conflict would comprise three stages.[14] The first "covers the period of the enemy's strategic offensive and our strategic defensive." The second stage will see the enemy consolidate his conquests and "our preparation for the counter-offensive." The third stage will be the period of strategic counteroffensive and the enemy's strategic retreat. As the war actually turned out, however, there seemed to be only the two first stages, the war ending because of the pressures brought to bear by the United States primarily, with a strong last-minute input by the Soviet Union. The first stage lasted from July 1937 to December 1938. The KMT also fought some brave battles in this first period and at times brunted the inexorable Japanese advance. Chiang K'ai-shek's decision to rupture the dykes of the Yellow River near Chengchow in Honan province also delayed Japanese mechanized divisions, but only at the cost of indescribable suffering for millions of Chinese peasants for several years thereafter because of the widespread flooding and destruction. After the fall of Wuhan in October 1938 and his retirement into the refuge above the Yangtze gorges in Szechuan province, Chiang mostly satisfied himself with the maintenance of a tacit truce with the Japanese. This stalemate would be broken only twice until the Japanese surrender in August 1945. There was the dramatic Communist Hundred Regiments Offensive of August 1940 and a Japanese offensive in the summer of 1944.

The celebrated Hundred Regiments Offensive remains an interestingly controversial adventure. By the summer of 1940, the Communists were coming under increasing criticism for not actually engaging the Japanese in heavy battle. There also may have been restiveness in their ranks, to take on the Japanese in a real test of arms. Whatever the reason, on August 20, 1940, 115 regiments of the Eighth Route Army suddenly attacked communications lines of the enemy throughout North China. This impressive, wide-scale campaign lasted until December and inflicted heavy damage and casualties on the Japanese. However, except for the element of surprise which it did include the effort is uncharacteristic of Mao, and it has been claimed that it was undertaken by P'eng Teh-huai without Mao's approval.[15] Whatever the explanation the campaign was probably counterproductive for it elicited from the Japanese fearful reprisals, particularly in the infamous "three-all" (burn all, loot all, kill all) policy. This scorched-earth program reduced populations of Communist areas, and a tight blockage was now imposed on the Communist bases, particularly on Shen-Kan-Ning.

Military cooperation in the second united front was strained from the beginning. Many skirmishes and pitched battles had already occurred between Communist and KMT forces before the famous New Fourth Army Incident of January 1941, but this event effectively ended any further cooperation. The New Fourth Army was formed in September 1937, composed of survivors of various guerrilla bases in central China following the Long March. Yeh T'ing who had been a leader of the Nanchang Uprising was commander, and one of his ablest officers was Ch'en Yi, who would later become a foreign minister. The New Fourth Army carried out its guerrilla mission south of the Yangtze River but also created apprehensions in the KMT regarding ultimate intentions. Chiang K'ai-shek ordered the entire New Fourth Army to move to the north of the Yangtze. This order was obeyed. In January 1941 most of the troops had already crossed the river. However, about ten thousand unprotected headquarters personnel who were still to the south of the river waiting to cross were suddenly ambushed by an overwhelming body of KMT troops. In the battle that lasted several days about nine thousand Communists were killed including the deputy commander, Hsiang Ying. Yeh T'ing was taken prisoner. Chiang K'ai-shek declared the New Fourth Army dissolved, for breach of military discipline! The wave of indignation and sympathy that swept the nation was some consolation for Mao's partisans. It once again highlighted a difference between the two parties that the Communists were eager to make clear, i.e., that they were leading the fight against the Japanese while the KMT persisted in killing other Chinese in the midst of national crisis. Mao capitalized on the sentiment by continuing to follow united front policies where this was possible. This patient attitude and cooperative stance did the image of the Communists no harm, and they remained the most patriotic and attractive alternative for increasing numbers of Chinese. The maintenance of the united front also served the purpose of keeping the KMT awhile longer at bay, for a joint KMT-Japanese move on Yenan could have been too much to handle.

Mao's interest in making a success of the united front, so long as the Communists did not lose control over their territorial base and military arm, seems to have been genuine. His concept of new democracy was never spelled out, but it referred to what he conceived of as a necessary period or stage in China's development. His important talk on "New Democracy," of 1940, places this stage in a fuller perspective of Chinese history.[16] The stage of new democracy, preceding as it did socialism, was one in which other classes could unite under the leadership of the Communists. Mao practiced what he preached in this regard. Various efforts were made to encourage participation by various social elements in the political processes and administration of the Communist-controlled areas. Elections were held in these areas in 1937 and in 1941, the most democratic phenomena in China during these years. Again the KMT's central government in Chungking suffered by comparison. The very act of elections held on the basis of universal direct equal suffrage by secret ballot was strongly reformist as well as democratic. It spurred interest and participation in several new institutions that represented a break with the past. Thus even if class struggle and land redistribution were temporarily eschewed, the political processes would never again be the same. Even if many of the former elite continued to participate, they would no longer do so exclusively.

Remarkable opportunities were extended to other progressive elements to participate in government. The best example of this was in the famous *san san chih* or "three-thirds system" instituted in early 1940 despite the general collapse of the united front by this time.[17] In this three-thirds system the Communists limited themselves unilaterally to no more than a third of the positions in all government organs and councils in the base areas. Surprisingly, this system seems to have been adhered to throughout the remainder of the war period even though it created certain difficulties for the Communists. Yet it indelibly underscored Communist sincerity about making concessions in order to enable all patriotic elements to concentrate on the war effort. It also enjoined the Communists to develop with patience techniques of persuasion in order to win support in these mixed councils.

The Communists succeeded in the years 1937-41 in establishing a sizable, functional bureaucracy throughout the border region. Civil, military, and Party affairs were integrated in highly articulated circuits. The civil administration was modeled after that of a regular province of the KMT central government. In Shen-Kan-Ning, with a population of about 1,400,000 there were an estimated 7,900 full-time salaried officials.[18] They enjoyed differentiated salaries based on rank or office. The entire establishment evolved in a rather orderly process and promoted stability in the border regions. However, except for the two election campaigns of 1937 and 1941 there had been very little experience in mobilization-style politics. In 1941 there was a new, most serious crisis in the air.

Could such a stable bureaucracy cope with the new challenge presented by the blockades and pressures imposed by both the KMT and the Japanese? Could such a bureaucracy succeed in stimulating production that would offset the effect of the blockade, its shortages, and the inflation it brought about? Could it relieve the effect that inflation and taxation policies were having on the poor in particular? Could it sustain the determination to endure such hardships and deprivations in order to realize the objectives of defeating the Japanese and continuing the revolution? Could it, under conditions of increasing decentralization and expansion, both continue to be responsive to central direction and yet capable of exercising needed initiative at local levels? Was it properly indoctrinated in order to undertake such initiative in reasonable conformity to the purposes and policies of the Party? This was a special problem under the conditions of united front policies in which so many intellectuals and students and others had been attracted to Yenan. These were well-intentioned, patriotic individuals but their commitment to the Party was uncertain or negligible. Some of these people tended to exhibit urban or elitist attitudes which offended old-line and peasant leaders. The sudden tremendous expansion of the Party membership alone (twentyfold, from 40,000 to 800,000 members between 1937 and 1940) raised questions regarding the real commitment and the adequacy of indoctrination of the new members.

And there continued to exist the problem of Party unity along ideological and policy lines. There remained in the Party a sizable opposition group that was identified principally with Wang Ming, the erstwhile leader of the Twenty-eight Bolsheviks who had returned to China from Moscow in 1939. This group still represented a dogmatic, foreign-brand of Marxism that pained Mao, and from his point of view, threatened the chances of the Chinese Revolution. Mao had criticized such opposition point-blank during the Party's Sixth Plenum in early 1939. There he emphasized the need for the Sinification of Marxism. He declared that "Marxism must take on a national form before it can be applied. There is no such thing as abstract Marxism, but only concrete Marxism. . . . If a Chinese Communist who is a part of the great Chinese people, bound to his people by his very flesh and blood, talks of Marxism apart from Chinese peculiarities, this Marxism is merely an empty abstraction. The Sinification of Marxism—that is to say, making certain that in all of its manifestations it is imbued with Chinese peculiarities, using it according to these peculiarities—becomes a problem that must be understood and solved by the whole Party without delay. . . . We must put an end to writing eight-legged essays on foreign models." [19] This advice was followed by a study movement in 1939 and 1940 in the immediate area of Yenan, but the success of this effort was limited. Opposition cadres controlled important positions within the Party and border government and often effectively prevented the publication of or proper use of Mao's writings and talks.

Mao's response to this vexing situation was a distinctive one that would ever after remain a hallmark of his political style. In the next couple of years, 1942-44, a series of policies and programs were implemented that taken together have come to be regarded as the Yenan Way. Here mass-mobilization politics, encouraging education, and consciousness-lifting participation were emphasized. This was in contrast to the heavy reliance on stable bureaucratic techniques in the earlier years of the Second United Front. The successful implementation of mass campaigns, along with the sense of danger, the provocation, and the scarcities afforded by the KMT and Japanese threat, led to the renewal of revolutionary commitment and the instilling of both spartan and socialist values—albeit within the limiting united front framework. Thus the Communists came to exhibit all the more pride in their hard, selfless work and simple but purposeful living. Larger numbers learned in adversity to realize the spirit that had animated the Long Marchers. Mao's political genius in these years made its finest and most creative showing. He achieved nothing less than a revolution within the revolution.

Characteristically the revolutionary new program began as, and in many respects remained an educational process. Mao assumed the comfortable and natural role of the patient, perceptive, and far-sighted teacher. For years Mao had counseled his followers and opponents, on shortcomings within the movement. He had pointed the way in many talks and essays to the resolution of these and to the necessary line to follow. In all such criticism and advice, however, he always managed to retain a sense of perspective, of the need to cultivate and marshal scarce revolutionary resources. Men who would risk their lives for the revolution were to be patiently dealt with, and their talents properly and economically employed. Class background was irrelevant in the face of such overwhelming need and opposition, and the deficiencies of such social origin could be rectified with proper education and revolutionary experience. However much this view departs from pristine Marxism, it made good sense in the Chinese revolution.

On February 1, 1942, speaking before more than a thousand Party members in Yenan, Mao officially launched the extremely important *cheng feng* or rectification campaign.[20] One week later, on February 8, he followed up with a second lecture. In the first speech he inveighed against the evils of subjectivism and sectarianism within the Party. By subjectivism he meant "an unorthodox tendency in learning." This referred mainly to the proper relationship in Party work of theory and practice. Mao criticized those who knew or pretended to have theoretical knowledge but neglected to apply it in practice in a way that was consonant with practical requirements. He was criticizing those who continued to study Marxism in the abstract or who failed to learn properly the requirements of the Chinese situation. Such persons were dogmatists. Mao declared: "We do not study Marxism-Leninism because it is pleasing to the eye, or because it has some mystical value, like the doctrines of the Taoist priests who ascend Mao Shan to learn how to subdue devils and evil spirits. Marxism-Leninism has no beauty, nor has it any mystical value. It is only extremely useful." Those who regard Marxism-Leninism as a ready-made panacea have a type of childish blindness, "and we must start a movement to enlighten these people." Such dogmatists must be told: " 'Your dogma is of no use,' or to use an impolite phrase, 'Your dogma is less useful than excrement.' We see that dog excrement can fertilize the fields, and man's can feed the dog. And Dogmas? They can't fertilize the fields, nor can they feed a dog. Of what use are they?" [21]

Mao also castigated those guilty of empiricism, a form of subjectivism that failed to be guided by theory. He used the simile of the target and the arrow. "In shooting the arrow, you must have a target to aim at. The relation between Marxism-Leninism and the Chinese Revolution is the same as between the arrow and the target." Some comrades shoot arrows without a target. Others "merely take the arrow in hand, twist it back and forth, and say again and again in praise, 'excellent arrow, excellent arrow,' but are never willing to shoot it." What was required was that "the arrow of Marxism-Leninism must be used to hit the target of the Chinese Revolution." [22]

By sectarianism Mao referred to the various divisions among cadres, such as between old cadres and younger ones who had recently joined the Party. Such intra-Party differences were to be resolved in the interests of Party unity. Similarly a like problem in the Party's external relations required attention. Recognizing that the Party constituted merely a tiny minority of China's population, Mao warned his followers that "we have an obligation to cooperate with all who are willing and able to cooperate with us; we have absolutely no right to reject them." He emphasized that there is "no basis whatsoever for any action leading to separation from the masses." [23]

Mao laid down an important guideline in the conduct of the coming campaign. Two principles were to be respected. The first was: "Don't repeat past mistakes." The second: "Save men by curing their ills." Mao held that "past errors must be exposed with no thought of personal feelings and face." A scientific attitude "to analyze and criticize what has been undesirable in the past" is to be used "so that more care will be taken in later work, and so that work will be better performed."

Regarding the second principle, Mao explained that "our object in exposing errors and criticizing shortcomings is like that of a doctor in curing a disease. The whole purpose is to save people, not to cure them to death. If a man has appendicitis, the doctor performs an operation and the man is saved. If a person who commits an error, no matter how great, does not bring his disease to an incurable state by concealing it and persisting in his error, and if in addition he is genuinely and honestly willing to be cured, willing to make corrections, we will welcome him so that his disease may be cured and he may become a good comrade. It is certainly not possible to solve the problem by one flurry of blows for the sake of a moment's satisfaction." [24]

One week later, on February 8, 1942, Mao gave a second address before about eight hundred Party workers, this time on the subject of "formalism" in Party work.[25] He assailed the formalistic writers of "eight-legged essays" whose writings are like "the foot-bindings of a lazy old woman, long and foul-smelling," and "fighting poison with poison" called his essay "The Eight Great Charges!" These "charges" included such practices as "mouthing empty phrases," or "making a false show of authority to instill terror," or using "insipid language, empty as the pocket, stomach, and head of a vagrant," or "categorizing thoughts like drugs in a Chinese medicine shop," i.e., not using thoughtful analysis. Mao recognized that such formalism is the "propaganda tool and form of expression" of subjectivism and sectarianism. Thus it is necessary to eradicate it as well as the other errors. Recalling his simile of curing the sick man, Mao suggested a psychological technique that goes beyond usual educational practices. "The task must be performed properly, which means that a reasonable explanation must be given. If the explanation is very reasonable, if it is to the point, it can be effective. The first step in reasoning is to give the patient a powerful stimulus: yell at him, 'You're sick!' so the patient will have a fright and break out in an over-all sweat; then he can actually be started on the road to recovery." [26]

Now a vast machinery was put into motion throughout the Party in order to deal with these errors. The Central Committee studied and discussed the issues and then other high level organs in Yenan did so. On April 3, the Propaganda Bureau announced that the movement would consist of three stages. First, there was to be a period of study and discussion for two months at all Party schools and three months at Party organs. At the end of these periods, a general examination was held on Mao's two keynote speeches and twenty other documents. Important among these was an essay by Mao of May 5, 1941, entitled "Reform Our Study," and two Central Committee resolutions of July and August 1941, entitled respectively "On Strengthening the Party Spirit" and "On Investigation and Research," both of which may have been written by Mao. There were at least four other essays by Mao, two reports by K'ang Sheng, one essay by Liu Shao-ch'i, and one by Ch'en Yun. Also included among the study documents was the "Conclusion" from the *History of the Communist Party of the Soviet Union* and an article by Stalin. There were no entries from the Wang Ming faction of the Party. Clearly, even though some attention was given to certain limited Soviet materials, the emphasis was on writings by experienced Chinese leaders who were concerned about the realities and specific needs of the Chinese Revolution. The period of concentrated study of such texts helped to Sinify the Chinese Communist Party.

After the period of study, discussion, and examination there followed a period of investigation of Party work. These investigations were conducted on a decentralized basis, i.e., they were conducted by the investigated organ or school itself and not by some central agency. A third and final stage was devoted to drawing conclusions on the quality of each other's work, with reports submitted to higher levels for action. While incorrigible comrades were dismissed from the Party, a second and third chance was extended to those who confessed and indicated willingness to reform.

As the *cheng feng* campaign actually unfolded it took much longer than originally planned. Several more months were needed to extend down to the lower levels in the various bases beyond Shen-Kan-Ning. But this only made for a more thorough educative experience. The campaign was more intensively educational than previous such efforts in its techniques too. Discussions were conducted through small study groups which utilized the method of criticism and self-criticism to fully assimilate the study material. These sessions were often intense, and as such were effective both in setting aside old leadership techniques and in evolving new ones. Leaders were now forced repeatedly to confirm their legitimacy by explaining to their subordinates the reasons for policies. No longer could they afford to remain leaders who were somehow above and beyond criticism.

The campaign was not permitted to go to extremes of criticism. There was after all a war on, and the Communist position was an endangered one. The principle of "unity-criticism-unity" was enjoined and respected. This meant that the participants ostensibly started from a desire to achieve unity and then by means of honest, open criticism and struggle resolved the outstanding contradictions or problems, therefore achieving the desired unity on an approved basis.

By all accounts the campaign was a smashing success, even though many dissidents undoubtedly kept their mouths shut rather than court further abuse. The campaign seems to have remained essentially an educational movement. There is little credible evidence that it was a purge, and it was not regarded as such. Certainly it differed remarkably from the Soviet purge. In the 1933–35 Soviet "cleansing" 270,000 Russian Communist members were brutally dealt with,[27] being subjected to terror, torture, imprisonment, and execution. Conversely, Mao's *cheng feng* campaign records no instance of such treatment, even of the known oppositionists. Wang Ming, perhaps the chief opponent of Mao, was demoted in these years to the position of principal of a girl's school in Yenan. But he retained his position on the Party Central Committee. Instead of the Party diminishing in size, it continued to expand.

As the *cheng feng* campaign settled into its first stage in May of 1942, Mao convened the famous "Talks at the Yenan Forum on Literature and Art." Intellectuals whose training in and commitment to Marxism-Leninism were uncertain were invited to participate on May 2 in an exchange of ideas on the relationship between work in the literary and artistic fields and revolutionary responsibilities in general. Questions of standpoint, attitude, audience, and study were raised in Mao's introductory speech.[28] Apparently a lively discussion ensued which revealed the suspected uncertainty and the differences of opinions current in the ranks of the revolutionary intellectuals. Mao suggested the proper answers to the questions raised in his introductory talk, but in his concluding remarks at a final meeting on May 23, 1942, he spelled out the answers in greater detail.[29] In so doing, he established the guidelines for revolutionary intellectuals for years to come. Even though there would be departures in practice, reflecting continued misunderstandings or basic subterranean disagreements, the Yenan Talks are celebrated even today more than thirty years afterward.

"The first problem is," Mao asserted, "literature and art for whom?" [30] Manifestly it is for the four kinds of people who constitute the overwhelming majority of the Chinese nation, the workers, peasants, soldiers, and urban petty bourgeoisie. In serving these broad masses, Mao reminded his listeners, it is important to take the standpoint of the proletariat. Even though all revolutionary artists and writers are sympathetic to the masses they still tend to use the petty-bourgeois standpoint and avoid living among and depicting the life and thinking of the masses. Artist and writers "must gradually move their feet over to the side of the . . . proletariat, through the process of going into their very midst and into the thick of practical struggles and through the process of studying Marxism and society. Only in this way can we have a literature and art that are truly for the workers, peasants and soldiers, a truly proletarian literature and art." This injunction is a clear enunciation of Mao's unorthodox Marxist belief that one's class consciousness can be changed through an act of will and by means of proper education. Proletarian consciousness is not dependent upon economic class origin alone, nor, by extension, is a revolutionary movement's consciousness necessarily reliant on the economic substructure of society. Else how could proletarians share national New Democratic leadership in a society that was still basically agrarian?

Having determined whom to serve, Mao raised the next problem of "how to serve." Should attention be devoted to raising standards or to popularization? Mao made it clear that both are required, but that since the starting point must be the workers, peasants, and soldiers, popularization takes precedence. "For them," he said, "the prime need is not 'more flowers on the brocade' but 'fuel in snowy weather.' " [31] Standards should be raised subsequently as the cultural level of the masses rises.

Mao made no bones about his view that art and literature served political ends. He granted that the study of Marxism would harm the creative mood. "Yes, it does. It definitely destroys creative moods that are feudal, bourgeois, petty-bourgeois, liberalistic, individualist, nihilist, art-for-art's sake, aristocratic, decadent or pessimistic, and every other creative mood that is alien to the masses of the people and to the proletariat." [32]

Mao proposed a couplet from a poem by Lu Hsun as a motto for writers and artists:

Fierce-browed, I coolly defy a thousand pointing fingers,
Head-bowed, like a willing ox I serve the children.

He challenged his colleagues never to yield to the enemy symbolized by the phrase "a thousand pointing fingers," and to be "oxen" for the "children," i.e., the masses, "bending their backs to the task until their dying day." But "intellectuals who want to integrate themselves with the masses, who want to serve the masses, must go through a process in which they and the masses come to know each other well. This process may, and certainly will, involve much pain and friction, but if you have the determination, you will be able to fulfil these requirements." [33]

Mao spoke with added conviction on the subject of art and literature because he was bolstered in his views by his beautiful young wife, Lan P'ing, who saw eye to eye with him in this critical area. Lan P'ing had been an actress in Shanghai and had been drawn to Yenan like so many other young, sensitive intellectuals and artists. Soon after her arrival in Yenan in 1937 she took the name Chiang Ch'ing—perhaps it was given to her by Mao. The two fell in love, but their romance was complicated by Mao's marriage to Ho Tzu-chen, whom Mao had married in 1931. There was much rumbling among Mao's comrades when the marriage was dissolved in 1938 and after Mao and Chiang Ch'ing were married in April 1939. However, the marriage obviously made Mao happy, and his new wife was to prove a real help to him in times of crisis.

Along with the *cheng feng* campaign of 1942–44, and the admonition to intellectual workers to study and integrate with the masses, there were other campaigns that collectively give the later Yenan period its distinctive character.

Between December 1941 and December 1942 there was held the significant campaign for "crack troops and simple administration," which reduced the number of organs and personnel in the military and in the government bureaucracy. The movement was a response to the intense economic blockade of the period and was designed to lighten the tax burden on the hard-pressed peasant. It overfulfilled its target of a 20 percent reduction of personnel. But more important, it proved to be a salutary attack on entrenched bureaucracy that strengthened lower-level leadership and increased popular participation in government. The independence of bureaucratic government organs was curtailed. District magistrates and party officials assumed broad coordinating powers. The focus of government shifted downward to the township and the village.[34]

The *hsia-hsiang* or "to-the-village" campaign began in July 1941 with cadres and students going to the countryside to help harvest grain. This practice of using "nonproductive" labor to help overcome seasonal labor shortages would continue in subsequent years. But this limited usage of visitors from the urban areas soon developed into a broader concept in which the visitors could perform other useful roles as well and learn from a wider experience with the masses. In conjunction with the *cheng feng* campaign, hundreds of intellectuals and students from Yenan began making extensive contacts with villagers in the spring of 1942. The objective was to provide shared experiences between peasant and intellectual that would reduce the enormous differences between them, to bridge the gulf between city and country, and erode the distinctions between manual and mental labor. The intellectuals could learn a great deal from the peasants that would both sober and enrich their life, but they had much to contribute as well. As educated outsiders they could help develop rural literacy. They could give fresh imaginative thought to endemic rural problems and impart a wider perspective leading to progressive programs. The experience often brought social friction and sometimes led to local power struggles, but it also generated enthusiasm and a sense of meaningful participation on the part of many. It was a concrete follow-through to the advice provided at the Yenan Forum on Literature and Art. It also reflected the personnel changes of the "crack troops and simple administration" campaign. The cadres shifted from various bureaucratic organs to the local scene played an especially vital role in forwarding the transformation of rural society.[35]

Another campaign promoted the reduction of rent and interest. This followed the issuance on January 28, 1942, of Mao's first major statement on land policy since the Japanese invasion. Still restricted by the restraints of the united front policy of nonexpropriation and nonredistribution of landlords' lands, the Party now began more vigorously to insist on a proper reduction of rent and interest. This was a tremendous relief to many peasants particularly in areas that had not previously experienced the land revolution. For all too many the tyranny of exorbitant rent and the usurious exactions of the moneylender were a greater hardship than the lack of land. Although care was taken to insure the collection of due rent and interest, the campaign helped to bring to the surface an activist peasant leadership that would go on to lead the way in restructuring village social and political relationships.[36]

An exceedingly important and significant movement was the mutual aid, cooperative campaign that began on January 25, 1943.[37] This was a risky adventure for Mao because it called for interference with accepted farming practice in the countryside. The campaign had to show positive results to skeptical peasants or be condemned as a failure. However, Mao experimented here in an extremely important area with profound implications. For only by initiating such a socioeconomic institutional change could serious problems of poverty and production be resolved. Mao was aware that cooperatives could not be imposed from above, that local conditions and sensitivities had to be taken into account. Mao reasoned that the organizational basis for mutual aid had to be social units of limited size; townships or any administrative units were too large and artificial. The natural village was the logical unit. The problem here, however, was that the traditional forms of labor cooperation in such units were bound up with complex social relationships, and these were not easily penetrated from the outside. Thus, the Communists were confronted with the dilemma of needing to work through natural social organizations yet still penetrate them in order to provide direction. This could only be done with great sensitivity, flexibility, and persistence.

The campaign had some success. Just prior to its launching in 1943 only 15 percent of the border region's full-time labor force was formed into mutual-aid teams. In 1944 reports claimed 50 to 75 percent participation, although in 1945 there was a period of retrenchment and consolidation, with only 28 to 45 percent participation. The creation of mutual-aid teams, a functioning socioeconomic organizational entity beyond the family unit, would be of great importance, it was hoped, in elevating the peasants' consciousness and in creating the possibility of further beneficial changes in society. The cooperative was to constitute a nongovernmental intermediary between the state and the family. In Mao's vision it would eventually become the focus of economic, social, political and military life of the community, in which wide popular participation would be encouraged and expected. This movement in 1943 was the first bold step in the direction leading ultimately to the commune of the late 1950s.

In 1943 a production movement, actually called a "production war," was launched on several fronts.[38] The purpose was to create a self-sufficient and more prosperous economy on the basis of cooperation and participation, in the face of the tight economic blockade. Several important experimental practices had an immediately salutary effect and would come to be integral elements of Mao's revolutionary model for the future.

One of these was the system of "organizational production." This technique, inspired by necessity, was predicated on the notion that men and women in all fields of endeavor could make direct contributions of productive, physical labor. In the military, the greatest reservoir of manpower, when the personnel were not soldiering, they did productive labor. The military was enjoined to attain considerable self-sufficiency, i.e., through raising its own food and producing many of its own necessities. Mao's injunction to achieve 80 percent self-sufficiency proved an impossible goal, but by 1944 the military did achieve an impressive measure of self-sufficiency and this proved to be a stimulus for the entire economy. Of course, this practice also helped relieve the tax burden of the peasantry and became one more feature of the Communist military that made it popular. It was a dramatic contrast to the unsavory behavior and reputation of the KMT military.

Such participation in productive, physical labor was not limited to the army. All cadres in the government and Party were similarly expected to engage in production. This economic form of participation was a counterpart of the cadres' political participation in small group discussions. The practice contributed to a sense of solidarity and camaraderie throughout society, and it effectively eroded the traditional distinction between mental and manual labor.

The production movement also used labor heroes as objects of emulation. Beginning in the summer of 1943 each village, township, and district selected, honored, and rewarded outstanding workers. The campaign concluded that fall with a conference in Yenan attended by 180 labor heroes from the border region. In his address to them Mao declared, "Among the Chinese people there are in fact thousands upon thousands of 'Chukeh Liangs,' every village, every town having its own." [39] This is a reference to the crafty and resourceful hero of the Three Kingdoms era, and Mao, with his knowledge of his people, recognized that there were always such resourceful individuals whose experience and services ought to be properly respected and used. Hence, Mao's articulation of the essence of the "mass line" rings of conviction. "We should go to the masses and learn from them, synthesize their experience into better articulated principles and methods, then do propaganda among the masses, and call upon them to put these principles and methods into practice so as to solve their problems and help them achieve liberation and happiness." [40] Thus the source of ideas and inspiration were those creative individuals among the people, and while the Party had the responsibility of mastering these ideas and generalizing them and acquainting others with their import and utility, and of providing adroit guidance, it was up to the people themselves ultimately to put the ideas into practice. It was the talent and leadership rooted in the community itself that in the end would determine how fast and how far social and economic practices would be transformed.

The "mass line" permeated the campaigns of the late Yenan period. It is the most distinguishing feature of Mao's program in these years. The active, conscious participation of the masses and of lower level leaders in the political, social, and economic matters that affected their lives was the key to spirited outreaches of effort, to raised production, and to needful changes if fundamental problems of society were to be resolved. But if the masses were to continue making such contributions to progressive change this would have to depend upon more than the enthusiasm generated by limited, temporary mobilization campaigns.

It was necessary to create permanent educational institutions that would provide continued learning opportunities for the masses, whose vision and capabilities were restricted by illiteracy and a low cultural level. Mao recognized that "unless the masses are awakened and willing, any kind of work that needs their participation will turn out to be an empty formality and end in failure." Only the long-term socialization process that education affords could provide the requisite learning and instill the desired values and attitudes that would successfully transform society. But changes were needed to begin with in the concept and the institutional structure of education itself. Education had to be provided extensively and economically throughout society. The curriculum had to be meaningful and relevant to the needs of the people. Hence new priorities and new experiments were implemented.

This effort in 1944 took on many of the features of the other campaigns.[41] Regular education was not ignored, nor was there any desire to sacrifice quality, but greater attention was now given to spreading the benefits of education rather than to further development of existing "elitist" institutions. Mao's strategy was to try to develop education along both mass and elitist lines in a kind of united front policy of education, another instance of his anxiety not to squander precious resources even while excitedly engaged in bold, idealistic innovations. Education became decentralized, with authority shifted from higher, professional levels of administration to local levels. Half-time schools were instituted, giving for many unprecedented opportunities. The curriculum was fused into the actual social and economic life of the local community. The popularization of education movement of 1944–45 did much to promote literacy and a new appreciation for health, hygiene, cooperative labor, and new art forms. Many mistakes were made, perhaps more than in any other endeavor as the Communists themselves admitted. Yet Peter Seybolt is probably right in saying that in "the process of learning and correcting these mistakes, it [the CCP] gained valuable experience in the application of a cardinal principle . . . a revolution for the people must be carried out by the people." [42] However, in the press of events over the next few years many of these reforms were not given the priority attention they received at the outset, and some fell into abeyance. Many would be resurrected in the future.

The success of Mao's programs and style of leadership was attested to in the accounts of most impartial visitors to Yenan, beginning with Edgar Snow's visit in 1936 to the reports of members of the American Dixie Mission in 1944–45. The latter was a military observation team which the Americans sent to the Communists partially because of their role in the fight against Japan.

Mao's leadership of the Party was resoundingly confirmed in the spring of 1945. On April 20, the Seventh Plenum of the Sixth Central Committee adopted the important document "Resolution on Some Questions in the History of Our Party," which provided an analysis of past correct and erroneous lines, clearly indicating the rectitude of Mao's own policies.[43] The resolution specifically hailed Mao's "integration of the universal truth of Marxism-Leninism with the actual practice of the Chinese Revolution." Three days later the Party's Seventh Congress convened and Mao's leadership received highest marks.

The Seventh Congress was held in Yenan from April 23 to June 11, 1945, with some 544 delegates and 208 alternates, representing a Party membership of 1,210,000. The Congress elected a new Central Committee and adopted a new Party constitution. Mao was made chairman of the Central Committee, and of its Political Bureau. He was also chairman in turn of the Political Bureau's Secretariat. Every major speaker at the congress praised Mao's achievements. Liu Shao-ch'i stressed Mao's accomplishments in uniting Marxist theory with Chinese realities and in the development of the theory and methods of the mass line. Liu said that Mao "is not only the greatest revolutionary statesman in Chinese history, but also its greatest theoretician and scientist." [44] The 1945 constitution codified Mao's clear-cut ascendancy. It regarded "the thought of Mao Tse-tung" and the theories of Marxism-Leninism from which it stemmed "as the guiding principles of all" of the Party's work.

Such lavish praise and the securing of his place as undisputed leader of the Chinese Communist movement appeared to be the apex of a Mao cult that had been underway for some years in Yenan. How much this was consciously manipulated is hard to say. There might have been some desire to exploit Mao's favorable image both in the interests of promoting unity about a father figure, a political technique that was familiar to the Chinese, in the face both of the remaining Japanese opponent and the alternative, somewhat tarnished national figure, Chiang K'ai-shek. There can be little question, however, that much of this regard for Mao was genuine. Many of the common people of the liberated areas must have responded positively to a leader whose policies so obviously had their interests at heart, a phenomenon that must have been especially unique in a country that in recent years had only known war, warlordism, and governmental inattention or exploitation. And most of Mao's colleagues must likewise have been genuinely persuaded of the validity and effectiveness of many of his innovative ideas and actions. As for those who disagreed, since Mao was so popular at the time, it would be necessary for them to dissemble for the moment, or to remain quiet. There would be opportunities later for such oppositionists to assert themselves.

The principal speech at the Seventh Congress, entitled "On Coalition Government" was delivered by Mao on April 24, 1945.[45] After eight years of terrible war the Japanese were on the verge of defeat. But China remained disunited and in grave crisis. Mao reviewed the differences between the Communists and the KMT both in their conduct of the war against the Japanese, and in the quality of government and the condition of the people in their respective areas. The KMT abandoned vast territories and populations to the Japanese and only passively resisted the Japanese while opposing its own people. The Communists, on the other hand, through people's war liberated vast territories and their people. The KMT forces "have shrunk to less than half their original size and most of them have virtually lost their combat effectiveness" . . . and in the KMT areas "there is a profound rift between this clique and the broad masses and a grave crisis of mass impoverishment, seething discontent and widespread revolt." On the other hand, Communist armed forces had expanded tremendously and they "set a heroic example in fighting Japan." They also set an example in carrying out the democratic policies of the united front. In fact, the Communists affirmed in 1937 that Sun Yatsen's Three People's Principles are what China needed, and these were "completely carried into effect in China's Liberated Areas."

Mao noted too that negotiations with the KMT had been unsuccessful. The KMT had rejected the Communist proposals for abolishing the one-party dictatorship, forming a coalition government, and instituting essential democratic reforms. The KMT had been "unwilling to introduce a single one of the urgently needed democratic reforms, such as the abolition of the secret police, the annulment of the reactionary laws and decrees that suppress the people's freedom, the release of political prisoners, recognition of the legal status of the political parties, recognition of the Liberated Areas and the withdrawal of the armies blockading and attacking them."

Nevertheless, Mao still hoped to attract support from some KMT members as well as from political independents. He still proposed a form of coalition government. This was necessary at this stage of history, when New Democracy was needed by the Chinese people, i.e., "a united-front democratic alliance based on the overwhelming majority of the people, under the leadership of the working class." It was still too early for socialism in China, but it was now too late for the old type of national-bourgeois state. The Communists, not the bourgeoisie, would lead the New Democratic coalition, whose politics would consist of overthrowing both external oppression and internal feudal and fascist oppression.

Mao outlined the democratic characteristics of the new state he envisioned. It even allowed for the growth of private capital and the protection of private property as long as this benefited the people. This program involved socialist factors, such as the political leadership and cooperative sectors of the economy, but its fulfillment "will not turn China into a socialist society." Mao was speaking of a stage of China's development.

So as not to be misunderstood, or regarded as deceitful or hypocritical, Mao immediately declared: "We Communists do not conceal our political views. Definitely and beyond all doubt, our future or maximum programme is to carry China forward to socialism and communism. Both the name of our Party and our Marxist world outlook unequivocally point to this supreme ideal of the future, a future of incomparable brightness and splendour." But for now, Mao explained, the democratic interlude is required. "It is a law of Marxism that socialism can be attained only via the stage of democracy. And in China the fight for democracy is a protracted one. It would be a sheer illusion to try to build a socialist society on the ruins of the colonial, semi-colonial and semi-feudal order without a united new-democratic state, without the development of the state sector of the new-democratic economy, of the private capitalist and the cooperative sectors, and of a national, scientific and mass culture, i.e., a new-democratic culture, and without the liberation and the development of the individuality of hundreds of millions of people—in short, without a thoroughgoing bourgeois-democratic revolution of a new type led by the Communist Party." Hence, Mao noted that Communists actually encouraged capitalism in certain given conditions. "It is not domestic capitalism but foreign imperialism and domestic feudalism which are superfluous in China today; indeed, we have too little of capitalism."

Mao pointed out the reasons for the strength of the Party at its present juncture. "Armed with Marxist-Leninist theory, the Communist Party of China has brought a new style of work to the Chinese people, a style of work which essentially entails integrating theory with practice, forging close links with the masses and practicing self-criticism."

Ideology, properly utilized, is important. Mao explained that "the universal truth of Marxism-Leninism, which reflects the practice of proletarian struggle throughout the world, becomes an invincible weapon for the Chinese people when it is integrated with the concrete practice of the revolutionary struggle of the Chinese proletariat and people."

"The people, and the people alone, are the motive force in the making of world history." This quote may be the best-known from Mao's speech "On Coalition Government." It underscores Mao's insight into the role and power of the masses and the need to relate the Party closely to this force. He reaffirmed therefore, that a "hallmark distinguishing our Party from all other political parties is that we have very close ties with the broadest masses of the people. Our point of departure is to serve the people wholeheartedly and never for a moment divorce ourselves from the masses, to proceed in all cases from the interests of the people."

Finally, "conscientious practice of self-criticism is still another hallmark distinguishing our Party from all other political parties. As we say, dust will accumulate if a room is not cleaned regularly, our faces will get dirty if they are not washed regularly. Our comrade's minds and our Party's work may also collect dust, and also need sweeping and washing.'' This point is indeed a distinguishing feature of Mao's management of the Party, for he went far beyond the Soviet party's practice in this regard. He realized that educative criticism and self-criticism were necessary to keep the Party responsive. The *cheng feng* campaign had been a notable innovation, and in future years he would make further innovations to maintain the effectiveness of such techniques. Always, the guiding principle would remain that of ''curing the sickness in order to save the patient'' and ''to learn from past mistakes to avoid future ones.''

Mao also outlined the specific program of the Party which was discussed under ten headings: the war, coalition government, people's freedom, unity, military, land, industry, culture, education and intellectuals, minority nationalities, and foreign policy. Moderation underscored Party work in each of these areas. For example, Mao again emphasized that agrarian reform would be limited for the time being to the reduction of rent and interest.

With regard to intellectuals, Mao acknowledged China's need for large numbers, but insisted that ''they must be imbued with the spirit of serving the people and must work hard.'' Mao also called for the establishment of China's ''own new national, scientific and mass culture and education.'' With regard to foreign culture, ''it would be a wrong policy to shut it out, rather we should as far as possible draw on what is progressive in it for use in the development of China's new culture; it would also be wrong to copy it blindly, rather we should draw on it critically to meet the actual needs of the Chinese people.'' Mao applied the same reasoning to China's own legacy: ''Similarly, ancient Chinese culture should neither be totally rejected nor blindly copied, but should be accepted discriminatingly so as to help in the progress of China's new culture.''

On foreign policy, Mao took pains to warn the United States ''to pay serious attention to the voice of the Chinese people and not to impair friendship with them.'' He said, ''if any foreign government helps the Chinese reactionaries and opposes the Chinese people's democratic cause, it will be committing a gross mistake.''

Mao had reason to be concerned about the United States. Despite the warmth of the relationship that prevailed between most Americans who visited Yenan and their Communist hosts there had already been unfortunate developments that threatened future prospects. Among the most unfortunate of these was the recall of General Joseph "Vinegar Joe" Stilwell from China at the insistence of Chiang K'ai-shek. The Communists had agreed to place their armies under the command of an American military commander-in-chief in China. But Stilwell's pressure on Chiang to fight the war led to the latter's implacable enmity and his own recall, and the end of the scheme for serious use of combined Chinese forces against Japan.[46]

The other unfortunate development was General Patrick Hurley's assignment to China in August 1944.[47] This man, a rich Oklahoma political appointee was singularly incompetent to handle such a delicate and complex job. En route to China via the Soviet Union he had reportedly learned from Molotov that the Chinese Communists were not genuine Marxists but "radish" Communists, "red on the outside, white on the inside." Lacking the wit to discern Soviet impatience with Mao in such an assessment, Hurley believed it. In China he tried to persuade Chiang K'ai-shek of this naive insight and pressed for a coalition government. On November 7, 1944, Hurley flew to Yenan, where he astounded Mao and his colleagues by giving an unexpected Indian war whoop as he emerged from his plane. Mao was further surprised to find that Hurley not only agreed to the Communist demands but actually strengthened them somewhat. Hurley signed the document stating the Communist position, then returned to Chungking. Mao had the measure of this man when after finding that Chiang K'ai-shek would not agree, Hurley reneged on his assurances and thereafter became a partisan supporter of Chiang's position. This turn of events ended Chinese Communist interest in fuller active relations with the United States. This was unfortunate, for in the preceding weeks there was even talk that Mao and Chou En-lai might visit the United States for high-level talks. However, on April 2, 1945, only three weeks before the Seventh Congress, Hurley declared that there could be no more American cooperation with the Chinese Communists. Mao's warning must be seen in this light.

Mao gave the concluding address of the Seventh Congress on June 11, 1945. In it he expressed his firm resolution and indomitable spirit by recalling the old Chinese fable called "The Foolish Old Man Who Removed the Mountains." [48]

> *It tells of an old man who lived in northern China long, long ago and was known as the Foolish Old Man of North Mountain. His house faced south and beyond his doorway stood the two great peaks, Taihang and Wangwu, obstructing the way. He called his sons, and hoe in hand they began to dig up these mountains with great determination. Another greybeard, known as the Wise Old Man, saw them and said derisively, 'How silly of you to do this! It is quite impossible for you few to dig up these two huge mountains.' The Foolish Old Man replied, 'When I die, my sons will carry on; when they die, there will be my grandsons, and they their sons and grandsons, and so on to infinity. High as they are, the mountains cannot grow any higher and with every bit we dig, they will be that much lower. Why can't we clear them away?' Having refuted the Wise Old Man's wrong view, he went on digging every day, unshaken in his conviction. God was moved by this, and he sent down two angels, who carried the mountains away on their backs.*

The story had immediate relevance in Mao's view: "Today, two big mountains lie like a dead weight on the Chinese people. One is imperialism, the other is feudalism. The Chinese Communist Party has long made up its mind to dig them up. We must persevere and work unceasingly, and we, too, will touch God's heart. Our God is none other than the masses of the Chinese people. If they stand up and dig together with us, why can't these two mountains be cleared away?"

This might have sounded like so much bravado coming from any other man. But any one by now who knew of Mao's achievements despite mountainous obstacles in the past should have been impressed and forewarned. Four years later Chiang's armies would be reeling under the final onslaughts of the People's Liberation Army, and Mao would usher in a new era in history.

FIVE
Completing the First Step of a Long March

After eight long years of terrible war in China, the Japanese surrendered on August 14, 1945. The Communists under Mao Tse-tung acquitted themselves well in the course of this national struggle and took full advantage of the opportunities it provided. From a state of near annihilation only months before the war began, they had, by the end of the war, acquired control over an effective and popular military organization of about 1.5 million men. Instead of being dispirited by the war, they emerged with buoyant spirits, confident of ultimate victory over their civil foes, the KMT under Chiang K'ai-shek. However, their estimate of the prospects ahead was a sober one. No one, including Mao, thought that the impending renewed civil war would take less than a decade to decide.

Even in this the Chinese Communists were optimistic in comparison to the assessment of others. The Soviet Union thought little of the prospects of their Chinese comrades and accordingly continued relations with the KMT government as if it would long endure. This was underscored by the Sino-Soviet Friendship Treaty signed on August 14, 1945. The Americans had few illusions about the quality of KMT governance, but few among them could see any chance of Communist victory. General Albert Wedemeyer, then commander of U.S. forces in China, said on October 17, 1945, that Chiang had "sufficient power to cope with the Chinese Communists provided they do not receive greatly increased aid from Russia. At present the Chinese Communists are not strong militarily as they have no air or artillery and no competent military advisers." [1] Such were the perceptions of the Russians, who incidentally never did give appreciable assistance to the Chinese Communists, and of Americans in those innocent days before Mao's awesome surge to power, and before the Vietnam disaster which would occur a generation later because the lesson that Mao would now provide was so inadequately comprehended. Nevertheless, looking at the situation in the conventional fashion that was then ingrained, the KMT did appear to have an overwhelming advantage. They possessed almost three-to-one superiority in fighting men, and at least five-to-one in terms of men in arms. The KMT also enjoyed an impressive absolute monopoly in air and naval forces. They had overwhelming superiority in firepower that could be brought to bear with artillery, air bombardment, and mechanized units. They had the advantage of being the legitimate government whose leader, Chiang K'ai-shek, was regarded as head of one of the five big powers, thanks largely to the insistence of President Franklin Roosevelt. Chiang's prestige was at an all-time high in the exuberance of Japan's defeat, and he had the important support of the United States.

This support was critical because it not only meant tremendous supplies of war material, financial assistance, and military advice, but it quickly made a great deal of difference in tactical terms. The Chinese Communists had the initial advantage at war's end of being in command of the situation in North China by virtue of their penetration and work in this part of the country during the war. In the scramble to extend territory when the Japanese suddenly surrendered they further improved their excellent position in order to consolidate their control and to handle the surrender of Japanese in north China. However, this squatter advantage was largely offset when the Americans intervened with decisions that clearly supported the KMT. General MacArthur, as supreme commander of the Allied Powers in Japan, directed the Japanese in China to surrender only to the KMT, while those in Manchuria were to surrender to the Soviet Union. In addition, the Americans

transported up to 500,000 KMT soldiers from their previously sequestered position in central China to the north and east. Thus the KMT
was able to disarm more than 1.25 million Japanese troops, compared
to 30,000 by the Chinese Communists within China Proper. In Manchuria the situation was less clear and the Communists may have
received many of the arms of the half-million Japanese there. Other
than this, however, the Russians seem to have been of little help to
their Chinese comrades. Stalin was bent on using the Chinese Communists in order to gain influence with the KMT government, not on
encouraging their desire for ultimate victory.[2]

Under these circumstances, it is understandable that Mao would
move cautiously and seek to use whatever political or military opportunities that were available. It would become clear years later during
the Cultural Revolution of the mid-1960s that he also had to contend
with and perhaps make concessions to colleagues, including Liu
Shao-ch'i, who supposedly cherished the "sweet dream of peaceful
transition" in the hope that the KMT would provide "peace and democracy." Mao complained that some were putting "their faith only in
political influence, fancying that problems can be solved only by influence." [3] The intra-Party debate was undoubtedly enlivened by the use
of the atom bomb on Japan and by the question of the role in China of
the United States and the Soviet Union. But while such considerations
might have given pause to some comrades and increased their pes-
simism, they only seemed to strengthen Mao's determination. Mao
claimed that it was a big mistake to believe that the atom bomb is all-
powerful. Such weapons would be of no avail without the struggles
waged by the people. As for the United States, Mao declared that its
"imperialism while outwardly strong is inwardly weak." It could not
stop the spread of revolution. A year later, Mao would coin the phrase
"paper tiger" in describing American imperialism. The new Soviet
treaty with the KMT must have disturbed the Communists, but Mao,
who ardently believed in self-reliance anyway, made no issue of it. All
people opposed to imperialism are our friends, he said, "Nevertheless,
we stress regeneration through our own efforts." [4]

It does seem clear that despite the undulations of Communist policy
and statements over the next few months, Mao remained firm in his
resolve to achieve victory. Mao acknowledged that the KMT would

take most of the large cities with American aid, but the Communists would contest control of medium and small towns. He said that certain areas would be given up for tactical advantage but that "our policy is to give tit for tat and fight for every inch of land; we will never let the Kuomintang easily seize our land and kill our people." Therefore, the Communists continued their program of territorial expansion, withdrawal from exposed areas, and war preparation. By the end of 1945 these activities are claimed to have resulted in their gaining control of about a fourth of China with a population of 149 million.[5]

However, simultaneously with this obvious beginning of the drive for power, Mao remained open to negotiations. The Communists used the phrase "Fight, fight, talk, talk," to describe this dual program. On August 24, 1945, Mao accepted Chiang K'ai-shek's third invitation to reopen negotiations in Chungking. On the twenty-eighth, Mao flew to Chungking, accompanied by Chou En-lai and Ambassador Patrick Hurley. Soon after his arrival Mao astonished observers by giving a toast to Chiang K'ai-shek's longevity.

The negotiations took forty-three days and covered the issues of political representation, the "nationalization" of armies, the manner of selection of local officials, the Communist base areas, among others. The Communists made concessions, such as the agreement to withdraw from exposed bases which was militarily advisable in any case and which additionally gave the appearance of seriousness in achieving a peaceful settlement. Mao may have become more optimistic of such a resolution, for he reported that the KMT "has accepted the principles of peace and unity." He explained later that if the KMT would launch "civil war again, it will put itself in the wrong in the eyes of the whole nation and the whole world, and we shall have all the more reason to smash its attacks by a war of self-defence." [6] This was an important position to have maneuvered the KMT into, because at the time, the KMT, aware of its apparent superior military strength, was probably more anxious than the Communists to have the full-scale test of arms. A political settlement, on the other hand, would leave the Communists free to carry on the work of "legal struggle" in the cities and even in the KMT army itself, which was precisely what Chiang would want to prevent. The October 10 agreement proposed the convening of a Political Consultative Conference, to represent all groups, to discuss questions of the democratic reorganization of government, and to approve a new constitution. A committee of three, composed of a KMT member, a Communist, and an American, was established to supervise military reorganization. Details were left to Chou En-lai to continue to negotiate. Mao returned to Yenan.

The continued negotiations proved especially difficult, and the question of the appointment of officials in the Communist liberated areas was insoluble. This along with continued hostilities on both sides made the October 10 agreement valueless. On November 26, 1945, General Hurley resigned as ambassador, claiming that his efforts had been undermined by several American foreign service officers in China, and thereby signaling the beginning of the unfortunate McCarthy witch-hunt period in post-World War II American politics. Actually the men Hurley referred to, particularly, John Stewart Service, provided amazingly accurate, perceptive, and balanced reporting of the situation. Unfortunately, their vindication would be delayed for a quarter-century. On the day following Hurley's resignation, President Harry S. Truman appointed America's greatest military hero, General George C. Marshall, as his special representative to China. The post of ambassador was taken up in July 1946, by J. Leighton Stuart.

The Chinese Communists showed renewed interest in negotiations almost immediately. They agreed to take part in the Political Consultative Conference, now scheduled for January 1946. They welcomed the arrival of General Marshall and President Truman's statement of December 15, 1945, calling for a "strong, united, democratic China," which was taken as indicating support for a coalition government. Chou En-lai proposed a cease-fire during the sessions of the PCC. With General Marshall's help this was agreed to on January 10, 1946, with the cease-fire to take effect on the thirteenth. Troop movements were to stop except in areas south of the Yangtze and in Manchuria. During its meetings of January and February, the PCC made provisions for the cessation of hostilities and for reorganization of the government. Both sides agreed to the convening of a National Assembly on May 5, 1946, which would have seven hundred delegates representing various parties, in addition to KMT delegates who had been selected in 1936. The KMT provisional constitution of 1936 was to be revised. The armies would be reorganized with the KMT enjoying a 5 to 1 superiority.[7] Apparently, a number of Communist leaders including Liu Shao-ch'i were hopeful that these agreements would be the basis for a general political settlement so that a test of arms might be averted.[8]

It is unlikely that Mao shared such optimism. Events would quickly justify his more realistic view. Surely the Communists were probably culpable of many of the violations that continued during this period, but Mao had succeeded in making the onus weigh more heavily on his KMT opponents. Far more important than the political dickering however were the military moves in the field. Chiang K'ai-shek was exasperated by Communist deployment in Manchuria, particularly the temporary occupation of Mukden, Changchun, and Harbin, in contravention of the January 10 agreement. On May 24, after the KMT had captured Changchun, Chiang yielded to American pressure and agreed on a two-week cease-fire, subsequently extended to the end of June 1945. But neither side made concessions, each asking what the other basically was not really willing to consider.

The Third Revolutionary Civil War, as the Communists term it, can be said to have begun in earnest from June-July 1946, even though the Marshall Mission would remain in China for several months longer. By late June, the KMT armies clearly began to move on an offensive in the Central Plains. In July there was considerable fighting in Shantung and in northern Kiangsu. KMT police became increasingly repressive and began executing middle-of-the roaders. Peace negotiations broke down, and even though political maneuvering continued into 1947 the test of arms had finally come. On January 8, 1947, General Marshall left China, his mission a notable failure.

The war was fought in three well-defined stages that bear the unmistakable stamp of Mao's military genius. As viewed by the Communists, the period from July 1946 to June 1947 was the defensive stage.[9] The Communists tolerated the full impact of the KMT offensive, allowing the KMT to extend their forces deeply into north China and Manchuria. In this policy of strategic withdrawal and mobile warfare, the Communists abandoned the cities and towns for the countryside. Lin Piao's troops withdrew to the north of the Sungari River leaving the rest of Manchuria to the KMT. Li Hsien-nien fought his way from central China to Shensi, out of harm's way. The Communist emphasis was on consolidation within the areas they did hold and on the fighting of a war of attrition. The peak of the KMT offensive was symbolized by their capture of Mao's capital of Yenan in March 1947, which Mao conceded without a struggle. Chiang was elated as his soldiers now pursued Mao in a hide-and-seek campaign in the rugged Shensi back country. Mao's confidence, however, was unshaken.

The second stage of the war began in the summer of 1947, a stage of limited counteroffensive.[10] Here the Communists continued to concentrate on mobile warfare, eroding the KMT's strength and extending the scope of engagements. Mao figured that Chiang had overextended himself by deploying most of his best troops in important, but remote Manchuria. This assessment was shared by American military advisers at the time who had counseled Chiang against the move. Hence, Mao's principle objective was to direct the counteroffensive at the soft underbelly of central China and at the major north-south railways in North China. During July and August of 1947 troops of the People's Liberation Army (PLA), the new designation of the Communist military, crossed the Yellow River in three separate areas and set up new base areas in central China. By the end of 1947 PLA units threatened railways running from north China into Manchuria, and they would soon cut the lines both north and south of Mukden. In November 1947 they captured Shihchiachuang in Hopei Province, linking together two base areas directly across the important Peking-Hankow railway.

On December 25, 1947, Mao gave a full explanation of his war strategy, and this was given considerable publicity. This confident propensity to reveal rather than conceal must have been disconcerting, even unnerving to sober KMT military leaders, who also were concerned at their many points of vulnerability despite the appearance of success. Mao ennumerated ten principles of operations for the impending counteroffensive.[11] The main objective was to eliminate the KMT's effective strength, not to acquire land or towns. The PLA would operate against dispersed and isolated enemy units, until the balance of forces swung to the PLA's favor. Operations against enemy concentrations and large towns would be deferred. Even battles of attrition that might end with equal losses were to be avoided; only when the PLA could bring a numerically superior force to bear was a battle to be joined. Mobile warfare was the principal form of combat. The PLA was to obtain its supply of arms and personnel from the enemy. "Our army's main sources of manpower and materiel are at the front." Mao would later refer to Chiang as his quartermaster! Short periods of rest were to be well-used, it was advised, but the enemy should not be permitted breathing space. Even American Ambassador Leighton Stuart regarded Mao's elaboration of tactics and strategy as remarkably candid, and commented: "It is perhaps a mark of Communist contempt for Nationalist military thinking and intelligence that the Communists have so little hesitation in explaining their strategy, which, it must be admitted, has to date not been without success." [12]

Mao's confidence and tactics did not depend exclusively on Chiang's military cupidity. Other factors were as important. Misgovernment and corruption began to catch up with the KMT during the civil war period. The population in general lost confidence in the KMT administration, and already weary of years of war, it was worried about the prospect of many more to come. Press-ganging of soldiers to fight such an unending, hopeless war was deeply resented, and contrasted with the voluntary service of Communist soldiers. After a brief respite before the civil war, the inflation worsened, and as the months went by, it became uncontrollable in KMT areas.

Every bit as important, however, were Mao's efforts to appeal for popular support during the conflict and to emphasize positive, effective governmental programs that lent substance to the appeals. The famous Three Rules of Discipline and Eight Points for Attention that emphasized civil treatment of the people was reissued, to be complied with by the PLA, now composed of many new, younger volunteers. The behavior of the PLA continued, therefore, to contrast with that of the many rapacious units of the KMT. It was this positive identification with and concern for the people that distinguished Mao's entire approach to politics and to war. Thus his "people's war" was, as he claimed, one that only the Communists could fight, and "no army opposed to the people," such as the KMT or American, however hard it tries, "can use our strategy and tactics." [13]

But the main weapon in Mao's arsenal was land reform, for this was an issue that had immediate and profound meaning for millions of

China's stolid peasants, who for the promise of a just share of the land that meant so much to them would undergo fearsome struggle. Communist statistics revealed that in the newly liberated areas the landlords and rich peasants constituted only 8 percent of the population but possessed 75 percent of the land.[14] Naturally the vast majority who had no land or too little land were desirous of change, and would support a Party that promised such change. Such statistics are disputed, some sources holding that the land tenure system was much more equitable than these extreme statistics suggest.[15] Certainly there must have been many variations in the land tenure system throughout such a vast country as China. Nevertheless, that Mao and the Communists were on to a key matter of concern to an absolute majority of the peasants can hardly be denied in the light of subsequent events. The amazing thing is not that Mao made such adroit use of the issue, but that Chiang K'ai-shek ignored it completely.

Thus in the spring of 1946 the Communists abandoned the moderate wartime policy of confining agrarian reform merely to rent and interest reduction. Now the more radical policy of "land to the tiller" was instituted, for this involved the redistribution of larger holdings. Such a policy can be considered radical only in terms of Mao's New Democratic politics, for it still fell well short of the ultimate goal of collectivizing agriculture. Nevertheless, even redistribution at this stage of development had to be approached with care for Mao was balancing important elements in the revolutionary social equation. On the one hand, the new reforms had to be sufficiently radical to satisfy the yearnings and the whetted appetites of the aroused landless and poor peasants, and this was important for marshaling support for "people's war." On the other hand, moderation was necessary to retain support from non-Communists for the New Democratic coalition government.

Such a balance was difficult, perhaps impossible to maintain, and was largely set aside by the peasants themselves. Between 1946 and 1948 some 178 million peasants in areas under Communist control obtained land under the new policy.[16] Land reform on such a scale took on a momentum of its own, and it would seem that what occurred was largely in the nature of a genuine "revolution from below." That is, regardless of Party directives to control the land movement the situation at times was beyond such control. Nevertheless, Mao persisted in his efforts to direct the course of events. In February 1947 Mao complained that the reform had been implemented in only about two thirds of their territories, and that it had not been thorough. On the other hand, he warned against excesses, saying that it was "absolutely impermissible to encroach on the interests of the middle peasants." [17]

In September 1947 the Communists held a National Land Conference in Hsipaip'o village in Hopei province, with some one thousand delegates in attendance. Mao at the time was still in northern Shensi, but the proceedings and its Outline Land Law were probably cleared with him, for the latter was not published until October 10, 1947.[18] The conference discussed and conducted "detailed research into conditions of the Chinese agrarian system and experience of the land reform." Subsequently, similar meetings were held throughout the liberated areas and the Outline Land Law was the chief text. The new law was radical and detailed. It called the present land conditions the root of China's "being the victim of aggression, poverty, backwardness and the basic obstacle to our country's democratization, industrialization, independence, unity, strength and prosperity." The village peasant associations, poor peasant leagues, peasant congresses, and subsidiary organs were designated to manage the land takeover. They would also supervise its equal distribution among the entire rural population regardless of sex or age. Land, equivalent to the peasants', would be given to Communist and Nationalist soldiers and landlords alike, but not to traitors, collaborators, and civil war criminals. People's courts were to be established to decide land disputes, and the peasant associations were charged with the maintenance of order.

Mao was obviously both pleased with and apprehensive over the progress of land reform, and he remained cautious. In a meeting of December 25–28, 1947, in Yangchiak'ou in northeastern Shensi, Mao discussed the topic. He praised the results of the movement, which was being directed to the east by Liu Shao-ch'i's land-reform work committee. But he again warned of "leftist" excesses, as he would continue to do in the months ahead. Of course, he was most immediately concerned about the effect of excesses on the war effort. He reminded his comrades that "Our policy is to rely on the poor peasants and unite solidly with the middle peasants to abolish the feudal and semi-feudal system of exploitation by the landlord class and by the old-type rich peasants." [19] Mao remained highly solicitous of the middle peasant in particular. He was annoyed at the "leftist" tendency of confusing well-to-do middle peasants with rich peasants and using both groups as objects of struggle. Middle peasants, in Mao's mind, were an important, productive element in China's socioeconomic scene. They were not to be alienated from the revolution. Instead, they represented the standard of achievement and of relatively comfortable, yet productive livelihood, that all peasants might some day attain. They were to be won over to the revolution and not made apprehensive of it. Their productive capacity was an asset not lightly to be disturbed or destroyed. Hence, Mao would remain anxious to make the distinction between middle and rich peasants. In January 1948 he defined a middle peasant as one who derived only 25 percent or less of his income from the exploitation of the labor of others; a rich peasant exceeded this percentage.[20]

Mao continued to counsel restraint in land reform as the year 1948 wore on, for he was deeply concerned that excesses not impede the thickening military situation in which the PLA was on the offensive. He demanded that proper discrimination be made among the different types of areas.[21] There were the "old liberated areas" which had been controlled as of mid-1945, where only a few adjustments of land conditions were required. There were the "semi-old" areas, taken over between 1945 and mid-1947, where the military situation had changed rapidly and widely in this period. Here, there had been a preliminary solution of the land problem but it was not thoroughly solved. He sensed that the middle peasants were still holding to a wait-and-see attitude, and the poor peasants, in the majority, were eagerly demanding land. He recommended that poor peasant leagues be formed and their leading position established. As for the "new liberated areas," those taken since mid-1947, land reform was not to be enforced at once, but in stages. There was another area, the "guerrilla zone" or "areas bordering on enemy territory and new liberated areas," in which work had to be confined to "propaganda, covert organizational work, and the distribution of a certain amount of moveable property." Here, mass organizations were not to be established openly, nor land reform implemented for fear of the masses being subjected to persecution. Mao also deplored brutality. He said, "reactionaries must be suppressed, but killing without discrimination is strictly forbidden; the fewer killings the better." [22] By late spring of 1948 he tried to slow the pace of land reform even further by declaring that it should not be attempted in an area unless the "overwhelming majority of the basic masses (the farm laborers, poor peasants, and middle peasants), not just a minority, must already be demanding the distribution of land." He added that "Party cadres must be adequate both in numbers and in quality to grasp the work of land reform and must not leave it to the spontaneous activity of the masses." [23]

Hence, even though land reform and massive peasant support that it brought about were important to achieving victory, as James Harrison has noted, "it also had to be keyed to victory, and the masses were allowed free rein only where the Party needed to arouse increased peasant support." [24] Even so, the results of the land reform program were spectacular. The program was slowed and stopped in some areas as victory approached and would not be started again on a large scale until after military victory, but by 1948 already about 100 million people of 168 million in the liberated areas had received land allotments. [25]

Mao was concerned in these months with marshaling maximum public support for the successful prosecution of the war in the years ahead. But he was equally mindful of the need to continue to consolidate his Party organization and insure its discipline if it was to remain equal to the formidable task. The complicated, overwhelming land reform program revealed deficiencies in this regard, and there had been dissent on other issues as well since the Seventh Party Congress. The need was all the more urgent because of the continued impressive expansion of the Party. From 1,210,000 members in April of 1945 the Party had grown to 2,700,000 members by mid-1947. This, Mao claimed, enabled many "landlords, rich peasants, and riffraff . . . to sneak into our Party." He said that "In the rural areas they control a number of Party, government, and people's organizations, tyrannically abuse their power, ride roughshod over the people, distort the Party's policies, and thus alienate these organizations from the masses." Such a grave situation, he declared, "sets us the task of educating and reorganizing the ranks of our Party." [26] Hence, Mao took advantage of the improving war situation in the winter of 1947–48 to conduct another of his distinctive *cheng feng,* or rectification campaigns. This campaign saw another of Mao's innovations, indicating his continuing anxiety to make such educational movements truly effective. Although this shorter campaign followed to some extent the model of the *cheng feng* campaign of 1942–44, this time it allowed for criticism from individuals outside the Party itself. Such indulgence did indeed reveal abuses and errors, but it is to Mao's credit that the Party did face up to such problems and seriously dealt with them. Once again, there was nothing even remotely similar to this regenerative exercise occurring in the ranks of the KMT party or government, where the need was so much the greater. Once again too, the rectification movement manifestly was not a purge in the dreadful Soviet style. Although some "bad" elements were certainly removed, the accepted technique of persuasion rather than coercion was employed. The Party continued to grow, rather than suddenly diminish in size.

The PLA experienced similar renewal efforts. On January 30, 1948, Mao drafted a directive for the "democratic" movement in the army.[27] The purpose was to achieve the three major objectives of a high degree of political unity, an improvement in living conditions and a higher level of military technique and tactics. Mao indicated that the techniques of "The Three Check-ups and Three Improvements" were already "being enthusiastically carried out" in order to achieve the first two objectives. "The Three Check-ups" refer to class origin, performance of duty and the will to fight, while "Three Improvements" meant organizational consolidation, ideological education, and rectification of work style. Mao's instinctive impulse to raise the consciousness of his fighting men and elicit from them a genuine sense of participation was yet another factor that aids the outside observer's comprehension of how the PLA managed the impressive accomplishments in the remaining months of the war.

The respite of stage two in the civil war was exceedingly beneficial to the Communists and Mao took full advantage of it. The land reform reached great proportions and some of its excesses were corrected. The Party expanded, streamlined, and reformed. Mass organizational work particularly among women, youth, and workers went forward.

The military also greatly expanded and found time both for fuller political indoctrination and for the practice of a new kind of warfare—the positional techniques that would be employed in the next stage of the war. Political and military leaders even began to study urban problems and administration, another new experience for China's proletarian revolutionaries. Industry and commerce behind Communist lines also was attended to and production increased. In contrast, the KMT was now clearly on the defensive. It had 300,000 of its best troops isolated in Manchuria, and another 100,000 tied down at Tsinan in Shantung province. Inflation was rampant and there was political unrest in Nanking, the KMT capital.

The third and final stage of the civil war began in the late summer of 1948.[28] His PLA now numbering over 2 million men had parity with the KMT for the first time. Mao launched his all-out strategic offensive. Most observers realized that the days of the KMT were numbered, but few could have foretold how soon this would be. Within four or five months in the fall and winter of 1948–49, in four major campaigns, the Communists made up for a quarter-century of oppression by the KMT military. For in this short space of time they broke the back of the entire KMT military organization.

In the first campaign, Ch'en Yi shocked the KMT on September 24, 1948, when he captured Tsinan, including its 100,000-man garrison and their 50,000 rifles.

In the second campaign, Lin Piao's Northeast China Field Army, now with twice the men of the KMT in Manchuria, moved in for the kill. The important rail junction and supply base of Chinchou was taken in mid-October, leading to the breakdown of command and coordination between KMT units. On October 19, Changchun, a former capital of Manchuria, fell. KMT troops defected in the thousands, and on November 2, Mukden, now known as Shenyang, was captured. The remaining KMT holdouts were taken a few days later.

The third campaign was perhaps the most decisive of all. It was the Huai-Hai Campaign, the winning of which cleared the way to the Yangtze River. It was a majestic, set-piece battle. Some 600,000 men of the East China and Central Plains Field Armies managed to surround the same number of KMT troops in a broad area north of the Huai River, centered on the city of Hsuchou. The KMT had generous air support, but the encircling Communists relentlessly closed the grip.

The battle lasted sixty-five days, from November 6, 1948 to January 10, 1949. The KMT lost another 500,000 troops.

The fourth of these smashing campaigns was the battle for the Peiping-Tientsin area. Tientsin fell on January 15, 1949, and one week later KMT General Fu Tso-yi surrendered Peiping to Lin Piao. The campaign lost the KMT another half million men and gave the Communists the city that would be their capital. The PLA entered the city by the end of January. Fu Tso-yi's action set a pattern that was oft-repeated in the weeks to follow. The Communist administration moved in during February and March.

Peace negotiations provided some respite from fighting in early 1949. Chiang K'ai-shek resigned as head of the Nanking government; the delegation was sent to Peking by Acting President Li Tsung-jen. But the talks broke down on April 20, 1949. The KMT rejected the Communist proposals which were tantamount to an ultimatum. On April 21, the Second and Third Field Armies of the PLA began the crossing of the Yangtze River. The demoralized KMT armies offered only token resistance. The major towns of the Yangtze valley fell quickly one after another. Nanking, the KMT capital on April 23, Hangchow on May 3, Wuhan on May 17, Shanghai on May 27. In the meantime, P'eng Teh-huai's First Field Army advanced into the northwest, capturing Lanchow in Kansu Province on August 26. The remaining northwestern provinces quickly surrendered.

Also in August, a new offensive began in south China. By fall the entire southeastern seaboard was taken. By December 1949 the western provinces of Kweichow, Szechuan, Yunnan, and Sikang surrendered. The island of Hainan would be captured in April of 1950, and Tibet would be taken later in the year. Only the province of Taiwan remained, and this became the refuge for the remnants of Chiang K'ai-shek's political and military apparatus.

Mao's tremendous victory could hardly have been more convincing and impressive. Characteristically, however, he did not lose his poise, nor indulge in self-congratulating rejoicing. Instead, he soberly surveyed the prospects ahead, remaining profoundly aware of the magnitude of future obstacles in going beyond military victory to the securement of the more important social revolution. He shared these thoughts with his colleagues at the Second Plenum of the Seventh Central Committee, which met in Hsipaip'o village in March 1949, just before moving to Peiping. "To win countrywide victory is only the first step in a long march of ten thousand li," he announced. "Even if this step is worthy of pride, it is comparatively tiny; what will be more worthy of pride is yet to come." Mao said that "after several decades, the victory of the Chinese people's democratic revolution, viewed in retrospect, will seem like only a brief prologue to a long drama. A drama begins with a prologue, but the prologue is not the climax. The Chinese revolution is great, but the road after the revolution will be longer, the work greater and more arduous." [29]

He warned his elated followers: "With victory, certain moods may grow within the Party—arrogance, the airs of a self-styled hero, inertia and unwillingness to make progress, love of pleasure and distaste for continued hard living. With victory, the people will be grateful to us and the bourgeoisie will come forward to flatter us. It has been proved that the enemy cannot conquer us by force of arms. However, the flattery of the bourgeoisie may conquer the weak-willed in our ranks. There may be some Communists, who were not conquered by enemies with guns and were worthy of the name of heroes for standing up to these enemies, but who cannot withstand sugar-coated bullets; they will be defeated by sugar-coated bullets. We must guard against such a situation."

Mao insisted that "comrades must be taught to remain modest, prudent and free from arrogance and rashness in their style of work. The comrades must be taught to preserve the style of plain living and hard struggle."

The warning took the form of a challenge. "The bourgeoisie doubts our ability to construct. The imperialists reckon that eventually we will beg alms from them in order to live." His prediction of the response was equally challenging: "We are not only good at destroying the old world, we are also good at building the new. Not only can the Chinese people live without begging alms from the imperialists, they will live a better life than that in the imperialist countries." [30]

In this report to the Central Committee, Mao noted the ending of an era in which the center of gravity of Communist work had been in the villages, "gathering strength in the villages, using villages in order to surround the cities and then taking the cities." Now, a new period had begun, where work would be centered in the cities.

Signaling this new orientation, the Central Committee moved into Peiping within days after the meeting. Here much attention was directed to the orderly construction of the new government, and to the problems and techniques of urban administration. In June, 1949, twenty-three "democratic organizations" sent delegates to Peiping where they met as a preparatory committee, in order to elect a standing committee and to set the rules for a meeting of the People's Political Consultative Conference. The latter body would then meet in Peiping from September 21 to 30, when it changed the name of the city from Peiping, "Northern Peace," to Peking, "Northern Capital," and decided upon the organization, composition, and initial program of the new regime. Mao was made chairman respectively of the CPPCC itself, of the Central People's Government Council and of the People's Revolutionary Military Council—in addition to his Party chairmanships.

On June 30, 1949 Mao commemorated the twenty-eighth anniversary of the CCP with another important article entitled "On the People's Democratic Dictatorship." [31] He succinctly summarized the valuable experience of the CCP, saying that "three main weapons" were used to defeat the enemy: "A well-disciplined Party armed with the theory of Marxism-Leninism, using the method of self-criticism and linked with the masses of the people; an army under the leadership of such a Party; a united front of all revolutionary classes and all revolutionary groups under the leadership of such a Party."

"To sum up our experience and concentrate it into one point," Mao declared, "it is: the people's democratic dictatorship under the leadership of the working class (through the Communist Party) and based upon the alliance of workers and peasants. This dictatorship must unite as one with the international revolutionary forces. This is our formula, our principal experience, our main programme."

" 'You are dictatorial,' " said Mao, repeating the rhetorical accusation. "My dear sirs, you are right, that is just what we are. All the experience the Chinese people have accumulated through several decades teaches us to enforce the people's democratic dictatorship, that is, to deprive the reactionaries of the right to speak and let the people alone have that right."

"Who are the people?" Mao asked the question. "At the present stage in China, they are the working class, the peasantry, the urban petty bourgeoisie and the national bourgeoisie. These classes, led by the working class and the Communist Party, unite to form their own state and elect their own government; they enforce their dictatorship over the running dogs of imperialism—the landlord class and bureaucrat-bourgeoisie, as well as the representatives of those classes . . . suppress them, allow them only to behave themselves and not to be unruly in word or deed. If they speak or act in an unruly way, they will be promptly stopped and punished." Mao explained: "Democracy is practised within the ranks of the people, who enjoy the rights of freedom of speech, assembly, association and so on. The right to vote belongs only to the people, not to the reactionaries. The combination of these two aspects, democracy for the people and dictatorship over the reactionaries, is the people's democratic dictatorship."

Mao explained that the power of the state would be used to protect the people and enable them to educate and remold themselves "by democratic methods on a country-wide scale, with everyone taking part," to shake off unwanted influences and "continue to advance—to advance towards a socialist and communist society." Mao emphasized that the method to be employed "is democratic, the method of persuasion, not of compulsion." Even the reactionaries, if they behave, will be given land and work "in order to allow them to live and remould themselves through labour into new people." Although if they are not willing to work, "the people's state will compel them to work." Education and propaganda work will be carried out among them, as with captured army officers in the past. When this program is accomplished, "China's major exploiting classes, the landlord class and the bureaucrat-bourgeoisie [the monopoly capitalist class], will be eliminated for good."

As for the national bourgeoisie, Mao believed that at present a good deal of suitable educational work could be done with many of them. Such educational work was to be carried a step further when the time came to "realize socialism, that is, to nationalize private enterprise." But this class is now "of great importance." "To counter imperialist oppression and to raise her backward economy to a higher level, China must utilize all the factors of urban and rural capitalism that are beneficial and not harmful to the national economy and the people's livelihood; and we must unite with the national bourgeoisie in common struggle.'' Hence, Mao explained: "Our present policy is to regulate capitalism, not to destroy it."

Mao acknowledged that "The serious problem is the education of the peasantry." This was because the "peasant economy is scattered, and the socialization of agriculture, judging by the Soviet Union's experience, will require a long time and painstaking work." But Mao firmly spelled out his intentions for all to note: "Without socialization of agriculture, there can be no complete, consolidated socialism."

Mao elaborated on China's international posture. " 'You are leaning to one side,' " Mao rhetorically put the accusation. "Exactly. The forty years' experience of Sun Yat-sen and the twenty-eight years' experience of the Communist Party have taught us to lean to one side, and we are firmly convinced that in order to win victory and consolidate it we must lean to one side." Therefore, China would "unite in a common struggle with those nations of the world which treat us as equals and unite with the peoples of all countries. That is, ally with the Soviet Union, with the People's Democracies and with the proletariat and the broad masses of the people in all other countries, and form an international united front."

Mao reiterated once again the need for humility in the face of the difficult job ahead. "We shall soon put aside some of the things we know well and be compelled to do things we don't know well." Looking at the damaged state of his country's economy and the need for economic reconstruction, he emphasized: "We must learn to do economic work from all who know how, no matter who they are. We must esteem them as teachers, learning from them respectfully and conscientiously. We must not pretend to know when we do not know. We must not put on bureaucratic airs." This was the essential Mao speaking, careful and anxious not to waste any precious resources that might help achieve an important goal. Again he singled out the Soviet Union, claiming that its Communist party "is our best teacher and we must learn from it."

He repeated the prideful warning that in the long period of the twenty-eight years of the Party, "only one thing" was accomplished, "we have won basic victory in the revolutionary war." This called for celebration because it was the people's victory. But, Mao again reminded his Party, "to use the analogy of a journey, our past work is only the first step in a long march of ten thousand li."

SIX
The People's Republic and the Lean to One Side

On October 1, 1949, Mao Tse-tung stood overlooking spacious T'ien An Men Square in Peking and proclaimed the establishment of the People's Republic of China. It was a moment of joy for him and for his doughty comrades who had sacrificed so much over the years and who had endured so much suffering. Their victory had been a triumph of will and of the human spirit that may be unprecedented in history. Yet Mao had already set the keynote over the past several months. The job ahead was so enormous, involving so much that was unfamiliar to the Communists, despite their years of practical experience in governing rural areas, and their ambition for social change was so great that efforts could not be relaxed. Yet Mao knew instinctively that people could not be rushed without respite, and that a dialectical pattern of progress would be the best course. Maximum effort required periods of rest or consolidation. In the years to come the Communist program would be characterized by one mobilization campaign after another with intervals of "normalcy" between. A period of relative quietude was in the offing immediately after the military victory. The first need was to consolidate that victory and to reconstruct the war-damaged economy.

Among the most important matters to be attended to was the securing of friendly relations with the Soviet Union. It is almost surprising, in the light of past treatment by the Soviet Union, that Mao would have put so much emphasis on this relationship. Stalin and his representatives had done great damage to the CCP in the twenties. In the forties Stalin had consistently underrated the CCP, preferring to strengthen his relationship with the KMT government. Ironically, the Soviet ambassador had been the only foreign diplomatic representative to accompany the fleeing KMT government to Canton while Communist armies were sweeping the north that spring. Nevertheless, Mao believed that his movement's best interests required an understanding with Moscow. His "People's Dictatorship" talk of June had affirmed the "lean to one side" policy. On December 16, 1949, Mao arrived in Moscow, six days before Stalin's seventieth birthday.

Mao spent more than nine weeks in Moscow and was undoubtedly disappointed at the length and difficulty of the negotiations that resulted in the Sino-Soviet Treaty of Friendship, Alliance, and Mutual Assistance on February 14, 1950. China gained by this instrument assurance of Soviet support in the event of an attack by Japan or by any other state cooperating with Japan. Another agreement provided Soviet credits to China of 300 million U.S. dollars over five years, a rather modest amount of assistance compared to American aid to the KMT government. And in return for such limited benefits Mao had to agree to continued Soviet presence in Port Arthur and Dairen in Manchuria until 1952, a deadline which, in fact, was not honored by the Russians. Mao also recognized the independence of the People's Republic of Mongolia and its implied inclusion in the Soviet sphere of influence, a bitter pill for the Chinese leader.

If Mao was disenchanted with the relatively hard line of the Soviet Union, he did not show it. In fact, on February 17, shortly before departing from Moscow, he referred to Sino-Soviet friendship as "eternal and indestructible." [1] He also indicated that Soviet achievements in economic and cultural fields would serve as models for China. Thus was confirmed an orientation, to be followed by other Chinese who would look to such models with more enthusiasm than Mao himself, which would cause China perhaps as much grief as benefit. At least, this is how Mao would come to view the experience.

Mao estimated in June 1950 that it would take three years to complete the program of reconstruction.[2] Land reform was to be completed, as well as the making of adjustments in industry and commerce. Large-scale reductions in government expenditures were planned, and a general demobilization of the army was scheduled. The emphasis in this period from 1950 to 1952 was indeed on recovery, but it is clear that the social revolution did in fact continue with considerable momentum.

The social revolution was abetted by the proclamation of a new marriage law on April 30, 1950, which was followed up by campaigns designed to implement it effectively. This commitment to the ultimate liberation of women in Chinese society was a long-standing one with Mao. He had argued for female equality as a student; and there had been an earlier marriage law in the days of the Kiangsi Soviet Republic. The removal of deeply ingrained social restraints on women over the next few years has come to be an extremely important dimension of the Chinese revolution.

Land reform also was crucial in furthering the social revolution. In June 1950 the Third Plenum of the Seventh Central Committee passed an agrarian reform law that was less harsh than the land laws of 1946–48, in that it guaranteed protection to the rich peasants. However, it went well beyond the rent and interest reduction programs of pre-1946 and 1948–49. Implementation of the new land reform program was forthwith, gathering momentum in late 1950, peaking in 1951, and basically completed in 1952. It was marked by considerable violence, particularly in south China where experienced Communist cadres were in short supply. However, cadres too, often encouraged violence and presided over the dispensation of summary justice. Mao would admit later, in 1957, that 750,000 persons were killed in the tremendous social upheaval.[3] The power of an entire social class, the traditional, powerful landlord-gentry, was completely eliminated. It would no longer constitute an obstacle or threat to Communist power. All Chinese peasants now owned a parcel of the redistributed land, and although the size and quality of the share in some areas did not spell release from extreme poverty, support for the new regime was understandably enhanced.

The Korean War, which began on June 25, 1950, soon presented unexpected problems for Mao, but some opportunities as well. While the war might have been as much a surprise to him as to the United States, President Harry S. Truman immediately jumped to the conclusion that it was part of a larger Communist plan of conquest. In his announcement that the United States would come to the aid of South Korea, therefore, he also again directly involved the United States in the Chinese civil war by placing the American Seventh Fleet in the Taiwan Straits. This was to prevent a possible Communist seizure of the last remaining province still in KMT hands. The action confirmed Communist assumptions regarding American intentions. The ruptured relationship was now sealed for more than a generation to come.

The war was also terribly costly to the Chinese. By October 1950 Chinese troops began to amass secretly in North Korea, following up on earlier Chinese warnings to the United States not to penetrate and thereby endanger the continued existence of North Korea. General Douglas MacArthur paid no attention either to these warnings or to his own intelligence reports regarding the presence of Chinese troops in the north. Thus in November 1950 the Chinese struck from their concealed positions, ambushing and inflicting a sizable defeat upon overextended American units in North Korea.[4] This was an impressive initial victory by the Chinese "People's Volunteers," but they subsequently absorbed terrific punishment from American aerial bombardment and firepower when their own lines of communication became overextended. The Chinese managed to bring about a stalemate in the war, thus achieving their purpose of maintaining the North Korean Communist regime. But this was at the cost of well over a half-million casualties and the additional strain on the recovering Chinese economy. Mao's own youngest son, Mao Anying, was killed in the war, by American bombs.

But there were compensations for Mao. Many of the Chinese troops expended in the Korean War were recently surrendered KMT veterans. The Soviet Union gave more credits and aid, although still only after long, hard negotiations, and everything given was reimbursable, with interest. More important, the patriotism awakened by a war fought so close to China's border enabled the Communist regime to mobilize the population in various campaigns and to make more rapid progress with programs than might otherwise have been possible. The war certainly facilitated the land reform already underway and contributed to its rapid completion. Six other campaigns were launched in the twelve-month period following China's entry into the war.[5] The Volunteer movement and the Resist-America and Aid-Korea movement began in November 1950. The former facilitated recruitment of new soldiers. The latter mobilized the patriotic sentiments of the entire population and translated this into concrete terms by appealing for increased production and the payment of taxes. It led to the signing of "patriotic pacts" by businessmen and industrialists who pledged donations for the purchase of heavy equipment and aircraft, among other needed military supplies. It also countered the doubts of those who wondered about the wisdom of fighting the United States while China was still recovering from long years of war.

The Suppression of Counter-revolutionaries campaign began in earnest in February 1951. The threat of foreign armies near China provided excellent opportunity to pursue all kinds of remaining armed opposition within the country, including remnant KMT units, warlords, and bandit gangs. The campaign was prosecuted vigorously and was essentially completed in the first half of 1951. Communist sources indicate that more than a hundred thousand lives were taken in this determined effort.

In the fall of 1951 three more campaigns were begun; the Three-Anti's (anti- corruption, waste, and bureaucratism) in September among cadres and government workers; and the Increase Production and Practice Economy and the Five-Anti's (anti- bribery, tax evasion, fraud, theft of state assets, and leakage of state economic secrets) campaigns in the business community in October 1951.

"Petty bourgeois" intellectuals, especially writers, social scientists, and humanists, were caught up in a series of campaigns that began in 1951 with criticisms of contemporary commentaries on a movie about Wu Hsün, a beggar who gave his savings for schools for poor boys in the late Ch'ing period. Mao was exercised at the uncritical praise lavished on the movie and its hero. He said that "people like Wu Hsün did not lift a finger to disturb the tiniest fragment of the feudal economic base or its superstructure. On the contrary, they worked fanatically to spread feudal culture, and moreover, sedulously fawned upon the reactionary feudal rulers in order to acquire the status they themselves lacked for spreading feudal culture." Mao was not referring only to bourgeois intellectuals. He asked, "Where on earth is the Marxism which certain Communists claim to have grasped?" [6]

Intellectuals underwent thought reform and special study programs to change their habits of thinking and world outlook to accord with Marxist conceptions and categories of expression.[7] Sources of foreign influence, such as missionaries and foreign-run schools were eliminated or severely restricted. All of these activities must have been onerous to many Chinese bourgeois. Yet it seems that many class advantages, such as preferment in school admissions for the children of bourgeois families, continued for years to come. This accorded with Mao's prescription for the New Democratic period, and with his instinct for continuing to make use of trained human resources in these transitional years of scarcity.

As the economy recovered and as the confidence of the new regime grew in dealing with the multifold responsibilities of a complex society, new measures were undertaken to centralize both government and Party operations. The first formal steps to establish a new national legislative body were taken in early 1953. Mao became chairman of a special committee to draft a constitution, which was adopted the following year. But before such reorganization could be completed it became necessary to resolve the first major intra-Party power struggle.

This was the celebrated Kao Kang-Jao Shu-shih case. The root cause of the Party split may have been in Mao's determination to move ahead more quickly with the program to collectivize the just recently redistributed land. This was opposed by many Party leaders, both in Peking and in the regional administrations which continued to operate during the recovery period. There was a strong feeling that China would have to industrialize first before the kind of mechanization would be available to make collectivization possible. Kao Kang and Jao Shu-shih both had powerful regional bases, Kao in the northeast (Manchuria) and Jao in east China based in Shanghai. Both were set on limiting Mao's power on this as well as other matters, and they were joined by others. Mao made his move against the pair after they had moved to Peking to accept new assignments. In Peking they were removed from their power bases. By singling out Kao and Jao, who had possibly offended other possible allies, Mao effectively split his opposition.[8]

Thus, Liu Shao-ch'i, a possible logical ally of Jao and Kao, led the way with an attack on them in February 1954 at the Central Committee's Fourth Plenum. Mao himself managed even to miss the meeting, the official explanation being that he had taken a holiday. Kao and Jao were accused of attempting to set up "independent kingdoms." It was not revealed until the spring of 1955 that both men had been expelled from the Party, and that Kao Kang had committed suicide.

This test of strength completed, Mao moved ahead with the reorganization of government and, to some degree, of the Party. In September 1954 the first National People's Congress (NPC) adopted Mao's constitution. The regional governments were abolished, as were for several years the regional Party bureaus. In the newly centralized government Mao continued as chairman of the PRC. As such, Mao was commander of the armed forces and chairman of the Council of Defense. All these leadership posts were in addition to the all-important Party chairmanship which he would always retain. Mao's position appeared to be more secure than ever. But basic policy differences remained within the Party leadership.

The first five-year plan was launched in 1953 but did not receive much notice until the chairman of the State Planning Commission, Li Fu-ch'un, made a major speech on it at the Second Session of the NPC in July 1955. Li outlined a program of economic development that stressed industry, particularly the extractive and heavy industrial sectors. The pace of development was rapid in these areas, and the results were by 1957 quite impressive. Steel production, for example, rose from 1,350,000 tons in 1952 to 5,350,000 tons in 1957. Coal output at least doubled. Petroleum production tripled. But this was the result of a forced pace and workers saw little of the compensation that might have derived from improving output from light consumer industries or the circulation of more agricultural foodstuffs.

In fact, increased demands were made of agriculture in order to supply raw materials for industry, to repay Soviet loans and to keep pace with a Chinese population that continued to grow from between 12 to 15 million persons a year. Hence the economic planners sought to avoid further alienation of the peasants by keeping to moderate land policies during this difficult forced march to industrialization. Any effort to socialize agriculture at this point, many felt, might endanger the desperately needed agricultural surpluses. Thus Li Fu-ch'un in his speech to the NPC specifically said that farm cooperativization would proceed slowly.

On the very next day, Mao dramatized the difference of views on the subject. Speaking to a meeting of Party secretaries from provincial and lower echelons, he sharply demanded faster collectivization. He angrily criticized those who tottered along like a woman with bound feet.[9] He was especially unhappy that some 200,000 cooperatives had actually been dissolved by Party authorities when he himself that April had warned not to make this "mistake." Mao was concerned about a reversion to capitalist agriculture. "The spontaneous forces of capitalism have been steadily growing in the countryside in recent years," he said, "with new rich peasants springing up everywhere, and many well-to-do middle peasants striving to become rich peasants. On the other hand, many poor peasants are still living in poverty for lack of sufficient means of production. . . ." Thus from this meeting the lower-level cadres were suddenly dispatched back to their local areas with Mao's personal, arbitrary instruction to speed up rather than retard the socialization movement.

The timetable was changed to accommodate this new objective. Already since 1951 mutual aid teams had been experimented with and were increasingly being implemented throughout the country.[10] Lower agricultural producers cooperatives (APC), consisting of units of from twenty to forty households, in which the income of members came from payment for labor services and payment for property contributed to the cooperative, were also already in existence. The APC represented a critical step from the mutual aid team because it changed the basic organization of the farm, with farming decisions now being made at a newly created level above that of the family. Following Mao's injunction, there was a sudden leap in the introduction of lower APCs.

The next stage came quickly. This was the higher APC, which consisted of one to three hundred households formed by amalgamating a number of lower APCs. Here payment for property contributed stopped, but animals taken over were paid for. The larger economic and social units had obvious advantages, including better utilization of labor, greater savings and investment potential, more rational use of resources, and improved social welfare possibilities. Disadvantages included uncertain administration until literacy had been adequately attained as well as inexperience with the larger, more complex organizations, and a possible loss of incentive to work for the collectivity.

Of critical importance in the shift from one stage to another were the continued increases in agricultural production and personal income that showed the peasant that collectivization was to his benefit. Apparently, production did increase steadily during the years of the first five-year plan; official statistics indicated that per capita food-grain production increased at an annual rate of about 1.5 percent. Thus conditions were good for implementing the stepped-up timetable. Consequently, whereas only about 14 percent of China's peasants were in lower-level APCs in early 1955, by the end of that year 60 percent had joined. By early 1956 virtually 100 percent were in lower APCs, while by the end of this same year almost 90 percent were transformed into higher APCs, the pace of developments having suddenly picked up spectacularly. By mid-1957 almost all peasants were in the higher APCs. The shift from lower to higher APCs was essentially the advance from cooperativization to collectivization, in which individual title to land, except for small private plots, was surrendered. But this was not as great a change perhaps as the earlier shift from mutual aid teams to the lower APCs, for the basic change in social organization and level of decision-making had occurred at that time. Obviously these major socioeconomic changes throughout a country as large as China encountered many problems. But it is remarkable that the programs did not cause more disruption than they did. There is little evidence that Chinese authorities resorted to the use of much physical force, which was a refreshing contrast to the Soviet experience with collectivization in the early 1930s.

Mao had had his way over considerable opposition in the socialization of agriculture. He also moved ahead to convert industry and commerce into socialist format, but here in contrast to agriculture he maintained a more moderate approach. Beginning in 1955, private firms were peacefully transformed into joint state-private enterprises. The original owner's capital was confiscated but he was paid interest on it and was usually retained as a well-remunerated adviser or manager.[11] This moderate handling of the "national bourgeoisie" was another contrast to Soviet experience. But the rapid success of the program might be attributed to the receptive political atmosphere as well.

This condition was brought about partly by the harassment of the bourgeois elements in a series of campaigns at this time. There was in 1955 another major campaign against counterrevolutionaries which undoubtedly inspired businessmen to be more cooperative than they might have wished. There also had been well-publicized campaigns that were instigated by Mao himself against certain prominent intellectuals. Thus Mao had vigorously attacked Yu P'ing-po's *Studies of "The Dream of the Red Chamber"* and the prominent scholar Hu Shih, whose "reactionary ideology" Yu's piece reflected. Most vociferous, however, was the campaign against the Communist writer Hu Feng. From May 13 through June 10, 1955, the *People's Daily,* the official Party newspaper, published three series of materials concerning the "Hu Feng counterrevolutionary clique" which purported to reveal "double-dealing tactics." Mao warned of the need to "maintain a high degree of vigilance," and to distinguish those "who disguise themselves as supporters of the revolution but are actually opposed to the revolution." [12] Mao was probably specifically warning others in the Party leadership that opposition to some of his basic policies might thus be construed as such double-dealing. The net effect of such campaigns probably did more to cow China's remnant bourgeois intellectuals and businessmen than it did the Party opposition.

With the socialist program both in the countryside and in the cities well underway, Mao sought to assuage the apprehensive intellectuals, hoping to win greater voluntary support from them and more active, contributory participation in the socialist program. This new effort was signaled in a speech entitled "On the Question of the Intellectuals" by Chou En-lai in January 1956, and followed up on by Mao in his celebrated speech of May 2, 1956 which included the famous slogan: "Let a hundred flowers bloom, let a hundred schools of thought contend." But he must have been disappointed at the results of this appeal. Other issues were intervening and the Hundred Flowers campaign had to be deferred for a time.

Mao's opponents had taken heart from Soviet Premier Nikita Khrushchev's famous secret speech denigrating the deceased Stalin at the Twentieth Congress of the Soviet Communist party on February 25, 1956. Concern was henceforth expressed about the desirability of avoiding a "cult of personality" in China and of using collective leadership. Such expressions were used to counter what was believed to be Mao's increasingly arbitrary use of power in order to have his way. In January he argued for and had adopted by a Politburo conference a twelve-year plan for agriculture.[13]

In April 1956 he delivered to the Politburo an important report "On the Ten Great Relationships," which urged "greater, faster, better and more economical results." The ten great relationships also constituted in Mao's view ten contradictions as well. The ten "problems" were the relationships between: (1) industry and agriculture and between heavy and light industries; (2) coastal and inland industries; (3) economic and defense constructions; (4) the state and productive units and individual producers; (5) the Center and the regions; (6) the Han and other nationalities; (7) the Party and others; (8) revolution and counterrevolution; (9) right and wrong; and (10) China and other countries.[14] In this comprehensive analysis Mao also called for a two-thirds reduction in the size of the government and Party bureaucracy, which must have prompted further apprehensions from those becoming accustomed to the perquisites of office.

As if to accentuate his physical ability to stand vigorously behind his programs Mao swam across the Yangtze three times that spring and summer. If he had been ailing in 1954 there was now no sign of disability.

The Eighth Congress of the CCP was held from September 15 to 27, 1956, with 1,026 delegates and 107 alternates representing a Party membership of 10,730,000. From outward appearances Mao seemed to be at the apex of power, presiding over a series of continuing successes both in developing the Chinese nation and in leading it toward socialism and communism. But Mao could undoubtedly see that formidable problems ahead were mounting. He could see busy hands at work using the occasion of the jubilant congress itself to curb his effectiveness, and perhaps even the possibility of continuing the social revolution. The congress was dominated by Liu Shao-ch'i and his Party-apparatus colleagues. In the new Party constitution now approved, all references to Mao and to his "thought" were deleted, in sharp contrast to the constitution of 1945. With the conferral of the reactivated post of secretary-general on Teng Hsiao-p'ing, Mao's effective control over the Party Secretariat was curtailed. There was even created the additional new post of honorary chairman of the Central Committee, perhaps pointedly in the expectation that Mao might soon be persuaded to take it, thereby removing himself from power altogether. Yet it was more realistic to expect that Mao would fight back. He did.

Almost immediately there was talk of the need for a new Party rectification campaign. In November, Mao called on "leading functionaries" to apply methods of rectification to their work. Agitation for a campaign from supporting sources continued over the weeks ahead.

Other issues were also tending to produce further concern within the Party. In the fall of 1956, rebellions in Poland and in Hungary reverberated widely. The Hungarian and Suez crises, along with continued discussion on the Hundred Flowers campaign had dominated the Eighth Central Committee's Second Plenum in November. An enlarged Politburo meeting in late December and a conference of Party secretaries in January 1957, were scenes of continued debate, and a growing resolution on Mao's part to implement a 1942-style rectification campaign. Turning from these intra-Party discussions, where support must have been less than enthusiastic about his plans, Mao now invoked a non-Party meeting in order to make one of the most important addresses of his career.

On February 27, 1957, before a secret enlarged Supreme State Conference Mao spoke "On the Correct Handling of Contradictions Among the People." [15] Here he acknowledged that contradictions in society still continued under socialism, although they were now primarily "nonantagonistic" contradictions and existed among the people, rather than being primarily "antagonistic" contradictions between the people and the enemy as had been the case before liberation.

Furthermore, Mao acknowledged that even though the people's government truly represents the people and serves them, still there did exist certain contradictions between the government and the masses and between the leaders and the led. Such candid admissions constituted a genuine breakthrough in both Marxist theory and political practice.

As a remedy for such contradictions, and to make the most constructive use of them, Mao argued once again for letting the hundred flowers bloom and the hundred schools contend. In this way might China avoid the distasteful upheavals of Poland and Hungary. In direct contrast to the assertions of Liu and Teng at the eighth Party congress the previous September, Mao contended that it would "take a considerable time to decide the issue in the ideological struggle between socialism and capitalism in our country." Mao insisted that ideological struggle remained necessary, but that it must be conducted correctly and with proper discrimination. He contended that Marxism "as a scientific truth . . . fears no criticism," and that Marxists should deal with their critics in the new dispensation by means of argumentation and persuasion; the use of force was rejected, except for dealing with outright counterrevolutionaries. Mao reiterated such ideas in another secret speech on March 12, 1957, before the National Propaganda Work Conference.[16]

Party apparatus leaders, such as Liu Shao-ch'i, Teng Hsiao-p'ing, and P'eng Chen, the mayor of Peking, were worried about such encouragement to non-Party intellectuals. They believed that class struggle was over, but they still preferred to run a tight ship, using the disciplined Party organization, state organs, and legal machinery to keep intellectuals in line and their criticism to themselves. The similarity of these *apparatchik* views to Soviet experience was evident.

But Mao did indeed "dare to struggle." He clearly believed that open criticism was essentially healthy, even beneficial. It was the essence of the mass line. Encouraged intellectuals, in better spirits and perhaps in gratitude after long months and years of remolding and silence, might be more inclined to cooperate with the regime and its programs. Mao finally persuaded his colleagues to go along with this experiment, and to do so within the format of a new rectification campaign that would subject themselves to the criticism that would be vented. Hence, Mao would kill two birds with a single stone, have the Hundred Flowers campaign implemented and also straighten out the Party detractors who had been aiming to clip his wings and frustrate his programs.

Hence the new rectification campaign, formally launched on April 27, 1957, incorporated the important feature of allowing for criticism from outside the Party. At the same time, so as to assure the probably apprehensive and doubtful Party dissidents, Mao declared that the campaign would be carried out "as gently as a breeze or a mild rain." Furthermore, criticism and self-criticism was to be carried "only to the proper extent." To insure this, only small discussion meetings were held; large struggle sessions were specifically ruled out. A guiding principle was provided of "telling all that you know, and telling it without reservation; blaming not the speaker but heeding what you hear; correcting mistakes if you have committed them and avoiding them if you have not." However, criticism was not to be imposed upon one who would not accept it, "the right to reserve differences must be permitted." [17]

Response from non-Party intellectuals was timid at first, but by June and July it became voluminous and astoundingly outspoken. Equally amazing was the very fact that the most candid of the criticisms were published in the national newspapers and were widely circulated. There were some fascinating, some predictable, and some incredibly foolish if not inane comments. One prominent figure asked whether the Soviet Union intended to reimburse China for the huge quantities of industrial equipment removed from Manchuria after the war against Japan. He also declared that it was "totally unfair" for China to have paid all the expenses of the Korean War, and made invidious comparison between the records of the United States and the Soviet Union on war loans. The former nation, he said, had canceled claims for loans given to allies during both the first and second world wars, while the Soviet Union "insists that China must pay interest on Soviet loans." [18] One can hardly wonder if the publicity given such remarks might not have been intended for Soviet ears as well as Chinese.

However, criticism began to transcend what were after all the bounds of reason in the China of 1957. One critic said that certain problems were keyed to the notion that "the world belongs to the Party," and he suggested that "a Party leading the nation is not the same thing as a Party owning a nation. . . ." Perhaps the extreme was reached in the injudicious comment of a lecturer at Peking University: "The masses want to overthrow the Communist Party and to kill the Communists. If you do not change, if you continue to degenerate, they will some day do so. This is the Law of Socialist Development. . . . When the Party needs a particular man, it will woo him even though he be a mortal enemy. It will cast off any man it does not need, though he has poured out sweat and blood for it. The Party members are inhuman; they address even their mothers as 'comrade.' The masses do not trust the Communist Party." [19]

Such intemperate remarks were considered outright treason, and even Mao came to believe that they must be halted, although he did not do so until such critics were given ample opportunity to compromise themselves thoroughly. On June 18, Mao's important speech on contradictions which had been delivered on February 27 was published for the first time. The published version contained an important addendum—six criteria by which legitimate criticism might be determined. Words and actions were to be considered right if they

1 | Help to unite the people of our various nationalities, and do not divide them;
2 | Are beneficial, not harmful, to Socialist transformation and Socialist construction;
3 | Help to consolidate, not undermine or weaken, the people's democratic dictatorship;
4 | Help to consolidate, not undermine or weaken, democratic centralism;

5 | *Tend to strengthen, not to cast off or weaken, the leadership of the Communist Party;*

6 | *Are beneficial, not harmful, to international Socialist solidarity and the solidarity of the peace-loving peoples of the world.* [20]

The most important of these, Mao stressed, was to follow the socialist path and to do so under the leadership of the Party. He made clear that these were political criteria only, and were not applicable to the sciences. He also declared that those who disapprove of his criteria "can still put forward their own views and argue their case," although it seemed clear enough that such dissidents could hardly hope to be regarded as anything other than "poisonous weeds." [21]

Mao seemed to be serious about liberalizing the intellectual atmosphere, but only to the degree he outlined. And he remained committed to the objective of enjoining, even if by ever-refining techniques, a real political conformity. He declared: "Not to have a correct political point of view is like having no soul. Ideological remolding in the past was necessary and has yielded positive results. But it was carried on in a somewhat rough-and-ready way and the feelings of some people were hurt—this was not good. We must avoid such shortcomings in the future." [22]

Apparently some persons did seek to capitalize on the liberalization policy to embarrass the regime and in some cases to marshal support against it. In the end they only fell into the "trap" which the Party acknowledged had been set. By permitting the expression of such criticisms, Mao had succeeded, whether intentionally or not, in demonstrating that his regime was confidently secure.

Now, however, Mao moved resolutely ahead with a new campaign against the "rightists" who had revealed themselves. Pains were taken to answer the major criticisms recently made, as in Chou En-lai's speech at the Fourth Session of the Fourth People's Congress in late June 1957. Many "rightists" were made to recant, some more than once. The entire campaign became much more serious when in the late summer a number of counterrevolutionary plots were exposed in various parts of China. In this atmosphere the hundred flowers were left to wither on the vine, although Mao may not have intended this result.

The antirightist campaign soon reached major proportions. By the fall of 1957 it spread throughout the ranks of the Party, where the rectification emphasis was laid most heavily on the higher-level leaders. The campaign also swept throughout society, reflecting Mao's penchant for mass mobilization and participation, as well as his stress on education rather than coercion.

Another major characteristic of this general rectification campaign that bore Mao's distinctive style was the *hsia-fang,* or sending down, to the countryside and to basic production units massive numbers of cadres. In 1957–58, 1,300,000 cadres were sent for such physical labor on a rotation basis. This was a practice reminiscent of the early 1940s, now again being vigorously experimented with. Such physical labor programs would eventually become more refined and by the late 1960s would be firmly institutionalized in Chinese society.

In November 1957, Mao was sufficiently satisfied with the progress of the rectification and antirightist campaigns and confident enough of his own position in the Party to leave the country for the second time, making another visit to the Soviet Union. In Moscow he participated in the celebrations of the fortieth anniversary of the Russian revolution. Mao was in a militant mood. He was encouraged by the success of such militancy within China recently, both in furthering the socialist revolution on all fronts and in unifying the Party behind the speeded-up timetable. Abroad, he had been encouraged by the recent technological achievements of the Soviet Union, including the launching of an intercontinental ballistic missile in August 1957 and the placement of Sputniks I and II into orbit in October and November. Mao believed that the socialist nations had achieved a strategic advantage over the West. He expressed this conviction with the phrase "the East Wind now prevails over the West Wind." [23] Under these more promising global circumstances, Mao was hopeful that he could get fuller Soviet support for future military actions, as in the possible taking of Taiwan. He also hoped to get increased military assistance.

However, Khrushchev had already come to believe that world conditions dictated a peaceful transition to socialism on the part of individual nations. He was not anxious to provoke the United States and incur the costs of nuclear conflict. Mao disputed this thesis in Moscow indicating that resort to armed force would in the end be necessary. He realized the risks of such a policy line and held that socialist countries would never be the first to employ nuclear weapons. But if the worst came "and half of mankind died, the other half would remain while imperialism would be razed to the ground and the whole world would become socialist." [24]

But Khrushchev would not be persuaded. Clearly his own calculations were out of phase with Mao's. Mao returned to China with real doubts in his mind. The Russians had agreed on October 15, 1957 to provide China with a sample atom bomb. But the misunderstanding between the two countries' leaders was very real. Khrushchev was upset at the militant analysis of the Chinese. He evidently already began to regret having committed himself to sharing information on nuclear weaponry with them.

In mid-1958 Mao put his Soviet allies to the supreme test. In May 1958 he began a series of military meetings that lasted for two months. These were serious enough to bring Khrushchev to Peking for a quick visit in August. The leaders momentarily appeared to be in agreement on major questions. However, on August 24, 1958, the Chinese began massive shelling of Quemoy, one of the offshore islands under KMT control. On September 4, the United States indicated it would help defend the offshore islands if necessary. Two days later Chou En-lai eased the crisis by offering to renew ambassadorial talks with the United States at Warsaw. The Soviet Union made belligerent statements directed at the United States, but these verbal blasts made it clear that it regarded the Taiwan matter a domestic Chinese affair and it would not intervene. Thus Mao had determined how much Soviet military backing meant in a real crisis.

Relations with the Soviet Union continued to deteriorate, as Mao decided that China could not depend on her ally. If Khrushchev believed he any longer could influence Chinese decisions by threatening to withdraw military aid he was mistaken. Thus on June 29, 1959, the Soviet Union tore up the agreement on nuclear weaponry and began in that year to cut back on the delivery of aircraft to China. In

1960, relations had become so strained that the Soviet Union suddenly withdrew all advisers from China and terminated its aid program. China was now on its own. But even before this necessity had come to pass the Soviet Union was no longer a model for China. Mao had already set his country on its distinctively own development program, one that was largely characterized by an emphasis on self-reliance.

SEVEN
A Chinese Way

During the winter of 1957–58 Mao thought long and hard not only about the relationship with the Soviet Union, but more fundamentally about the course on which China was set domestically. His challenge to the Soviet Union's international policies was now to be matched by a bold new conscious departure from Soviet development norms and models. The novel Chinese experiments in turn would exacerbate even further the differences between the two countries and their respective leaders.

The turn away from Russian tutelage cannot be attributed only to the differences of opinion between Mao and Khrushchev. China had gained much from Soviet assistance and had made notable progress particularly in industrial development by following the Soviet-style program and techniques. Nevertheless, there were clear differences between the two countries. Under the best of circumstances and with the best of intentions this necessitated appropriate adaptation, which often went against the cultural grain. Moreover, it eventually seemed that the two Communist leaderships had in mind different objectives, or visions of attainable social orders. But even in the more immediate future, Mao was apprehensive that the tried and true procedures of Soviet development, while productive, did not promise change quickly enough to make the crucial difference in China.

Mao's response to China's desperate need again revealed the essential great leader, an experienced leader who had already overcome numerous obstacles using the resources at hand with determination and with a profound belief that if man's spirit is properly aroused he can achieve anything. Already in the preceding summer and fall, Mao had been urging further radicalization in agriculture. This received support at a meeting of Party secretaries in Tsingtao in July 1957, and at Politburo and Central Committee meetings that September and October.[1] Now Mao unfurled the famous "Three Red Banners" comprising the general line for building socialism, the Great Leap Forward, and communization. This sudden, pervasive, and intensive total adventure made 1958 one of the most exciting years of Chinese history.

The new plans were partly spelled out in a report of February 19, 1958, entitled "Sixty Points on Working Methods." [2] The fifth session of the National People's Congress that month began to publicize the Great Leap Forward. In March, at a Central Committee meeting in Chengtu, Mao called for the freeing of the mind of restrictive ideas.[3] In April he declared that China was "poor and blank" and this was "a good thing," because "poor people want change, want to do things, want revolution." Also, "the newest and most beautiful pictures can be painted on" a clean, blank sheet of paper.[4] In May 1958 the Second Session of the Eighth Party Congress was held, and this was a real contrast to the moderately keyed First Session in 1956. Mao challenged his comrades "to dare to think, speak out and take action." The session approved Mao's revised twelve-year agricultural plan and accepted his exhortation of 1956 "to go all out and aiming high to achieve greater, faster, better and more economical results." The program had the apparent support of leaders such as Liu Shaoch'i, who now conceded incidentally that class struggle would be around for a long time to come.[5] The extreme criticism, i.e., the "poisonous weeds," of the Hundred Flowers campaign had ostensibly convinced him of Mao's correct analysis, but Liu may have been only speaking for Mao while concealing his own opinion.

Perhaps recognizing the continued opposition, albeit now a largely silent one or in seeming agreement only, Mao moved to strengthen his hand organizationally. The clearest indicator of this came at the Fifth Plenum of the Eighth Central Committee on May 25, 1958, when Lin Piao was elected a vice chairman of the Central Committee and a member of the Politburo's Standing Committee. Lin's support of Mao seemed unquestionable. During meetings of the Military Affairs Commission at this time Lin, who was the second-ranking military man after aging Chu Teh, began speaking his and Mao's mind. He excoriated the heavy reliance on the Soviet Union. He deplored the way in which the military was developing under P'eng Teh-huai with its emphasis on professionalism and modern arms rather than on men and morale which had traditionally distinguished the PLA.[6]

The Great Leap Forward generated for a time unbelievable enthusiasm and unleashed many innovations. The idea was not only to overtake England in fifteen years in steel production, but to get the entire population involved in the act of conscious development. The backyard steel furnaces were not simply to produce more steel, but to extend the consciousness of industrialization throughout the population. In this way might unsuspected talent be discovered and creative ideas generated. The resulting sense of common discovery and increasing awareness, pride and participation would hopefully lead to a genuine leap in production and development in many areas. At the least, certain iron and steel products locally made would help satisfy limited local needs and free larger factories to meet other requirements.

The Great Leap Forward program undoubtedly succeeded in much of this essential purpose. It did indeed make an indelible impact upon the consciousness of most Chinese. They did indeed have a sense of common adventure and of purposeful accomplishment. The most important product was in this elusive area of awareness, which for a country as backward as China is a factor that should not be forgotten. Yet it often has been lost sight of in Western accounts of the Great Leap Forward. There were also concrete achievements in the many public works and buildings that were constructed with amazing speed during this year and a half or so. The Great Hall of the

People in Peking is just one symbolic example of this kind of accomplishment.

Of course, there were mistakes made and some of these were serious. Inexperience and overambition combined to cause economic dislocations and bottlenecks. Sometimes useful objects were melted down in the primitive smelters only to become useless low-grade metal. Too many overenthusiastic and improperly trained and supervised cadres failed to report accurately and honestly. Workers and peasants were overworked, and their accumulating fatigue caused mistakes, accidents, and disenchantment. Any evaluation must take into account the lack of genuine cooperation on the part of cynical oppositionists and even the possibility of sabotage.

The population took on a military aspect, especially in the "everyone a soldier" campaign, in which the militia expanded enormously. But people already tired from longer hours on their jobs could not have been overly enthusiastic about spending additional hours in military formations and drill. Too many experiments were underway at one time, with too little planning and too few trained leaders. For all its successes, the Great Leap Forward was overly ambitious and went beyond the reasonable limits that it might have respected.

And yet China's need was so great and so urgent and Mao's faith in the awesome power and creativity of an aroused populace so strong that the "irrational" somehow seemed rational. This is particularly true in the communization movement, the further logical step in the socialization of agriculture. Since land reform was completed in 1952, the socialization process had already gone through the establishment of mutual aid teams followed first by the lower, then the higher APCs. These APCs were basically the equivalent of the natural or several small natural villages where resources and land had come to be pooled and worked in common. This had already been a major step, but what was considered ultimately most desirable was the creation of a more rational way of utilizing manpower in the countryside. By constricting labor basically within the confines of the natural village, i.e., by using the same social group doing the same traditional work routines in this limited framework, whether socialized or not, only certain limited absolute gains could be realized. However, by considerably expanding the APC, labor resources within the larger unit could be used much more rationally, and more creative opportunities could be exploited. It would be an effective way of dealing with the problems of underemployment during certain periods of the agricultural cycle and actual manpower shortages at other times.

The way was already suggested by the successful, massive water conservation projects that had been underway over the past couple of years.[7] This was nothing new in the Chinese experience since peasants had been used en masse to build dikes, canals, and walls for thousands of years in China. But the Communists had the most immediate successes to go by, such as the construction of the impressive Ming Tombs Reservoir, and the answer seemed at hand. The APCs would be expanded into a much larger unit to be known as the people's commune. The term "commune" recalled the earlier militant communard adventures, even though those had been in urban centers. It had connotations of an armed citizenry, and indeed the military aspect of the population at the time, with the greatly expanded militia, made the term seem somehow appropriate. The communes even came to be organized along military lines. The use of this cherished Communist term, and the bold agricultural socialization program itself both confounded and angered the Soviet Union.

In the spring and summer of 1958, with obvious encouragement from Peking's new radicalization line and concurrently with the militia movement, communes began to form spontaneously in different parts of the country. In July and August, top Party leaders, including Mao, made wide-ranging investigations to observe this phenomenon firsthand. The Politburo then met in Peitaiho for thirteen days beginning on August 17, 1958, to discuss the commune movement. At the conclusion of these deliberations a communique was issued which rather cautiously announced the high tide of communization already in progress.

Words of caution went unheeded. The movement went ahead full speed. At the end of August 1958 there were 8,730 communes that included 30.4 percent of the peasant population. Only one month later there were 26,425 communes that now embraced 98 percent of the peasants of China. Clearly the movement had progressed far too rapidly to make sense administratively or practically. So too had the accompanying rhetoric which proclaimed that final communism was around the corner, and that after only three years of suffering a thousand years of happiness would ensue.

The concept of the commune was an intriguing one for China, and many excellent features were to be incorporated into it that would ultimately improve the quality of life for denizens of the countryside, as well as raise production. The notion of spreading small industry down into the communes was part of the general decentralization scheme of the time. The new plants to be developed would make use of available labor in the countryside as well as provide new work experiences and other accompanying benefits. Exhortations to plow deeper and to plant more intensively were meant to increase productivity as such techniques proved to do under proper conditions. Commune dining halls might indeed have led under the right circumstances to a better diet, more efficiently produced. The commune emerged too at a time of military exigency, for the Taiwan Straits crisis might have led to war. The militarization of the peasant population and the general decentralization of decision-making in several fields would have made China better prepared.

However, as with the Great Leap, too much was done too soon, and the results were too often disappointing. Benefits gained from the new economies of scale were offset by the departure from more effective Party leadership techniques that were based largely on personal relationships within natural social groupings. There turned out to be severe labor shortages as manpower was used in novel enterprises. Overworked available labor resources were exhausted.

Of course, the dizzy pace of developments and the disturbing dislocations led to intensified intra-Party debate. By the end of the year important corrections were decided upon. The Sixth Plenum of the Eighth Central Committee meeting in Wuchang from November 28 to December 10, 1958 resolved to ease restrictions on peasant ownership of private property, made the size of the communes more manageable, and slowed the pace of development. The demands on labor were eased and more attention was given to material incentives. Backyard steel furnaces were largely abandoned. No longer was participation in communal mess halls or nurseries obligatory. Rhetoric was toned down.[8] Curiously, the moderate tenor and realistic assessments of this meeting were marred by the continued claim of extraordinary grain harvests for the year and the setting of an even less realistic target for 1959. That such estimates were grieviously in error was finally recognized, faced up to, and publicly acknowledged in 1959.

Another major decision made at the Sixth Plenum was that Mao would not be a candidate for another term as chairman of the PRC, although he would retain his more important chairmanship of the Party. This move suggested to many that Mao was compelled to turn away from economic programming as a result of the alleged fiasco or that he regarded it as prudent to do so. To be sure, his opponents made good use of the opportunities thus provided for them. Mao may also have been offended by the apparent alacrity at which his offer to step down was accepted. Certainly he later expressed dissatisfaction with this meeting and resented having been treated subsequently as "a dead man at his own funeral." [9] But it is reasonable to accept that he wished to be free from the burdens of that office, particularly its ceremonial responsibilities. Mao did want to give more attention to theoretical work and to deal with questions of overall policy, especially in the debate with the Soviet Union over fundamental issues before a worldwide audience. He explained his reasons in the final point of his "Sixty Points on Working Methods" as early as February that year.[10]

The next few years were to be especially trying ones for Mao, and it is perhaps just as well that he had the extra time to give to the mounting new problems, both domestically and internationally. The spring of 1959 saw renewed violence in Tibet, as restive tribesmen, encouraged from abroad, again openly revolted. This led to tension and deteriorating relations with India. The first months of bad weather began, a burden that would continue to stretch mercilessly for a period of three years. This natural complication confused the uncertain progress of the commune movement. Mao's critics, the proponents of the opposition line (the second of the "two lines"), again improved their positions and promoted their own policies. Liu Shao-ch'i was elected chairman of the PRC in April 1959, thus gaining further influence, along with Teng Hsiao-'ping, over China's extensive bureaucracy.

More immediately threatening to Mao was the attitude and behavior of Defense Minister P'eng Teh-huai. This doughty, outspoken old veteran had for some time irritated Mao with his brand of professionalizing and modernizing of the PLA, with his sympathetic attitude toward the Soviet Union, and with his criticism of the Great Leap and communization programs. P'eng's conception of the new PLA required continued Soviet support, a domestic economy that would sustain the PLA's program, and an avoidance of mass movements that allegedly would dissipate the PLA's professional integrity and morale. Employment of the PLA for public works projects or the requiring of officers to join the enlisted ranks occasionally for physical labor were examples of such detrimental policies, as viewed by P'eng.

But Mao's ire was further aroused when in the course of a seven-week visit to the Soviet Union and Eastern Europe beginning in late April 1959 P'eng shared with Premier Khrushchev his critical views. To Mao's mind this was behavior approaching treason. On July 14, 1959, P'eng issued a circular letter attacking the Great Leap Forward, the communes, and the "habit of exaggeration" and "petty bourgeois fanaticism" that led to the excesses that had been committed. P'eng implied criticism specifically of Mao's style of leadership.[11] Only four days later Khrushchev made similar assertions and this served as further evidence of collusion between the two.[12]

On July 23, 1959, Mao rebutted P'eng and other critics in a long informal speech at a Central Committee work conference.[13] He took exception to charges that he was divorced from reality or from the masses—especially searing criticisms. He acknowledged that mistakes had been made, and that "too high a price" had been paid. The trouble that had come about was "a big one," he acknowledged, "and I hold myself responsible for it." On the other hand, Mao indicated that he was not as far to the left as some have suggested, that in fact he was a "middle-of-the-roader." He also said that the setbacks should not be regarded as a failure of the proportions of the defeat of the Kiangsi Soviet. The "people of the whole country have learned a lesson," he said. In fact, the experience had been a vast educational campaign in which several million cadres and hundreds of millions of peasants received an education. His point in admitting responsibility carried the implication that others might also analyze their own responsibility. He did not mention P'eng Teh-huai by name.

However, at the important Eighth Plenum of the Central Committee held at Lushan from August 2 to 16, 1959, the debate with P'eng was joined squarely. P'eng, obviously speaking for many others, now attacked Mao directly. However, this personal confrontation with Mao, along with the compromising association with Khrushchev, placed P'eng in a very weak position. Mao counterattacked vigorously, even warning that if the PLA should follow P'eng, he himself would conduct a guerrilla war. The Party backed Mao and condemned P'eng and his "anti-Party clique." In September 1959, P'eng was dismissed as defense minister and was succeeded by Lin Piao. Considering that P'eng was representing an "antagonistic contradiction" and might well have been charged with treason for having collaborated with the Soviet Union, he seems to have suffered no further punishment than removal from power and the abuse that has since attached to his name. He would remain for many other dissidents something of a hero, and would even be defended allegorically by writer-critics and others over the next couple of years, an undercurrent that escaped detection by China-watchers at the time and was not realized until the advent of the Cultural Revolution in 1965. P'eng was even called upon to make an investigatory tour of agriculture in 1962.

Having won this critical test, Mao persisted over the next several months in trying to make the communes work on a relatively innovative basis. Estimates of achievement and of what was possible were drastically scaled down, but Mao felt that the most should be made of the bold socialization experiment at this time despite the difficult problems being encountered. A new *hsia-fang* program was aimed at lower-level cadres who had misinterpreted earlier directives, and for a time some of the more radical commune features were again instituted. However, this bucking of the tide was given up by the summer of 1960.

A decisive factor in this was the sudden recall by Premier Khrushchev in July 1960 of all of the 1,390 Soviet technical advisers then in China and the termination of the Soviet aid program. This dramatic move could not have been made at a worse time for the Chinese development program, for despite the terrible weather situation and the difficulties engendered by the pervasive experimental program of the past year, the Chinese were counting on rather large imports of capital equipment from the Soviet Union in 1960. The new crisis left China isolated internationally. Coupled with another bad harvest in 1960 it contributed to the disheartening situation in China which included near-famine conditions on a widespread basis and isolated instances of outright starvation. China's industrialization program was dealt a severely damaging blow. Under these circumstances, it is understandable that further socioeconomic experiments of any magnitude were curtailed for the time being.

Retrenchment and restorative measures were now undertaken on an emergency basis. Production was given first priority. Agriculture was given equal attention with industry. Some of the measures that were now worked out not only helped the country to weather this protracted national disaster, but led to a patterning of agriculture that has resulted in many years of successful harvests ever since 1961. Demands on peasant labor were reduced. Communes were reduced in size, and therefore increased in number from the twenty-four thousand in 1959 to seventy-four thousand in 1963. Within the communes something of a rational division of functions was worked out. The production team, or the original smaller APC, came to be responsible for the actual conduct of farming. It became the unit of production management and of the distribution of profits. The production brigade, or the original natural village or villages and the later higher APC, coordinated farming but had limited authority to enforce policy. The production brigade also contracted with state trading and procurement organs. The third and highest tier, the commune administration itself, planned and implemented the establishment of small factories, the coordination of water-conservation plans and the provision of certain social overheads. Each collectivity in this arrangement seems to do what its scale best fits it to do.[14] Restored was the trusty CCP leadership technique of face-to-face contact with local people and the comfortable feeling and the joy of working with one's neighbors in basic work groups that approximate the original mutual aid teams within the production teams. Restored too were private plots, on which peasants could grow fruits and vegetables to supplement communally grown crops. Such privately grown produce could be sold, although sometimes only occasionally, in free markets.

The traumatic experience of these difficult years of the early sixties produced deep scars, as well as the needed successful economic response. For one thing, it guaranteed a long-standing distrust of and resentment against the Soviet Union by the entire Chinese nation, and the Sino-Soviet dispute would become China's foremost international preoccupation for many years to come.[15] This problem was of sufficient gravity that it would occupy even more of Mao's time. Such preoccupation on his part gave his political opponents additional opportunities to strengthen their positions in order to promote their own domestic policies. This was related to the other painful legacy of these years—the widening of the gap and the intensification of the struggle between the so-called two lines. The proportions of China's economic difficulties seemed so enormous to them that Mao's opponents resolved all the more to avoid a repetition of some of Mao's programs which they held to be the root cause of the disasters. They sought to use the occasion of the emergency retrenchment measures to secure a more orderly, better managed economic development that relied basically on experts, professionals, and the bureaucracy. These men were Communists and were dedicated to the eventual attainment of communism in China, but they clearly opted for a different route from that espoused by Mao.

Mao repeatedly declared his responsibility for the mistakes of the adventurous policies of 1958 to 1960. He acknowledged that he was unfamiliar with economic decision-making. But he had a deep and abiding instinct as to what was necessary to prevent the revolution from dying out. He believed that the road his opponents desired to follow was not an optional approach to communism, and would only result in the undermining of revolutionary goals, even if economic progress was made. For him the revolution was meaningless if it did not continue to elicit the full, conscious participation of all the people. This route demanded unorthodox, unprecedented methods and experimentation—because no people had ever attempted such an ambitious undertaking before. Only in this way might all of the people be assured of sharing the ultimate benefits of development. Thus Mao resented the exploitation by his opponents of the difficulties during 1959-61 to discredit his ideas. But even more, he feared that China might also travel the road the Soviet Union had already gone, as he saw it, to revisionism and capitalist restoration. These were thoughts and apprehensions that undoubtedly beset Mao as his critics became bolder, and as the intensifying debate with Soviet leaders caused him to reflect on the Soviet revolution and its apparent demise.

Therefore, the legacy of the Great Leap period and the retrenchment that followed was the emergence in exaggerated profile of the struggle between the two lines. Ultimately the conflict would come to a head and burst into an open free-for-all. That day of reckoning was set for the mid-sixties. In the meantime, the opposing forces prepared in one way or another for the decisive event. On the one side, anti-Mao elements asserted themselves increasingly in the state and Party bureaucracy. These were positions of great strength and influence in the Communist system, given its mechanisms of propaganda and the practice of democratic-centralism that could enjoin discipline throughout the ranks. But Mao, the wily guerrilla fighter of vast experience against great odds, was not to be underestimated. Through Lin Piao, he saw to it that the PLA was being prepared to exercise the final determination. His basic insight of the early thirties, "political power grows out of the barrel of a gun," was not forgotten.

Lin Piao set to work preparing the PLA. The general political department of the PLA began in 1960 an intensive program of ideological revitalization in the ranks and among relatives of PLA men. Lin Piao maintained the "four firsts" principle as the key to political work, i.e., man first over weapons, political work first over other work, ideological work over administrative, and practicing ideology over book ideology. An October 1960 resolution of the Military Affairs Committee quoted Lin's injunction: "Read Chairman Mao's works, listen to his words, do as he instructs, and become a good soldier of Chairman Mao." Great Leap Forward themes, such as the mass line, democracy in politics, in the military, and in economics, and the "three-eight work style" were reaffirmed. Efforts were made to simplify administration, with one third of the cadres above the regimental level ordered down to the companies. By December 1960 the "five-good soldiers," i.e., good in politics and ideology, military techniques, three-eight style, doing one's duties, and steeling oneself, campaign was underway. This was followed in 1961 by the "four-good company" campaign, i.e., good in politics and ideology, three-eight style, military training, and management of living. These campaigns were intensive and between July 1960 and February 1961, 85 percent of all PLA Party branches were rebuilt.[16] All of this strengthening was clearly in the Maoist vein. It was diametrically opposed to the kind of policy reviewing and adjustments that were being made in the Party and government.

Between the Ninth Plenum of January 1961 and the Tenth Plenum of September 1962, the Party put out a series of comprehensive retrenchment directives. In agriculture the so-called Sixty Articles document was drafted without consulting Mao. This led him to ask testily, "Which emperor decided this?" The comprehensive document gave detailed and helpful guidance on commune management, but contained provisions which Mao found objectionable. Mao felt strongly enough about this to believe that their inclusion could lead to the very denial of the principle of collectivism. He therefore halted further debate on the subject by invoking at the Peitaiho work conference in August 1962 the call for class struggle. A revised draft was approved by the Tenth Plenum the following month.[17]

Similarly, in the field of industry a Seventy Articles document was drawn up which contradicted many aspects of Mao's own famous 1960 Constitution of the Anshan Iron and Steel Company. The Anshan Constitution would later be referred to as being both a result of and a weapon in the struggle between the two lines and the two roads. Specifically, it had repudiated the Magnitagorsk Constitution (named for the giant steel complex in the Soviet Union), which allegedly had been the model for those who would later be called "revisionists." The Magnitagorsk Constitution consisted allegedly of five principles: (1) putting profits first; (2) relying on a one-man management-responsibility system; (3) allowing the domination of experts; (4) using bourgeois legal rights in order to control the workers; and (5) the keeping of techniques in the hands of experts only. The Anshan Constitution responded with principles of its own: (1) putting politics first, with the slogan of "politics in command"; (2) strengthening Party leadership; (3) promoting mass movements "in a great way"; (4) using the "two participations," i.e., the participation of workers in administration and the participation of leading cadres in productive labor; (5) implementing "the one transformation," i.e., the transformation of irrational rules and regulations into rational ones that were relevant and sensible; and (6) using the "three-in-one combination," i.e., the formation of working groups of leading cadres, technicians, and workers who together resolve problems and implement the technical revolution.[18] The Seventy Articles sought to reverse this mass line in industry, and was only one prominent instance of such opposition during the early 1960s.

Developments contrary to Mao's views were especially noticeable in the fields of culture and education. Leading figures in the Party's Propaganda Department made no secret of their opposition to Lin Piao's campaign for the study of Mao's thought in the PLA. In the eased atmosphere of 1961 the Propaganda Department issued several "revisionist" regulations designed to encourage artists and intellectuals. Similar reforms were carried out in education. A document entitled "Sixty Articles on Universities" became in November 1961 a Party directive. It restored to practice the three principles: (1) that the main task of universities was teaching and research; (2) that specialized training and research were necessary; and (3) that the teaching staff was relatively autonomous from Party control.[19]

Such indulgence gave rise to a modified Hundred Flowers campaign that blossomed in 1961–62. The writer-critics who now appeared were mindful of the six restrictive criteria on political expression that Mao had imposed in 1957. Hence they resorted to a new kind of satirical literature characterized by themes and expressions laden with double meaning. Perhaps the most famous of these critics was Wu Han, the deputy mayor of Peking and a well-known Ming Dynasty historian. He chose to write a play about a famous Ming official. It was entitled *Hai Jui Dismissed from Office,* and was published in January 1961. The implication of this play, to those knowing oppositionist cadres and intellectuals, was that just as Hai

Jui had been unjustly removed from office as a result of his courageous behavior so too had P'eng Teh-huai in 1959.[20] Teng T'o began
a newspaper column in February 1961 called "Night Talks at Yen-
shan," and then joined Wu Han and another author in October to
begin another column, "Notes from the Three Family Village," using
a pen name.

One example, among many such essays, was a column titled
"Great Empty Talk." The piece complained about those who talk
endlessly on any subject, yet one cannot remember what they've
said afterwards. Any explanations by the speaker only result in more
confusion. As an example of such a person, the essay referred to a
"neighborhood boy" who imitated the expression of great poets and
who has written many "great empty talks." One of his poems, full of
such empty talk, was this poem:

The heaven is our father,
The earth is our mother,
The sun is our governess,
The east wind is our benefactor,
The west wind is our enemy.[21]

The reference to Mao's own slogan of the east wind prevailing over
the west wind was obvious to those in the know.

This bold, intensifying criticism was not detected by outside observers of Chinese developments. But Mao realized their import and
he chafed, although patiently, under what he considered their unfair-
ness. It is not known whether he was aware at the time of more important secret discussions designed to thwart his policies. One such
meeting in December 1961 was held at the Peking Zoo (!) under the
supervision of Teng T'o and produced a long report delivered to
P'eng Chen, the chairman of the Peking Party Committee.[22] In essence, the report agreed with P'eng Teh-huai's earlier criticisms.

In January 1962 an important debate took place at a conference of
seven thousand cadres.[23] Liu Shao-ch'i held that the Great Leap
Forward had been a failure and that the economy was still in bad
shape. He continued to maintain this evaluation for several more
months. Mao, on the other hand, told the conferees that the difficult
years were over. He again acknowledged responsibility for the fail-

ures, but indicated that he and the Party lacked experience in construction and needed to learn from practice, just as they had mastered revolution over a period of twenty-eight years. Liu argued suggestively that Mao's style of leadership—his personal decision-making—disrupted the normal Party procedures. Mao agreed that collective leadership was desired. He also held that the minority had the right to persist in their views and said that sometimes the majority could be wrong.

Liu proposed that everything possible must be done to restore the economy, implicitly suggesting compromises that Mao could not tolerate. Teng Hsiao-p'ing at a meeting later in the year best expressed Liu's conviction, saying that "Whether cats are white or black, so long as they can catch mice, they are all good cats." [24] At an enlarged meeting of the Politburo in February 1962, Mao's economic critics continued their dismal evaluation, and concluded that the economic situation constituted a national emergency.

Mao did not need to defend himself alone. Both Lin Piao and Chou En-lai argued against the criticisms. Lin declared that the Three Red Banners of the Great Leap Forward had been correct. He held that the thought of Mao Tse-tung was "the soul and root of life," and that the Party had to follow Mao's instructions.[25] But Mao was on the defensive during this period. The criticisms and the "revisionist" programming continued through the summer. They were perhaps topped off symbolically with the publication of a new edition in August 1962 of Liu Shao-ch'i's work *How to Be a Good Communist*. This book would later be condemned as a "big poisonous weed" and a "bourgeois book" whose "revisionist program opposed the Thought of Mao Tse-tung." Mao would look back at this period in 1962 as one of the series of events that made him decide on the frontal assault on the Party in 1965. But first, he was still to be further provoked.

Mao began to counter the "adverse wind" in Party meetings of August and September 1962.[26] At the Tenth Plenum of the Central Committee in September he succeeded in halting further concessions in the agricultural socialization program and reminded his comrades of the need for continued class struggle. There was the need as well, he said, to guard against Soviet-style revisionism and to guarantee that genuine "revolutionary successors" were cultivated among China's younger generation. How were they to be cultivated? Mao did not have in mind the moderated atmosphere and educational system that was currently being experienced. "Successors to the revolutionary cause of the proletariat," he announced, "come forward in mass struggles and are tempered in the great storms of revolution." [27] To these ends, the Tenth Plenum was persuaded by Mao to provide for a new rectification campaign. This would comprise a socialist education campaign, a crackdown on divisive intellectuals, and a new five anti-campaign among cadres. With this authorization in hand, Mao dispensed with any further large formal Party meeting for a period embracing the next four years.

The comprehensive socialist education campaign proceeded in stages.[28] The first phase, from late 1962 to mid-1964, began by concentrating on errors among basic-level cadres, particularly on the communes. The emphasis was on education and indoctrination, and the campaign was to be conducted with patience. By mid-1963, however, it was apparent that a major split had developed within the Party as to the best means of implementation. During 1963 there were held three Central Committee working conferences on the campaign. The second meeting, in May, still reflected Mao's guidelines and wishes. It produced a draft resolution known as the "first ten points," which followed Mao's insistence on relying upon the poor and middle peasant associations for leadership in rural work. Thus by going outside the Party and encouraging mass participation relations between the Party and masses were to be improved. It was noted that some 95 percent of lower-level cadres were all right, but there were 5 percent who had to be weeded out.

By the third meeting in September, however, Mao's opponents seem to have got the upper hand. This meeting adopted a revised program, known as the "later ten points." This program now emphasized lower-level Party leadership, rather than the peasant associations. It also reintroduced material incentives in order to bolster response and enhance production.

Fascinating debates continued among intellectuals, fascinating both in terms of the topics under consideration and of their signification for the intra-Party split.[29] One historian, Liu Chieh, was criticized for holding that the Confucian concept of *jen,* i.e., benevolence or human-heartedness, transcended class affiliations. Lo Erh-kang was criticized for insisting that Li Hsiu-ch'eng, "the loyal prince" and last commander of Taiping forces in the 1860s, was a hero. Lo's critics maintained that Li had betrayed the Taiping Revolution by means of his confession to his captors shortly before his execution. Thus, whatever the justice of the actual case, through his surrogates Mao could refer to a famous negative example in stressing the contemporary need "to continue the revolution to the very end." [30] Another scholar, Shao Chüan-lin, was criticized for depicting the average peasant as something less than a revolutionary paragon.

Yang Hsien-chen, a senior Party theoretician and former director of the Party's advanced cadre school, also came under attack. He had propounded the notion of "two into one" a conceptual slogan which meant that opposites were in fact permanently united. This implied that problems only required study to identify the relevant opposing contradictions and that solution followed with the further determination of the common ground between the opposites. Such an interpretation emphasized resolution and unity. In society this would mean deemphasizing class struggle in the interests of compromise and conciliation. Yang's views provided theoretical justification for the Party bureaucrats who opposed Mao's mobilization approach to development. But such views were so utterly opposed to Mao's own interpretation, reflected in the contrary slogan "one into two," which insisted on the need for class struggle, that Yang was discredited, and indeed may even have been made a scapegoat by sympathetic Party leaders.

Thus, by the end of 1963 and during 1964 the tension and the jockeying between the two lines intensified. In 1963 the "four clean-up" (rectifying politics, ideology, organization, and economy) campaign was gradually introduced. By the end of the year, the Maoists were asserting themselves again by joining this campaign with Lin Piao's well-publicized program for the "whole country to learn from the People's Liberation Army." In the spring of 1964 there was established a political commissar system in all government departments and increasing military representation throughout the Party.

But Liu Shao-ch'i and his supporters seem to have maintained their ground during 1964. In June, a directive entitled "Organizational Rules of Poor and Middle Peasant Associations" confirmed that they, along with all other activities, were to be under the control of local Party organizations. Under the circumstances, this meant the effective control of mass mobilization politics and the thwarting of Maoist objectives. Party work teams sent down from higher echelons consolidated the apparatus over which Liu Shao-ch'i and Teng Hsiao-p'ing held sway. A rectification campaign in cultural circles began in June 1964 at Mao's direction, and went through the established motions of such a campaign. It was unusually moderate, however, and finally petered out before year's end—before reaching possible high-ranking targets.

In January 1963 Mao had penned a poem expressing his ire, but in the same indirect manner as much of the recent criticism of himself. When it was published a year later, his opponents cleverly turned the thrust of his barbs away from themselves by interpreting the "insects" referred to therein as being references to Soviet revisionists. In fact, Mao probably had his domestic detractors primarily in mind:

In this small globe there are several flies crashing against the wall
They hum in a bitter tune and sob once and again
The ants taking their abode inside the ash tree claim their place is
  a large kingdom
It is not easy for the ants to take a tree
The direct Westerly wind tears down the leaves and passes
  Ch'ang-an
  Howling like whizzing arrows
  So many things happened; they happen always fast
  The earth is revolving; the time is too short
Ten thousand years is too long; we only seize the morning
  and the evening
The four seasons are in a fury and the clouds and water in
  a rage
The five continents are in eruption under strong gales and
  loud thunder
It is necessary to wipe out all harmful insects to become
  invincible. [31]

Two years after this expression of Mao's feelings the "insects" were still as troublesome to him as ever. In fact, they were soon to be elevated to the status of "monsters and demons," thereby requiring extraordinary measures of disposal.

At an important Central Committee work conference held December 1964 to January 1965, Mao made several momentous decisions. He criticized the handling of the socialist education campaign. A twenty-three-point document basically reaffirmed earlier procedures that had been overturned by the "later ten points." [32] With various modifications, the socialist education campaign would continue for months longer. But it was apparent to Mao, as to others, that such a campaign was not the answer to the deep division in the ranks. It was this divisiveness, this opposition to his concept of the revolution, that was responsible for the campaign's ineffectiveness. His insistence on uninterrupted revolution was being ignored flagrantly. The Chinese revolution, Mao believed, was seriously endangered. Different, sterner measures were required.

Therefore, Mao also decided at this conference to launch a thoroughgoing overhaul of the Party, to be called a "cultural revolution." He undoubtedly knew at this time, that among its ultimate purposes would be the removal from power of Liu Shao-ch'i. To this end he established a Group of Five to make plans for the unprecedented type of campaign. With cold calculation he saw to it that some of his principal antagonists were in this preparatory group. Of the original group, P'eng Chen as its head, Politburo member K'ang Sheng, Propaganda Director Lu Ting-yi, General Office Director Yang Shang-k'un, and *People's Daily* Editor-in-Chief and New China News Agency Director Wu Leng-hsi, were purged; only K'ang Sheng would remain unpurged a few months later.

Mao's concept of the Chinese way to revolutionary development was emerging in fits and starts. It had to evolve in the face, not only of the unknown since it was an exploratory and unprecedented approach, but also against powerful domestic and international opponents as well. Even the impending Cultural Revolution which had so much of the black and white about it was confused from beginning to end because of the stratagems of these opponents, and the complications of intervening international considerations.

The relationship with the Soviet Union in particular had gone from bad to worse since 1960 when all the experts had been withdrawn and aid was terminated. This alone was a most traumatic experience for China, but relations became further strained by Soviet aid to India during the Sino-Indian border war of 1962 and by the Cuban Missile Crisis of October 1962. China supported the Soviet Union during the latter crisis, but when the Soviet Union backed down from her position and promised to withdraw her missiles, China denounced the decision as an example of the "cowardice" of modern revisionism. The Soviet Union, in China's eyes, was guilty successively of "adventurism" and then of "capitulationism." [33]

The final break, however, came in July 1963 when the Soviet Union signed the Nuclear Test-Ban Treaty.[34] China denounced the new treaty and postponed indefinitely Sino-Soviet bilateral talks. There began totally unrestrained polemical exchanges between the two Communist parties, although much of this had already been going on during the winter of 1962-63. There was a lull in the dispute following Khrushchev's resignation in October 1964. However, by March 1965 the clash was on once again; the Moscow Meeting of that month was a failure from the Chinese point of view.[35] China's behavior with respect to the finally postponed Second Afro-Asian Conference that was to have been held in Algiers, June 1965, was widely criticized and may have been partly out of kilter because of the preoccupation with an anti-Soviet policy. However, Chinese foreign policy was considerably marred by yet other developments during the impending Cultural Revolution.[36]

In July 1964, Mao issued a stinging polemic entitled "On Khrushchev's Phoney Communism and Its Historical Lesson for the World." The essay traced the dilution of communism in the Soviet Union since the death of Joseph Stalin. It was a clear warning to his Chinese comrades not to permit a similar drift toward "revisionism" to continue in China.[37]

The Vietnam War, now intensifying would prove only to exacerbate differences between the Soviet Union and China, rather than provide a rallying point for possible resolution of them. The Vietnam War became serious enough in 1965 that it also served to create a new concern for the Chinese that had to have at least equal weight for a time with the Soviet threat. This was the rapidly escalating involvement of the United States in the war. This was serious, especially if, as the Chinese had been claiming since the Nuclear Test-Ban Treaty of 1963, the Soviet Union and the United States were in fact "colluding."

EIGHT
Reaffirming
the Chinese Way

Developments in the months preceding the launching of the Cultural Revolution are partially obscured by the escalation of American participation in the Vietnam War. This produced tremors within China that affected Mao and Lin Piao's refurbishing of the PLA along the lines of its erstwhile "people's army" image. Lo Jui-ch'ing, who up to this point had cooperated in this program, now balked as he perceived the increasing American threat to China itself. Lo began to argue both for some degree of professionalization within the PLA and for a more aggressive stance toward the Americans, including perhaps active military entry into the Vietnam War. Mao and Lin's program went ahead nonetheless. By May 1965 the PLA was sufficiently reformed so that ranks of insignia and distinctions between officers and men were abolished. In September 1965 Lin Piao gave his famous address "Long Live the Victory of the People's War" in commemoration of the defeat of Japan that clearly indicated that China would not enter the Vietnam War.[1] "Self-reliance" had been the essential ingredient in China's own revolutionary war and this is what was indirectly proffered in advice to the Vietnamese Communists and to other liberation movements elsewhere. As if to document this position China could point to the essentially defensive character of the now transformed PLA. Lo could not accept this policy, and in December 1965 he was purged. Thus, the intensifying war near China's southern border which involved increasing numbers of troops from the world's leading capitalist power, and the consequent division among the military and policy-makers on this account, forms a vivid, omnipresent, and ominous background factor to the Cultural Revolution itself. It helped produce an atmosphere that Mao could capitalize upon.

In the meantime, the Cultural Revolution that Mao had called for at the beginning of the year had not materialized. At a joint meeting of the Politburo and regional Party secretaries in September-October 1965, Mao continued to press for action. He wanted action on two levels. He wanted basic changes in the institutions of socialization—those institutions that transmitted and implanted the values of society. Thus he called for radical changes throughout the educational system. He regarded Peking University as a "rotten" institution, and suggested that full-time courses of study throughout the nation's universities be set aside in favor of part-work, part-study programs.[2] Teng Hsiao-p'ing is said to have opposed any such changes in the system, for it was geared to producing the professionals and technicians ostensibly required by the nation's industrialization program. Once again, Mao was rebuffed.

On a more immediate and urgent level, Mao wanted to begin a direct assault on revisionism within the Party. He suggested that this start with a critique of Wu Han's play *Hai Jui Dismissed from Office*. Evidently, Mao's opponents realized that such an attack would undoubtedly lead to Wu Han's immediate protectors in the Party's Propaganda Department and the Peking Municipal Party Committee. Again, Mao's suggestion was turned down. The "watertight kingdom" which his opponents had established in Peking "could not be penetrated even by a needle," as Mao later exclaimed.[3] Frustrated by the organizational strength of his foes, Mao left Peking to begin a flanking operation elsewhere. During this period, Mao was, as he himself put it, very much "alone with the masses." Six months would pass before his return to Peking.

On November 10, 1965, the attack on playwright-historian Wu Han finally began, with the publication in the Shanghai *Wen Hui Pao* of Yao Wen-yuan's critique of the play *Hai Jui Dismissed from Office.* But even this was to prove a hesitant beginning, for the authorities in Peking refused to republish the critique there for another nineteen days. Yao's attack on Wu Han was direct and gave no quarter. Yao accused Wu Han of coining a false, beautified historical figure, Hai Jui, in order to publicize his own point of view. One theme of the play had been the Ming official's returning of the land to the peasants. But Yao disputed this, saying that Hai Jui had done no such thing. And if Wu Han's suggestion was that the present regime return the land, Yao asked how this could be done since the land now belonged to the people of the communes. "To whom was it to be returned?" Yao puzzled. The attack led to an intensive countrywide discussion campaign that saw many successive criticisms of Wu Han and two confessions on his part, but surprisingly it revealed a great deal of support for him as well.[4]

Reflecting this support for Wu Han and his colleagues, P'eng Chen issued an "Outline Report" on behalf of the Group of Five that was supposed to be managing the Cultural Revolution on February 12, 1966, which attempted to deflect the emerging and intensifying campaign away from political leaders by emphasizing academic issues. P'eng was clearly out of sympathy with Mao's intentions and remained opposed to the kind of thoroughgoing rectification program that Mao had in mind.

Contrastingly, Chiang Ch'ing presided over a Forum on the Work in Literature and Art in the Armed Forces in February 1966. The Summary of the Forum which was finalized after being personally examined and revised by Mao three times, was altogether different in tenor and in purpose. A *Red Flag* magazine editorial (No. 9, 1966) stated that P'eng's report "is a black banner" whereas the Forum Summary is a "red banner representing the general counterattack launched by the proletariat on the handful of Party persons in authority taking the capitalist road."

The Maoists ignored P'eng's evasive effort and now turned heavy verbal guns on Teng T'o and others. Teng was accused of hating the Party and socialism "to his very bones." He was to be "grabbed, have his words rooted out and impaled." In May and early June,

Teng's writings and those of his "clique," comprising at least two hundred articles, were publicly analysed almost daily in the press and in broadcasts.[5]

On May 16, 1966 the Central Committee denounced P'eng's "Outline Report" of February and the original Group of Five was replaced by a new Cultural Revolution Group.[6] This new organ included K'ang Sheng and Mao's wife Chiang Ch'ing, and was chaired by Mao's long-time personal secretary, Ch'en Po-ta. This move had been prefaced by two important developments in the preceding ten days. One of these was the issuance on May 7, 1966, of a directive from Mao to Lin Piao that the PLA and other sections of Chinese society ought to move beyond their normal responsibilities and also engage in "economic construction," "mass work," and active "criticism of the bourgeoisie." [7] This directive eloquently expressed the spirit of the impending Cultural Revolution. Of more permanent significance, it is regarded as the charter which established the unique May Seventh cadre schools in the next few years. Two days later, on May 9, 1966, China conducted its third nuclear test, providing a dramatic backdrop for Mao's imminent return to Peking.

Even after May 16, 1966, considerable political maneuvering continued in Peking. P'eng Chen was not actually removed from office until later in May or in June, probably with some pressuring from Lin Piao. Liu Shao-ch'i, with Teng Hsiao-p'ing, attempted to make the best of a deteriorating situation, now that the Peking Municipal Party Committee and the Party Propaganda Department were in shambles. Liu was aware that he was the ultimate target. He had returned from a visit to South Asia in April to a cold reception at the Peking airport where no leading dignitaries were on hand. There is a possibility that Liu and Teng tried in June and July to put together a Central Committee meeting that would confirm their leadership and actually remove Mao from power. Such a move, however, was precluded by the presence in Peking of Lin Piao's PLA in some force. By early June too, the *People's Daily* was taken over by Mao supporters. Lu Ting-yi, referred to as the "king of hell" by Mao, was replaced as propaganda director. The replacement, T'ao Chu, would last only several months before himself being disgraced.

Liu Shao-ch'i was also busy trying to quell the rising tide of the

Cultural Revolution at the grass-roots level as well. Already at Peking University faculty and students, with encouragement from Mao and his supporters, had begun mass demonstrations. On May 25, 1966, they erected a huge poster criticizing the university's officials. This received Mao's personal approval on June 1. The great activity that ensued became confusing because some students and faculty members continued to support those being criticized. On July 16, it was announced that the university would be closed during the coming academic year. Liu tried to settle the turmoil by means of a technique that had become familiar during the earlier socialist education campaign. He sent in work teams in which his wife participated to discuss matters. But it soon turned out that such work teams were there to support the officials under attack.

Mao had again absented himself from Peking, leaving on June 2 just as things were warming up at Peking University. He was gone for more than six weeks, perhaps this time giving Liu Shao-ch'i ample opportunity to compromise himself directly. Because Mao had been out of sight for so much of late 1965 and early 1966 rumors had become rife that he was ill or otherwise incapacitated. Observers recalled that he had spoken with foreign guests in months prior to his absence of soon going "to see God." Mao set aside all such speculation on July 16, 1966, by making a spectacular swim on the Yangtze River. Reportedly, he swam a distance of ten miles with the current in only one hour. Whether the champion performance was accurately reported or not, the event had the desired effect of informing the world, and in particular his opponents in Peking, that he was in excellent health and robust enough to take on *any* challenge.

The celebrated and controversial swim on the Yangtze was part of a now crescendoing cult that extolled Mao to the high heavens. Mao was referred to in the most grandiose terms, for example, as "the reddest sun in our hearts," or the "Great Helmsman." [8] Mao was the only hero in the four-hour epic musical extravaganza "The East is Red," which tells the story of the entire Chinese revolution. So too, Mao's thought was singled out for unparalleled attention. It was called "the sun in our heart . . . the root of our life . . . the source of all our strength" [9] and was even regarded by some as a magic weapon that might accomplish miracles. Indeed, many claims would be made that the use of Mao's thought did, in fact, produce wonders, even miracles. Some of this was undoubtedly nonsense, and some such publicity may have been as much the work of clever detractors as much as naive devotees. In any case, Mao buttons, slogans, busts, and portraits soon saturated Chinese life at every turn. It is undoubtedly true that much of this spectacle sickened even Mao himself. He intimated as much later. However, at the same time it is clear that Mao was making use of the cult in his political struggle with oppositionists entrenched in the Party and elsewhere. He conjectured with Edgar Snow that Khrushchev may have fallen because he had no such cult.[10] Mao's popularity, especially in its immensely exaggerated form, was a factor that neutralized his enemies despite their numbers or their positions of power and influence. As a matter of fact the real point was who would control the cult, Mao or the Party.[11] Mao won this struggle. The cult was a distasteful weapon to be wielded in an hour of need. Along with the mobilization of the masses and the ultimate power of the PLA it gave Mao the decisive hand.

The Eleventh Plenum of the Eighth Central Committee from August 1 to 12, 1966, signaled Mao's victory over Liu Shao-ch'i, although Liu would not be personally identified and subjected to public calumny for some time to come. Lin Piao was named the exclusive vice chairman of the Party and Mao's heir-designate. P'eng Chen and his group were formally dismissed. On August 5, Mao composed his famous wall poster "Bombard the Headquarters." [12] This was the signal to carry the Cultural Revolution to the highest levels of the Party. On August 8, the Eleventh Plenum issued the "Sixteen Articles," which provided the initial guidelines for the Cultural Revolution that was now to get underway in all seriousness. It was to be a movement that was to "sweep away all monsters" and "touch men to their very souls." [13]

A principal characteristic of the Great Proletarian Cultural Revolution (the full title) was the mobilization, organization, and use of young people who now came to be known as the Red Guards. These youngsters attacked with relish the "four-olds," i.e., old ideas, culture, customs, and habits. This phenomenon directly reflected Mao's long-expressed concern that the younger generation become proper revolutionary heirs through personal steeling in the rough and tumble struggles and the soul-searching of mass mobilization politics. The Red Guards were a highly visible element of the Cultural Revolution, but they were not intended to be its principal ingredient. However, the uniqueness of the phenomenon along with its scale and its abuses have given it a perhaps disproportionate amount of attention.

The Cultural Revolution Group provided political guidance for the Red Guards while the PLA helped with organization, logistical, and travel support. In the fall of 1966 about 10 million Red Guards converged on Peking to participate in a series of eight huge rallies between August 18 and November 26. Mao made an appearance at each of these massive demonstrations, as did Lin Piao and Chou En-lai. Such "long marches" to Peking were discouraged after November 1966, partly because the nation's transportation had become disoriented from the traveling hordes and partly so that the young people would now carry on the Cultural Revolution within the Party organizations at provincial and lower levels. By late 1966 the Party center in Peking had already become docile; in October both Liu Shao-ch'i and Teng Hsiao-p'ing made self-criticisms, although these were not considered acceptable.

It was otherwise in the provinces. Here the Red Guards soon ran into trouble. Party chieftains, bureaucrats, and some military leaders who regarded themselves as natural allies of the Liu-Teng Group in Peking used a variety of wiles to blunt and deflect the rampaging Red Guards, many of whom were especially zealous now that they had made their own "long march" and had seen Mao with their very own eyes. Local and provincial power wielders employed "Red Guard" groups of their own, and these gave the appearance of supporting Mao themselves. It was the technique of "waving the red flag in order to undermine the red flag," as the Maoists quickly recognized. As a result of such tactics tremendous confusion reigned.

Assistance from the Cultural Revolution Group in Peking through the mobilization of groups such as the Revolutionary Rebels, composed of workers, only elicited from the opposition similarly designated groups of their own. The struggle became intense in some areas, and violence ensued.

In some areas where the Maoists had enjoyed considerable support already, the Red Guards and Revolutionary Rebels were able to make the necessary "power seizures" swiftly. In Shanghai, for example, events moved so quickly that the enthusiasm of the Maoists led them to establish an urban commune in February 1967. Their thinking was certainly in the right direction, for Mao himself probably desired such bold experimentation, if circumstances were conducive.[14] However, desirable circumstances were lacking at this time so that by the end of the month the adventure had to be abandoned. In its stead, however, there was created a governing body that would help set the pattern for other areas, as they similarly completed their power seizures. A Revolutionary Committee was established that comprised representatives of a "three-way alliance," i.e., of the three constituencies: the "revolutionary masses" such as the Red Guards and the Revolutionary Rebels; PLA men; and Party cadres who were loyal to Mao, or who had transformed themselves. By April 1967, Peking recognized six legitimate power seizures throughout the country—Shanghai, Heilungkiang, Shansi, Shantung, Kweichow and Peking—each of which now had such revolutionary committees. Those areas which had only pretended to have a power seizure were compelled to continue the Cultural Revolution. In the next several months progress slowed to a snail's pace as developments became exceedingly confusing.

Mao wanted a thorough shaking down of the system, and he believed that a degree of disorder, disruption and destruction was necessary in order to accomplish this objective. But surely he did not want the chaos that was threatening, and that did come about in some parts of China during 1967. However, in order to forestall an unnecessary undesirable state of affairs Mao called upon the carefully groomed PLA in late January 1967 to intervene in the working-out of the Cultural Revolution. The PLA was expected to support "left revolutionaries" in the confusing factional struggles throughout the land, as well as to assure a modicum of order and the functioning of vital public services. But this was an extremely difficult assignment for the PLA. In the confusion of the early weeks, the PLA often seemed to err on the side of conservatism, opting for providing order rather than adequately support pro-Maoist revolutionaries. By early April 1967, Lin Piao had to order his hard-pressed commanders not to use force against pro-Maoist elements.

Developments became increasingly confusing. In Peking, the Politburo's Standing Committee seems to have stopped functioning in March 1967. Liu Shao-ch'i, still not identified personally, was now indirectly attacked with great fanfare as "China's Khrushchev." The Cultural Revolution Group in Peking seemed to be in charge and it kept encouraging the making of revolution. As a result, the turmoil continued and there were many instances of excesses both within and without China. Chou En-lai was called upon frequently to mediate among feuding factions. His task, and that of the PLA commanders and others, was made difficult not only by the tactics of devious oppositionists, but also by the extremists on the left. The latter, in their rambunctious ways, were as much a threat to the attainment of Mao's objectives as the original targets of the Cultural Revolution were alleged to be.

A particularly dramatic example of how such extremist elements goaded a military commander into overplaying his hand was the Wuhan incident of July 1967.[15] For some time, Ch'en Tsai-tao, commander of the Wuhan military region, had been leaning rather hard on the apparently more Maoist of the Red Guard factions in Wuhan. Two prominent visitors from Peking, Hsieh Fu-chih, former minister of public security and now chairman of Peking's Revolutionary Committee, and Wang Li, a member of the Cultural Revolution Group, investigated the situation and upheld the oppressed Maoist factions. Ch'en Tsai-tao then connived in having Hsieh and Wang seized and beaten. The serious situation was relieved only by the deployment of forces by Lin Piao and the direct intervention of Chou En-lai. Ch'en was later removed from his important position for such defiance, but was not punished severely. Mao could see that the provocations of extremists were undermining his objectives.

But the activities of extremists were not easy to control, apparently partly because many were part of an organized plot, implemented to a large extent by a group known as the 516 Group (or May 16 Group). Ultimately, Lin Piao himself would be accused of having connections with this disruptive program. It is not clear to what extent such an organized group was involved in many of the irrational manifestations of the Cultural Revolution, but the 516 Group has become a convenient way to explain away some of the embarrassing incidents. China's prestige did suffer from the antics of foolish ultraleftists in Hong Kong, Rangoon, London, as well as within China itself, where the Soviet Embassy was under siege early in 1967 and the British diplomatic compound was seized and burned in August 1967, among other such atrocious acts.

By September 1967, some of the ultraleftists, like Wang Li, were removed from the scene. The PLA was authorized to use force, albeit defensively, in order to protect itself against Red Guard raids. China enjoyed a respite from the confusion for several months. Enough stability was provided that from January until May 1968, fifteen provincial revolutionary committees were formed, compared to the nine completed during 1967.

However, following the replacement of Acting Chief of Staff Yang Chen-wu by Huang Yung-sheng in March 1968 there was a renewed upsurge of Red Guard activity. Some of this was encouraged by Chiang Ch'ing. Again there came to be open violence between opposing factions. In Kwangsi, trains carrying war material to North Vietnam were pilfered for arms in order to support the internecine conflict, which now reached major proportions. Stories of torture and executions abounded. By midsummer the use of weapons had spread to Peking. On July 3, an armed clash took place at Tsinghua University (China's M.I.T.) in which fifteen students were killed.[16] All such violence was in direct violation of Mao's own warnings not to take up arms. The Red Guards became emboldened enough to hold a secret conference in Peking later that month at which plans were discussed for a national organization that would have its own radio network.

Mao got wind of these plans and at 3 A.M. on July 28 he had the Red Guard leaders before him to receive his scolding firsthand. Reportedly with tears in his eyes, Mao told them that they had let him down and disappointed the workers, the peasants, and the soldiers.[17] The Red Guards had served a function in the Cultural Revolution, and some young new leaders had invariably been identified. However, the youth movement had been found wanting in certain respects and this was a consequence, Mao reasoned, of faults in the educational system. Mao would turn to a new instrumentality with which to replace the Red Guards. This new instrumentality was a force as elemental as the young people, but better experienced and more mature.

Two days later, thousands of PLA-men, workers, and peasants moved in on Tsinghua University. A Worker-Peasant Mao Tse-tung Thought Propaganda Team took over control of the school. Similarly designated teams soon assumed the administration of schools at all levels in urban areas throughout China. In rural areas the poor and middle peasant associations took control of schools. The new "teams," which would have as many as hundreds of participants at times, worked in conjunction with the PLA. On August 5, Mao sent to the Tsinghua University Worker-Peasant Mao Tse-tung Thought Team a gift of mangoes, which had that day been given to him by the Pakistan foreign minister.[18] The gift signified Mao's approval of the new teams and the event was given tremendous publicity throughout China.

By early September, the last of the twenty-nine provincial and metropolitan revolutionary committees had been formed. The last five of these were in sensitive border areas, and their formation in August and early September may have been an indicator of Chinese alarm at Soviet armed intervention in Czechoslovakia on August 21, 1968.

The Cultural Revolution was not declared ended. Some of the programs it inspired would continue for many months to come. Following the formula of "struggle-criticism-transformation" it was now generally a time for transformation. However, at the Twelfth Plenum of the Eighth Central Committee, held October 13–31, 1968, it was made evident that at least some of the goals of the Cultural Revolution were achieved. Mao's principal adversary, Liu Shao-ch'i, was removed from all offices and expelled from the Party as a "renegade traitor and scab." [19] A new draft Party constitution was adopted, for submittal to an expected new Party congress in the next several months. Also approved were two mass line programs that were soon put into effect. The first of these was a massive shift of urban dwellers, mostly young people, to the countryside. By the spring of 1969 this had involved a movement of 30 million people. The other program included the restoration in some places of certain elements of

Great Leap Forward economic policies. Thus some communes again abolished such material incentives as private plots and work points.

The Party congress that would formally approve these changes was held in early April 1969, but before that event, two momentous developments occurred in the field of foreign relations that seemed to prefigure the shape of things to come. The first was Chou En-lai's overture to the United States for a resumption of the Sino-American Warsaw talks. The offer was made on November 25, 1968, but Chou suggested the opening date of February 20, 1969, which was designed to give President Richard Nixon time to settle into his office, a conciliatory gesture with promising implications. Unfortunately, however, the session was canceled at the last moment, apparently due to the temporary ascendancy of a militant leftist viewpoint in Peking.[20] An internal debate was raging, and Mao gave it full rein.

The other development was profoundly disturbing. On March 2, 1969, Chinese and Russian forces engaged in heavy fighting on an island in the Ussuri River.[21] A second clash on March 15, according to the Chinese, resulted in a Russian defeat. Some claim the Chinese started the incident, perhaps to provoke a crisis that would make the forthcoming Party congress patriotically less critical of domestic policies. Others would say that the Russians provoked the incident as a warning to the upcoming congress.

The Ninth Party Congress met in Peking from April 1 to 24, 1969. Mao gave two brief speeches at this "congress of unity and of victory," while Lin Piao delivered the principal address. The 1,500 delegates adopted the new Party constitution, and elected a new Central Committee of 170 members and 109 alternates. The now popular three-way alliance was reflected in the membership composition, with a decided weight in favor of the PLA. Thus about 45 percent were PLA-men, about 28 percent were "revolutionary cadres" and 27 percent were representatives of the "revolutionary masses." Only about one-third of these members were carryovers from the Eighth Central Committee.[22]

The Ninth Central Committee elected a new Politburo of twenty-one members and four alternates, with Mao as chairman and Lin Piao as vice chairman. Only nine of these men had been on the Politburo before the beginning of the Cultural Revolution. About half of the members of the new Politburo were military men. Fourteen of the Politburo members had been members also of Mao's *ad hoc* "proletarian headquarters," an organ that had supervised civil administration over the past several months.

From all appearances the Ninth Party Congress was a victory for Mao. He and his thought were praised to high heaven, in contrast to the First Session of the Eighth Congress in 1956. Lin Piao's political report alone contained no less than 148 references to Mao.[23] The report recounted the preparations for the Cultural Revolution, reaffirming Mao's contention that it was "absolutely necessary and most timely for consolidating the dictatorship of the proletariat, preventing capitalist restoration and building socialism." Lin then reviewed the "crimes" of the rejected Liu Shao-ch'i, indicating that "it has now been proved through investigation that Liu Shao-ch'i betrayed the Party, capitulated to the enemy, and became a hidden traitor and scab as far back as the first revolutionary civil war period, that he was a crime-steeped lackey of the imperialists, modern revisionists, and Kuomintang reactionaries, and that he was the arch-representative of the persons in power taking the capitalist road." The catalog went on to astonishing lengths, and one wonders that it did not strain the credulity even of the most devoted Maoist.

Lin reviewed the course and the policies of the Cultural Revolution, liberally quoting Mao at every turn. Lin asserted that a great victory had been won in the Cultural Revolution, but referred to Mao's own word of caution: "We have won great victory. But the defeated class will still struggle. These people are still around and this class still exists. Therefore, we cannot speak of final victory. Not even for decades. We must not lose our vigilance." Mao had reminded his comrades that "according to the Leninist viewpoint, the final victory of a socialist country . . . also involves the victory of the world revolution. . . ."

In this vein, China's foreign relations were also aired. The tone was militant. Mao's description of the general trend in the world was quoted: "The enemy rots with every passing day, while for us things are getting better daily." Several current armed struggles were singled out as evidence of the "vigorously surging forward" of the worldwide revolutionary movement. This was taken to affirm that

Mao's old adage, or as Lin put it, the "truth that 'political power grows out of the barrel of a gun' is being grasped by ever broader masses of the oppressed people and nations." Lin noted that "an unprecedentedly gigantic revolutionary mass movement has broken out in Japan, Western Europe and North America, the 'heartlands' of capitalism." Perhaps it was this phenomenon that encouraged militancy toward the United States and the Soviet Union simultaneously, despite the recent armed flare-up on the Soviet border. Lin struck out at both superpowers, noting that both "are always trying to 'isolate' China." He again quoted Mao: "Working hand in glove, Soviet revisionism and U.S. imperialism have done so many foul and evil things that the revolutionary people the world over will not let them go unpunished. The people of all countries are rising. A new historical period of struggle against U.S. imperialism and Soviet revisionism has begun."

The Ninth Party Constitution was the briefest such document to date.[24] It also extolled Mao and some of his basic precepts. It declared that the Party "takes Marxism-Leninism-Mao Tse-tung Thought as the theoretical basis guiding its thinking." It elaborated: "Mao Tse-tung Thought is Marxism-Leninism of the era in which imperialism in heading for total collapse and socialism is advancing to world-wide victory." "For half a century now . . . Comrade Mao Tse-tung has integrated the universal truth of Marxism-Leninism and has brought it to a higher and completely new stage."

The constitution recognized that "Socialist society covers a considerably long historical period." During "this historical period, there are classes, class contradictions and class struggle, there is the struggle between the socialist road and the capitalist road, there is the danger of capitalist restoration and there is the threat of subversion and aggression by imperialism and modern revisionism. These contradictions can be resolved only by depending on the Marxist theory of continued revolution. . . . Such is China's Great Proletarian Cultural Revolution." Members of the Party were enjoined to "Study and apply Marxism-Leninism-Mao Tse-tung Thought in a living way."

A most unusual feature of the Ninth Party Constitution was its naming of Lin Piao as Mao's successor. There is little question that Lin had been a loyal and an important supporter of Mao for many years, and particularly when Mao most needed support prior to and during the Cultural Revolution. Mao's gratitude was undoubted. But the selection of Lin as successor was premature. It made the Ninth Congress an even greater success for Lin than it did for Mao. In reflecting back on the salient features of the congress and what it approved, it actually seemed to be as much, or perhaps even more, Lin's congress than Mao's. While many of the sentiments and the objectives of this congress would endure, it was otherwise with some of the key people whose prominence and power along with Lin Piao were confirmed by it.

The Cultural Revolution, and the Ninth Party Congress that seemed to signify its success, represented a confirmation of Mao's unique Chinese Way for national and social revolutionary development. This Chinese Way is a Sinified Marxism-Leninism, as suggested by the assertion that Mao has brought this Communist ideology "to a higher and completely new stage," implicitly on the basis of the experience of the Chinese Revolution. This was a process that had begun in the 1930s and it reached one high-water mark in 1945. It was down-played and largely abandoned in the early and mid-'50s during the period of leaning to the Soviet side. But beginning with the Three Red Banners of 1957–58 and culminating in the Cultural Revolution, the Sinification process, with Mao's own distinctive stamp upon it, was intensified. The ebbtide of the early sixties was merely a temporary one that heightened the clash and the drama of the Cultural Revolution. Thus it is uninstructive to concentrate only on the surface political development of the confusing Cultural Revolution period. To understand the meaning of this tremendous upheaval, and to gain insight into Mao's revolution, one must plumb somewhat deeper.

The Cultural Revolution was more than a political power struggle, for it was fundamentally a revolution in values and attitudes.[25] Mao sought to implant more deeply a new consciousness in the Chinese people, a consciousness informed by genuinely socialist values that were to be practiced now rather than allowed to become embalmed by rhetoric for a never-to-be-realized future. Mao enjoined an ideology of "service to the people" that entailed dedication, self-sacrifice, selflessness, self-reliance, and struggle.

Such an ideology was the substance of the literature of the Cultural Revolution, a literature that saw record-breaking publication statistics, universal distribution and serious reading and internalizing by vast numbers of the huge Chinese population. Aside from the relevant pithy passages in the Little Red Book of Mao's Quotations itself, perhaps the articles that best exemplified this ideological thrust were the "three most constantly read articles" of the Cultural Revolution. They are "Serve the People," "Remember Norman Bethune," and "The Foolish Old Man Who Removed the Mountains," all written by Mao at various times. Bethune was a Canadian medical doctor who had given his life while selflessly ministering to the wounded and ill among the Chinese Communists during World War II. The third piece was quoted on page 86 and encourages a spirit of undaunted persistence in the face of "impossible" obstacles.

Other positive, more recent heroes were given intensive nationwide publicity. Such PLA-men as Men Ho and Lei Feng were said to have lived astonishingly virtuous and selfless lives, even going to their death fearlessly in the service of their comrades.

Institutional models that exemplified a particularly desirable collective spirit and enviable achievements received massive publicity. The Eleventh Plenum of the Eighth Central Committee instructed industry to follow the example of the Taching oil field in Manchuria, agriculture to follow the example of the Tachai production brigade in Shansi, while the entire country was encouraged to "learn from the PLA." At both Taching and Tachai workers and peasants had accomplished almost unbelievable achievements in the face of most unpromising circumstances and uncooperative terrain.[26] However, through heroic feats of persistence, endurance, and social cooperation, the rather miraculous results were obtained.

Complementing this heavy dose of positive individual and institutional models that the Chinese people were to emulate, there were negative models that personified the kinds of attitudes, values, and behavior that were regarded as anathema to the new society struggling to be born. Thus we noted that Li Hsiu-ch'eng, the erstwhile popular Taiping hero, was revealed as a traitor for allegedly having failed to carry out the revolution to the end. Liu Shao-ch'i fared even worse, for he came to personify a whole range of undesirable thinking and practices. Such wholesale attribution of "towering crimes" to a single individual when clearly the truth is being twisted in the process is repugnant to many outside observers, as indeed it must be to many critical minds within China. But, whether acceptable or not, such use and abuse of negative models has been standard practice in China long before the present revolution. It fulfills the function today of adding in its way to the implantation of new values. The justice and the effectiveness of the technique in China must be left to time and to the Chinese people to determine, although outsiders will likely retain their doubts and disagreements.

But Mao is hardly one to entrust the instilling of new values exclusively to the use of campaigns, propaganda, or to the discussion of models of one sort or another. The all-important values and attitudes are to be insured by necessary changes in the institutions and practices of society. Thus there were sweeping changes implemented in the educational system and in the Party and government bureaucracies. The means of bringing about these changes, and the purposes in doing so, were reminiscent of the Yenan Way from the Party's proud civil war days.

The government organization was urged by Mao to achieve greater administrative efficiency with his call for "better troops and less administration." Accordingly, central government offices in Peking sharply reduced their staffs. Many Peking personnel were transferred out to the provinces and to local posts as part of the simplification and decentralization program. Others were sent to the now famous May Seventh cadre schools. The government bureaucracy and its organizational structure underwent a general housecleaning and the structure would be rebuilt by means of a process that would take several years to complete.

An important element in this shakeup of government administration was to eliminate not only revisionist thinking, but the more common offensive, bureaucratic patterns of behavior as well. The May Seventh school, called into being by Mao in his famous directive of that date in 1966, was ingeniously devised to serve these ends.[27] Here, professionals and administrative cadres were encouraged to go beyond the study and practice of their own professional pursuits, and "to raise levels of education and to engage in agriculture and side-occupations, to run small or medium-sized factories, to engage

in mass work, and to participate in the struggles to criticize and re-
pudiate the bourgeoisie." The schools were built from scratch,
usually in very hard or marginal countryside terrain. They were
built by the "students," i.e., the cadres temporarily assigned to the
schools. The students made the soil yield crops, usually with the advice and help of neighboring peasants, and eventually made themselves largely self-sufficient. As the schools prospered, the students
constructed small factories to manufacture products of use in the
local economy. Aside from such productive labor, the students spent
much of their time in political study. The length of assignments to a
May Seventh cadre school varied from place to place but normally a
student could expect to spend three to six months. He or she would
be allowed to visit families for a couple of days every ten days or so.
Usually about a sixth of the total professional population of a given
district might be assigned to their district school. This meant that administrative staffs in town were smaller in size by that proportion at
any given time. It meant too that personnel could expect to be ro-
tated out to the cadre school on a regular basis every few years. The
system seemed to work, at least in places observed by many visiting
foreigners. The exercise served the purpose of maintaining and improving political responsiveness, cultivating an appreciation for the
value of physical labor and of what life is like for those who do such
work on a permanent basis, raising the level of health of those who
tended to work at desks all the time, and deterring officious behavior. The newly designed government structure was staffed by rededi-
cated and reinvigorated personnel. Bureaucracy, its merits and its
evils, have had a long experience in China. It is said too that undue
bureaucratization is one of the major problems of other socialist
bloc countries. Clearly, no other Communist leadership has done
more to deal with the problem.[28]

In education, the spirit of Yenan was revived as the entire system
underwent a revolutionary overhauling.[29] The Ministry of Education,
which had been the apex of a highly centralized educational bureaucracy, was abolished. In its stead there was established a Science
and Education Group under the State Council that would operate for
several years until a new ministry would come into being and which
only formulated educational policy and guidelines for recommen-

dation to the country. The devising of textbooks and much of the curriculum was now left to the provinces to determine. Even at the local level there was latitude allowed for using local experience and materials in order to improve the effectiveness of teaching. All hiring, firing, transferring, and promotion of teachers was placed in the hands of local or community authority rather than in a local or district office of the former Ministry of Education.

The number of courses in schools was reduced and the content of courses was often greatly revised. Much greater emphasis was placed on productive labor and the relating of curriculum to practical life and work experience. Examinations were for a time abolished. No longer did students proceed automatically from middle school to college; there was now a two or three year hiatus during which all youngsters engaged in some form of productive labor in factories or on the farm. In order to be admitted into college or university the prospective student had to be selected by his work group on the basis of his political and work attitude as much as his academic qualifications, promise, and health. This has resulted in a much changed social composition among students in higher education. Where before the Cultural Revolution the sons and daughters of the officials and "bourgeoisie" had a real advantage, such children were now limited to a small percentage quota. The bulk of students now came from the ranks of the worker and peasant families of China, with a quota from the military as well. University instruction was shortened, and again regular productive labor either by work in school workshops or in a local factory or commune was made part of the new routine.

Revolutionary committees that were established in all organizations and institutions saw to it that practices were followed that guaranteed fuller participation by all members in work and in decision-making. This was to forestall a reemergence of elitism and bureaucratism and also to help cultivate the emergence of the well-rounded socialist man. Hence, in factories and shops throughout China the principles of the Anshan Constitution were implemented, particularly the "two participations" and the "three-in-one combination." [30] It is possible that in many places such practices were followed only grudgingly, and sometimes merely given lip service.

However, it is also likely that in many more places they were practiced in the hoped-for spirit of cooperation with resultant benefits in morale and productivity. It is a fact that despite some economic slowdown in some parts of China during certain periods of the Cultural Revolution, the pace of China's economic development did not suffer noticeably from the implementation of these social reforms. Of course, one cannot read into these reforms more than what they actually comprised. There remained other problems such as wage and salary differentials that still have ratios of 5 or 6 to 1, between the most experienced and best-trained managers and skilled workers and the youngest, unskilled personnel.

China's intentions to socialize and to spread social benefits equitably was perhaps best illustrated in the field of medicine and public health.[31] Emphasis was placed during the Cultural Revolution on the training of paramedics, known as "barefoot doctors," who with minimal training of up to six months, were distributed evenly throughout the countryside. By the end of the sixties just about every production brigade could boast of a health clinic with at least one such barefoot doctor in attendance. Most minor, routine ailments could be handled by means of this service, which was available to all commune members as part of an inexpensive health plan. Serious illnesses or ailments are treated at hospitals at the commune level where better-trained staff normally serve. Similar medical service is available to workers in the cities, except that it is usually free and there are likely to be even more better-trained doctors. The vastly improved health of China's citizens, and their ready access to medicine and medical treatment regardless of the individual's position in life is concrete evidence to all Chinese that Mao's revolution is serious about its rhetoric of spreading benefits equitably.

Similar evidence can be seen in the distribution of industry throughout the country where the aim is not to maximize efficiency, production, and profitability [32] but to achieve a better balance between heavily urbanized areas and the countryside, thereby equalizing a bit more the opportunities for urban and countryside denizens. Mao's program was spelled out in September 1969 in a *Red Flag* magazine article entitled "The Road to China's Socialist Industrialization." [33] The article reaffirmed the principles earlier expressed in Mao's essays of 1956 and 1957—"On the Ten Great Relationships" and "On the Correct Handling of Contradictions among the People." Self-reliance, the mobilization of the labor and the wisdom of the people, and full and planned use of all natural resources were principles to be implemented swiftly but at the lowest cost. Learning from abroad was permissible, but not unmodified imitation of foreign technology. "Politics in command" was to remain an absolute injunction. Heavy industry was to take the lead, but both industry and agriculture and both light and heavy industry were to develop simultaneously. By means of centralized leadership, overall planning and the division of work, both central and local industries were to be expanded simultaneously and both foreign and indigenous production techniques were to be employed. Heavy industry, while leading the way, had to be based upon the expansion first of light industry and farming. In this way would the people's needs be satisfied and the needed capital be raised for the heavy sector. Also a prosperous agriculture was deemed necessary in order for heavy industry to have outlets for its products. Thus, agriculture and the peasantry received the assurance that they would get maximum support from all other sectors of the economy.

Each county was instructed to set up an industrial network which would manufacture and repair farm equipment. Each region, province, and city was to establish an independent industrial system that would not only further distribute industrialization advantages but provide a dispersed system that would be a safeguard in the event of an attack from the Soviet Union. The division of labor of these networks was logical. County factories build the hard-core industries which manufacture the means of production to equip commune and brigade factories and also supply agricultural inputs. Commune level factories make agricultural implements, process foodstuffs, and make available raw materials to county factories. At the brigade level, workshops assemble and repair agricultural implements, mill flour, and help mine ores for higher level factories.[34]

Mao's development strategy does seems to be working for his country. It is a program that he had to struggle to implement, against the advice and the opposition of many others who supposedly represented more professional or rational schemes. However, Mao persisted, especially against notions that would have depended more exclusively upon experts and professionals, or upon government bureaucracies whether at the central or provincial levels. His dislike of Liu Shao-ch'i's scheme to establish "trusts" that would have monopolistic control of the manufacture and distribution of their products was a case in point. These trusts would have destroyed small-scale industries. Likewise, tractor stations, prominent in the Soviet Union, were enjoined by the Liuists to show a profit as a measure of their effectiveness, or (in 1962) be abolished if they did not do so within two years.[35] Mao returned the tractors to the communes where their ownership by the people could be perceived more directly and where they would accordingly receive much better care. The emphasis in Mao's strategy has been not on profitability but on getting people involved in the experience of development. This involvement must be on a very intimate, personal, and direct basis. Then the naturally aroused interest must be channeled into cooperative work patterns that produce results that can be seen and that have a meaningful return for their livelihood and for their own calculations of the future.

China's decentralized economy, built basically upon agriculture and light industry and supported by a network of rural industries, is expected to make a leap , as public awareness and expertise increase, towards becoming a modern, advanced, and balanced economy. By succeeding in this patterning of industry throughout the country China also is resolving employment and regional problems that are endemic among the developing and underdeveloped nations of the world.

China paid off her external debt to the Soviet Union by 1965, so that she is unique among countries of the world in having neither an external nor an internal national debt. The controlled and growing economy has experienced no inflation since the early fifties, so that hard-earned wages are not affected by that affliction. There is a sense of purposefulness among the Chinese people and a pride that comes from all the hard work and the self-reliance and the willingness to serve the people and the nation. There is an awareness that someday the technological revolution may succeed and that China will have the modern conveniences and comforts that other nations and peoples today enjoy. In the meantime China must work to achieve such benefits. It is the mark of success of Mao's revolution thus far that the Chinese people are already realizing some basic benefits and that they are doing so on a more or less equitable basis. It is testimony too, to Mao's success thus far that his people are willing to continue the struggle and self-sacrifice to make the capital investments today that will make China a better place to live tomorrow.

NINE
The Continuing Need for Revolutionary Renewal

Entering the 1970s China's record of achievements was impressive. Despite the gloomy assessments and forecasts of anti-Communist and anti-Maoist detractors, and in spite of the years of relative isolation and embargo imposed by the United States, of the increasing enmity of the Soviet Union, and of the occasional disequilibrium wrought by such massive and unprecedented campaigns as the Great Leap Forward and the Cultural Revolution, the economy did move forward. There was clear and abundant evidence of overall material progress. Even more important, in Mao's reckoning, was that the momentum of the social revolution had not been sacrificed in the process. That this revolution continued to succeed was reflected in the spirit and the morale of the now unified and healthful populace. This spirited ethos, the badge, and the product of China's Maoist revolution was a frequent object of admiration by many visitors to China in the early seventies.[1] The Cultural Revolution had made a difference, apparently, in helping to produce this heady buoyancy in the vast population.

But for all the positive features that one might identify in the post-Cultural Revolution period, it was also evident that serious problems continued to exist. And some of these gnawed at the very vitals of the Chinese system. Within months of the seemingly triumphant Ninth Party Congress, Mao was threatened by ex-comrades from across the vast northern border who wielded the largest concentration of armed power in the world. Perhaps even more ominously he was also threatened within China itself by a man who had been his closest comrade. These grave threats to the Chinese revolution were of extraordinary magnitude and urgency. They required special measures to deal with successfully. Yet as serious and menacing as these two threats were, they were only in addition to the omnipresent usual problems besetting the revolution, the alleged pernicious influences of the "bourgeoisie" whether consciously exerted or not, and the human failings that result in bureaucratism and other forms of backsliding. Vigilance and class struggle remained prerequisites for maintaining the viability of the Chinese revolution. The more ordinary and routine threats were to be struggled against by means of the new institutional structures, such as the May Seventh cadre schools and the revamped educational system, and through the reconstituted propaganda mechanisms.

The Soviet threat, however, was immediate and overwhelming. By mid-1969 the Soviet Union had amassed an intimidating array of military units along the Sino-Soviet border. Such pressure necessitated the moderation of domestic revolutionary time-schedules. This is one reason why mass campaigns were not employed intensively in this critical period. Organization and regularization of activities and processes took precedent in the face of possible foreign attack. But the threat was so great as to require additional measures as well. The greatest of these was the beginning by mid-May 1969 of a diplomatic offensive that soon won acclaim and recognition throughout the world. The purpose was to counter the Soviet armed threat by means of involvement with other nations whose support might help deter a sudden attack from the north. Under heavy Soviet pressure, the Chinese agreed on October 6, 1969, to hold border talks with Moscow,[2] but diplomacy elsewhere proceeded apace.

These responses to the external threat were not approved by a militant leftist element in the Chinese leadership. Lin Piao, the most prominent of these leftists, seemed intent on maintaining tense relations with both the Soviet Union and the United States simultaneously. Apparently, Lin's belief in the efficacy of "people's war" or the use of the PLA defensively in order to wear down any Soviet invasion, made him oblivious of the danger China was in and of the need for other kinds of support under the circumstances. Lin was being true to Mao's military precepts, but these were intended by Mao to be employed only if there was no alternative.

Hence, Chou En-lai enjoyed Mao's backing in his effort to secure support through diplomacy. This included renewed overtures to the United States. In January and February 1970, Sino-American talks were again held in Warsaw. At the second of these meetings the Chinese seemed interested in sending an invitation to President Nixon to visit China inasmuch as he had expressed a willingness to do so. However, this prospect was set aside for the time being by the sudden American incursion from South Vietnam into Cambodia. This action sharply divided the American people themselves. It upset Mao too, and served to reinforce his own perception of the danger of imperialism in the modern world. On May 20, 1970, Mao publicly denounced American imperialism and affirmed optimistically that "revolution is the main trend in the world today." [3] But such a declaration of position, as straightforward and principled as it was, did not close the door on the possibility of negotiations with the United States. The Soviet threat assured such pragmatism on Mao's part.

But the new diplomacy and its domestic counterparts of temporarily playing down mass mobilization campaigns and easing off on Great Leap Forward-type economic policies led to further tension between leftists and moderates. This came to a head at the Second Plenum of the Ninth Central Committee, which was held between August 23 and September 6, 1970, at Lushan, Kiangsi province. Here the moderates under Chou En-lai vigorously defended the new policies. They concentrated their own attack on Ch'en Po-ta, and succeeded in having him removed from positions of influence. It would be revealed later that Ch'en was actually purged. He was, in fact, part of a plot being laid to take power. He had become increasingly objectionable to Mao for a long time, for having pushed the Mao cult to extremes, perhaps to gain advantage for himself. Lin too was guilty, according to Mao, of thus using the cult against Mao's wishes.[4] Mao may have suspected for some time Ch'en's sincerity. There were further clashes at the Second Plenum, including a confrontation between Mao and Lin Piao. This was referred to in later documents as the "struggle between the two headquarters." [5] However, this tension subsided for the moment. Lin Piao apparently tried to arrange for his elevation to the chairmanship of the People's Republic, the post vacated by Liu Shao-ch'i. Mao was annoyed at this impatience and opposed the move. Lin was confirmed as Mao's successor in the draft of a new state constitution which still required approval by the next national people's congress. But Mao may have already decided in his own mind by this time that Lin was hardly a suitable successor.

In the next several months the divergent courses of the moderates and the leftists widened, and would become antagonistic contradictions during 1971. On the one hand, the trend toward a new relationship with the United States continued, as symbolized perhaps by Edgar Snow standing beside Mao during the October 1, 1970 National Day celebrations at T'ien An Men Square. Also that October, President Nixon for the first time referred to China as the People's Republic of China. On the other hand, Lin Piao and his coterie of supporters, sensing that events were going against them and that Mao was becoming increasingly disappointed with Lin, began to crystallize an outright conspiracy to take the reins of power.

The plotting began in earnest during the winter of 1971. By February Lin, with his wife, Yeh Chun, and his son, Lin Li-kuo, were actively working on the "counterrevolutionary coup" in Soochow. From there, Lin Li-kuo was sent to Shanghai and to Hangchow to seek out comrades and to discuss and draft a plan for the coup. The plan was finally drafted by Lin Li-kuo and Yu Hsin-yeh, the Air Force deputy director of Party affairs. The coup was dubbed "Project 571." [6]

The conspirators affirmed the use of "revolution by violence to stop any counter-revolutionary evolution which takes the form of peaceful transition." Knowing that Mao was suspicious of their activities, they decided that "instead of waiting passively for our fate," to "take the great gamble." Their original plans called for the capturing of Mao, whom they gave the code name "B-52," and compel him to accept their terms. Realizing the difficulties inherent in their all-or-nothing enterprise, the plotters allegedly hoped for Soviet support. However, this allegation is inconsistent with their known anti-Soviet position. They also considered the use of "extraordinary measures, such as poison gas, germ weapons, bombing, car accidents, assassination, kidnapping, small urban guerrilla teams" and what was referred to as "Five-Four-Three," a code name for secret weapons.[7]

Tension was becoming acute by the summer of 1971, for the conspirators realized that time was running out for them. The ultrasecret debate over relations with the United States continued even while Henry Kissinger, President Nixon's foreign affairs adviser, secretly visited Peking in July. The discussions were all but concluded, however, when Kissinger hand-carried to President Nixon the invitation to visit China. The debate was ended. The contradictions among China's leaders turned antagonistic.

Mao, anticipating Lin's move against him, made a tour of key military regions in the late summer of 1971. He discussed with some of his loyal military commanders the conspiracy that was being put into motion, and he secured their support. Lin Piao was unable to make serious inroads into the ranks of the key regional military organizations. His adherents remained associated principally with the top levels of the central military command in Peking.

The conspirators now decided to assassinate Mao, for there was little prospect of persuading him to change his views. The assassination could be blamed on others. Lin Piao would take power and with feigned righteous indignation eliminate Mao's dastardly "enemies." The deed was to be accomplished on September 12, 1971, during the course of Mao's return train trip from Shanghai to Peking. Arrangements were made to blow up the train at two separate points along the line, the second one to be activated in case the first one misfired.[8] Mao was thus condemned by his erstwhile "closest comrade in arms" to the same fate that the Japanese had provided for the Manchurian warlord Chang Tso-lin in 1931.

But fate took an unexpected turn and the entire plot failed. The PLA officer who was entrusted with setting off the first bombing, torn between conflicting loyalties, found a way to miss the assignment. His wife informed authorities who quickly removed Mao from the train only minutes before the second fateful rendezvous.[9]

For Lin Piao the game was up. His son, for whom Lin had secured a rapid promotion to the post of deputy director of operations of the Chinese Air Force at the age of twenty-four—a familial indulgence that must have disturbed Mao who gave his own progeny no such preferment—used his connections to arrange for an escape flight. This was done in such haste that it is speculated that insufficient fuel was taken aboard. As a consequence, the plane went down in the early morning of September 13 in Mongolia killing all occupants. Apparently, the plane had been headed for the Soviet Union.

This was a shocking and deplorable incident, and given the public's belief that Mao and Lin were closest comrades, given the evolving new relationship with China's erstwhile number one nemesis, as well as the unknown extent of Lin's sympathizers, the event had to be handled with much delicacy. The October 1 National Day celebrations at T'ien An Men Square were cancelled. Celebrating was confined to smaller gatherings at public parks throughout China, but it was now evident to all that something drastic had occurred. Yet it would be the following July before an official explanation of the Lin Piao affair was made public.

In the meanwhile, Mao's new policies were implemented. On October 5, 1971, it was announced that Henry Kissinger would pay another visit that month. Also in October, China scored a major diplomatic victory by her admission to the United Nations as Taiwan was expelled. At the first of the year an advance party to the Nixon visit was in Peking, led by General Alexander Haig. Then, for seven days, from February 21 to 28, 1972, President Nixon, his wife and a substantial retinue spent a well-publicized, historic stay in China.[10] That Mao was behind this dramatic policy switch was made clear when he met with the visiting President hours after his arrival. The exchange between the two world leaders was termed "serious and frank." [11] Chou En-lai was entrusted to handle the several following discussions with President Nixon that touched on a wide range of topics.

The Sino-American joint communiqué of February 27, 1972 affirmed that the talks were beneficial.[12] Each side stated its positions on various matters and acknowledged that there "are essential differences between China and the United States in their social systems and foreign policies." Both "agreed that countries, regardless of their social systems, should conduct their relations on the principles of respect for the sovereignty and territorial integrity of all states, non-aggression against other states, non-interference in the internal affairs of other states, equality and mutual benefit, and peaceful coexistence." Disputes were to be settled on this basis, without resort to force or threat of force. The communiqué said that progress toward normalization of relations between the two countries was in the interest of all countries, that both countries wished to reduce the danger of international military conflict, that neither should seek hegemony in the Asia-Pacific region, that each is opposed to efforts by anyone else doing so, and that neither is prepared to negotiate on behalf of any third party or enter into agreements or understandings with the other directed at other states. Both sides agreed that collusion between countries against others or division of the world into spheres of interest by the major countries would be against the interests of all.

Each side stated its position on Taiwan. China's position was reaffirmed: "The Taiwan question is the crucial question obstructing the normalization of relations between China and the United States; the Government of the People's Republic of China is the sole legal government of China; Taiwan is a province of China which has long been returned to the motherland; the liberation of Taiwan is China's internal affair in which no other country has the right to interfere; and all U.S. forces and military installations must be withdrawn from Taiwan. The Chinese Government firmly opposes any activities which aim at the creation of 'one China, one Taiwan,' 'one China, two governments,' 'two Chinas,' and 'independent Taiwan' or advocate that 'the status of Taiwan remains to be determined.' "

The United States, for its part, acknowledged "that all Chinese on either side of the Taiwan Strait maintain there is but one China and that Taiwan is a part of China." It went on to say that it "does not challenge that position. It reaffirms its interest in a peaceful settlement of the Taiwan question by the Chinese themselves. With this prospect in mind, it affirms the ultimate objective of the withdrawal of all U.S. forces and military installations from Taiwan. In the meantime, it will progressively reduce its forces and military installations on Taiwan as the tension in the area diminishes."

Both sides also undertook to facilitate people-to-people contacts and exchanges in various fields and to develop trade relations.

Both sides agreed to stay in touch through various channels. This was done initially by visits of American representatives in Peking and through ambassadorial exchanges in Paris. By 1973 each country would have established a liaison office in the other's capital.

Mao's "revolutionary line in diplomacy," which emphasized negotiation and played down confrontation, and ably managed by Chou En-lai, had scored its greatest triumph. The years of isolation and embargo imposed by the United States were over. From the depths of the highly questionable diplomacy and excesses in the treatment of foreigners of the Cultural Revolution period, which was partially the irrational consequence of such enforced isolation, and the ultra-leftist paroxysms perpetrated, perhaps by Lin Piao elements, China's stature now soared in the international community. Having President Nixon, who had his own purposes in mind, make the dramatic visit to China was replete with meaningful symbolism for the Chinese people and for much of the rest of the world. Mao's own stature and prestige were enhanced by Nixon's gesture; his role was even legitimized thereby for yet others. But more important for Mao was that by means of this creative breakthrough China was relieved in large measure of a major threat from the United States. Mao could now face the Soviet Union more squarely, and with less distraction. The Soviet Union, for its part, would now have to consider, when confronting China, the less certain role of the United States.

But as majestic an accomplishment as this détente with the United States was, it required rather delicate domestic handling given ideological strictures and the past image of the United States, as well as the charges of still-remembered Lin Piao oppositionists. Mao made the new reality more palatable for his people by repeated references to an essay he had written in 1945 entitled "On the Chungking Negotiations." [13] That earlier experience provided the rationale for the present remarkable turnabout. The moral was simply that under certain circumstances, i.e., when the priority among contradictions has shifted, it may be desirable to negotiate, even with the enemy, in order to gain certain advantages.

With Chou En-lai's masterful management, this sensible diplomacy continued to achieve successes. In the following months a steady succession of distinguished foreign statesmen and prominent personalities visited Peking, many meeting with Mao personally. In June and July Mao disclosed to Sri Lanka's visiting prime minister and France's visiting foreign minister the heretofore confidential story of the Lin Piao affair. Japan's Prime Minister Kakuei Tanaka made his historic visit to Peking and to Mao in September 1972, conveying his nation's apologies for past behavior and bringing about a normalization of relations.

In the meanwhile, domestic stabilization proceeded apace. In the months preceding the public disclosure of the Lin Piao affair the entire Chinese people were being instructed about it and its meaning. It remains an incredible feat that during those months of late 1971 and 1972 (before late June), despite the large numbers of visiting foreigners, there does not seem to have been a breach of this national secret, even though the general population was informed about it! [14]

Party-building continued, and the rebuilt Party gradually reasserted its dominance in the political life of the country. By early 1972 the slogan "Learn from the PLA" was complemented by another, "The PLA learns from the People." The effect of this was seen in the omnipresent revolutionary committees where the PLA members now asserted that they were there to learn from society rather than provide stability. To some degree, however, they could still guarantee a properly leftist orientation and provide reminders of the need to study the thought of Mao Tse-tung.[15] But gradually the reconstituted Party committees in all organizations took precedence over the revolutionary committees.

Mao's successful new diplomacy did not exclude the Soviet Union, even though it may have further irritated the Russians and skewed their option for a less uninhibited assault upon China. It would appear that Mao, through Chou En-lai, was anxious to avoid provoking the Soviet Union beyond endurance, and was even aiming in the direction of an eventual accommodation in the future. In the meantime, Mao felt constrained to criticize the Soviet Union on points of principle, on policy, and on certain practices. This remained the case with regard to the United States as well. Both "superpowers" are often taken to task by Chinese spokesmen at the United Nations, where China has emerged as the principal advocate of the Third World. But the Soviet Union has, by and large, as the "apostate" from Mao's point of view, been the recipient of the heaviest and most bitter of China's critical comments.

This has been for China a very dangerous course of action. The Russians have backed up their own anti-Chinese polemics, particularly since 1969, with more than a half-million soldiers aggressively poised on the Sino-Soviet frontier. Soviet psychology has appeared paranoid at times on the subject of China. There has been talk of a preventative armed strike—"while there is still time." (!) Mao has been mindful of this danger. He has not trusted to diplomacy alone for defense. The Chinese people have engaged in massive excavation work in all major cities, constructing a maze of air raid shelters. It has been a national exercise that expresses more eloquently than words the danger, and the fear which the Sino-Soviet rift has produced.

Following Lin Piao's demise, Mao shifted his overall defensive posture along the border. Lin had deployed poorly equipped militia and paramilitary units on the border, in order to draw Soviet troops deep into Chinese territory before they would engage PLA regulars and after which guerrilla units would attack from the rear. Instead, Mao has moved several first-line PLA divisions and air force squadrons to forward positions, apparently in order to challenge more seriously and much sooner. This shift of posture was made possible in part by China's successes in nuclear and missile development. The use of nuclear weapons, if the need should arise, would require that Soviet forces be kept in major concentrations in sparsely settled border areas. This would reduce nuclear fallout and other damage to large population centers deeper in China.[16]

For many months during 1971, 1972, and 1973 observers wondered aloud about China's top leadership situation. The leadership that had been selected at the Ninth Party Congress, which showed so heavily the marks of Lin Piao's influence, was rendered asunder by Lin's disgrace. In the meantime, Mao operated with a severely truncated Politburo, implementing his imaginative new policies almost without regard to the formal top decision-making structures. In tandem with Chou En-lai, a great deal was accomplished. Yet many wondered about the legitimacy of the new policies, and it was apparent that a new Party congress and a new national people's congress would be necessary in order to reconstitute the top leadership and to provide the missing formal sanctions for the new policies. There were signs by midsummer of 1973 that such a large meeting of one kind or another was in the offing, but Chinese security was very tight on further details.[17]

It came as some surprise to the world therefore when on August 29, 1973, there was suddenly released the press communiqué of the Tenth Congress of the Communist Party of China. The communiqué revealed that the congress had already been held between August 24 to 28.[18] The large meeting of 1,249 delegates was held in secret sessions in the Great Hall of the People on T'ien An Men Square. Despite the presence in Peking of many foreigners and foreign newsmen, not a single word seems to have given away this well-kept secret. This was of interest particularly since journalists were expecting a large meeting of some kind and had been keeping watch on the Great Hall of the People for evidence of increased traffic. The journalists were to be disappointed, however, because the delegates to the congress used underground passages in order to congregate within the Great Hall.[19] These passages were part of the air raid shelter system that had been built in expectation of possible Soviet attack. The unstated reason, in fact, for the secrecy of the Tenth Congress was to reduce the risk of tempting the Russians with undue publicity about such a large assemblage of principal Chinese leaders in one vulnerable building.

The Tenth Congress was billed as a congress of unity, of victory and as being "full of vigour." Chou En-lai gave the important political report. A surprising newcomer at the top leadership level, Wang Hung-wen, delivered a report on the revision of the Party constitution. The congress adopted the new Tenth Party Constitution. It also elected a new Central Committee. Mao had used the occasion to clarify a number of outstanding issues and to convey an image of an enlarged and reconstituted Party that was committed to essential revolutionary goals that were to be pursued resolutely and with vigor, yet without the embarrassing and counterproductive extremist manifestations which characterized some of Lin Piao's contributions.

The communiqué revealed that there were now 28 million Party members, the first official figure given since 1961 when the total membership stood at 17 million. The Party had indeed been expanding in the intervening twelve years, despite the thoroughgoing rectifications that marked the period. The newly elected Tenth Central Committee was composed of 195 members and 124 alternate members. The membership was said to embody the combination of the old, the middle-aged, and the young. This was a new form of "three-in-one combination" that reflected Mao's determination to have the three generations of leaders work together in a way that demonstrated that while experience was still respected and used there was "no lack of successors."

Expelled from Party ranks were Lin Piao and Ch'en Po-ta. Lin was termed a "bourgeois careerist, conspirator, counter-revolutionary double-dealer, renegade and traitor." Ch'en was called a "principal member of the Lin Piao anti-Party clique, anti-communist Kuomintang element, Trotskyite, renegade, enemy agent and revisionist." This kind of unrelenting criticism left no doubt that those who might sympathize with the cashiered clique should avoid any sympathetic expressions or actions. The communiqué made it clear that "at present, we should continue to put the task of criticizing Lin Piao and rectifying style of work above all else." To do this, "full use of that teacher by negative example," Lin Piao, is to be made. Above all, it would be necessary to continue to adhere to the basic principles: "Practise Marxism, and not revisionism; unite, and don't split; be open and aboveboard, and don't intrigue and conspire," and "unite to win still greater victories!" [20]

Chou En-lai, in his report to the congress, made the perfunctory acknowledgment that the "correctness" of the political and organizational lines of the Ninth Party Congress had been proven.[21] He then went on to describe the "Victory of Smashing the Lin Piao Anti-Party Clique." Chou recounted that Lin and his followers were people who "never showed up without a copy of *Quotations* in hand and never opened their mouths without shouting 'Long Live' and who spoke nice things to your face but stabbed you in the back." An unbelievably long list of crimes was ascribed to Lin, and his "machinations" were traced back over several decades. In this respect, Chou also recalled Mao's teaching that one tendency covers another. Thus "opposition to Ch'en Tu-hsiu's Right opportunism which advocated 'all alliance, no struggle' covered Wang Ming's 'Left' opportunism which advocated 'all struggles, no alliance.' The rectification of Wang Ming's 'Left' deviation covered Wang Ming's Right deviation. The struggle against Liu Shao-ch'i's revisionism covered Lin Piao's revisionism." There have been many such instances, and there may be more, Chou cautioned. "When a wrong tendency surges towards us like a rising tide, we must not fear isolation and must dare to go against the tide and brave it through." Again, Mao's statement was quoted: "Going against the tide is a Marxist-Leninist principle."

The most surprising feature of the exposé of Lin Piao's crimes, however, was that they allegedly were designed to bring about another form of revisionism. Chou revealed more of the background of Lin's political report to the Ninth Party Congress. He said that prior to that congress, "Lin Piao had produced a draft political report in collaboration with Ch'en Po-ta. They were opposed to continuing the revolution under the dictatorship of the proletariat, contending that the main task after the Ninth Congress was to develop production. This was a refurbished version under new conditions of the same revisionist trash that Liu Shao-ch'i and Ch'en Po-ta had smuggled into the resolution of the Eighth Congress, which alleged that the major contradiction in our country was not the contradiction between the proletariat and the bourgeoisie, but that 'between the advanced socialist system and the backward productive forces of society.' " Chou said that "Naturally, this draft by Lin Piao and Ch'en Po-ta was rejected by the Central Committee." Lin secretly supported Ch'en Po-ta in the latter's open opposition to the political report drawn up under Chairman Mao's guidance, and it was only after his attempts were frustrated that Lin Piao grudgingly accepted the political line of the Central Committee and read its political report to the Congress." This is an exceedingly interesting revelation for what it tells of both Lin and Ch'en, but it is also scarcely credible. Mao and Chou apparently had determined that the worst attribution that could be made to Lin and Ch'en and the one that best served their revolutionary purpose in the climate currently prevailing in China was that the two disgraced men were on a revisionist orientation. The ultraleftist manifestations of their activities were allegedly directed to a rightist end. An argument can be made for this line of reasoning in the interests of simplicity and symmetry, but it appears to be a real strain on whatever was the actual truth of the matter.

Chou then discoursed "on the Situation and Our Tasks," quoting liberally from Lenin and from Mao, but nowhere near the extent of Lin Piao's report to the Ninth Congress. Chou said that the "present international situation is one characterized by great disorder on the earth," and noted that "relaxation is a temporary and superficial phenomenon, and great disorder will continue." This is a good thing, he maintained, because it "throws the enemies into confusion . . ." and it "arouses and tempers the people. . . ."

Chou noted the growth and increasing unity of the Third World. The "great victories" of the people of Vietnam, Laos, and Cambodia "against U.S. aggression," he said, "strongly encouraged the people of the world in their revolutionary struggles against imperialism and colonialism." "Countries want independence, nations want liberation, and the people want revolution—this has become an irresistible historical trend."

Chou noted that the two superpowers are contending for world hegemony. At the same time they collude with each other but the "contention is absolute and protracted, whereas collusion is relative and temporary." The key point of contention is Europe, and the West is always trying to divert the Soviet Union toward China. "China is an attractive piece of meat coveted by all. But this piece of meat is very tough, and for years no one has been able to bite into it. It is even more difficult now that Lin Piao the 'superspy' has fallen." Chou doubted the future prospects of either of the two superpowers, but inveighed particularly heavily against the Soviet Union. He noted that internally it had "restored capitalism, enforced a fascist dictatorship and enslaved the people of all nationalities, thus deepening the political and economic contradictions as well as contradictions among nationalities." Meanwhile, "externally, it has invaded and occupied Czechoslovakia, massed its troops along the Chinese border, sent troops into the People's Republic of Mongolia, supported the traitorous Lon Nol clique, suppressed the Polish workers' rebellion, intervened in Egypt, causing the expulsion of the Soviet experts, dismembered Pakistan and carried out subversive activities in many Asian and African countries.'' Chou declared that this ''series of facts has profoundly exposed its ugly features as the new Czar and its reactionary nature, namely, [quoting Mao] 'socialism in words, imperialism in deeds.' ''

Chou asked that if the Soviet Union is so anxious to relax world tension, why doesn't it show good faith ''by doing a thing or two—for instance, withdraw your armed forces from Czechoslovakia or the People's Republic of Mongolia and return the four northern islands to Japan?'' He pointed out that ''China has not occupied any foreign countries' territory. Must China give away all the territory north of the Great Wall to the Soviet revisionists in order to show that we favour relaxation of world tension and are willing to improve Sino-Soviet relations?'' Chou said that the boundary issue must be settled peacefully through negotiations that are free from any threat. Quoting Mao again, ''We will not attack unless we are attacked; if we are attacked, we will certainly counter-attack. This is our consistent principle. And we mean what we say.''

Chou believed that it was possible to prevent world war but cautioned on the need for vigilance. ''We must uphold Chairman Mao's teachings that we should 'be prepared against war, be prepared against natural disasters, and do everything for the people' and should 'dig tunnels deep, store grain everywhere, and never seek hegemony.' . . .'' This was necessary ''particularly against surprise attack on our country by Soviet revisionist social-imperialism.''

Chou also reaffirmed the aspiration of unifying Taiwan province with the Chinese motherland.

Chou reaffirmed Maoist precepts for developing the economy, restating Mao's general line of ''going all out, aiming high and achieving greater, faster, better and more economical results in building socialism,'' and of ''taking agriculture as the foundation and industry as the leading factor.'' He said that in order to ''learn from Taching in industry and to learn from Tachai in agriculture we must persist in putting proletarian politics in command, vigorously launch mass movements and give full scope to the enthusiasm, wisdom and creativeness of the masses.'' This was qualified somewhat by the additional comment that ''On this basis, planning and co-ordination must be strengthened, rational rules and regulations improved and both central and local initiative further brought into full play."

Also affirmed was the central role of the Party once again. Chou quoted Mao: "Of the seven sectors—industry, agriculture, commerce, culture and education, the Army, the government and the Party—it is the Party that exercises overall leadership."

Chou concluded his report with two more Mao quotes in the final brief paragraph: "The future is bright, the road is torturous," and "be resolute, fear no sacrifice and surmount every difficulty to win victory!"

The report was a straightforward expression of Mao's own views, although it might have been weighted on the conservative or moderate side on some of the points, for example by restraining militancy in foreign relations and referring to rules and regulations in economic programing. But there was nothing in such qualifications that Mao would take exception to necessarily.

Wang Hung-wen's report on the revision of the Party constitution similarly expressed essential Maoist views.[22] If Chou is somewhat moderate, Wang would be regarded more a radical among Mao's close associates. Wang had risen quickly in Party ranks. Only thirty-two years old in 1973, he was originally a textile worker who rose to power during the Cultural Revolution. He became a leader of the Shanghai workers' revolutionary rebel general headquarters, the major mass organization in Shanghai during and following the Cultural Revolution. He was elected to the Ninth Central Committee, and in January 1971 was appointed one of the five secretaries of the Shanghai Municipal Party Committee then established. He has been a protégé of Chang Ch'un-ch'iao and Yao Wen-yuan, the nationally prominent Shanghai radicals since the Cultural Revolution, and in their absence Wang was the de facto resident chief in Shanghai. In April of 1973 he was also named political commissar of the Shanghai garrison.[23] Now at the Tenth Party Congress Wang was made a vice chairman of the Party, listed as number three man in the Party after Mao and Chou, and was given the honor of making this important report. The new Party constitution did not name a successor to Mao, but by implication Wang Hung-wen seemed to be an appealing and logical prospect.

Wang explained that the new constitution differed from the previous one mainly by having a "richer content with regard to the experience of the struggle between the two lines." He pointed out that "under the leadership of Chairman Mao, our Party has been victorious in the ten major struggles between the two lines and accumulated rich experience of defeating Right and 'Left' opportunist lines. . . ." He noted Mao's injunction: "To lead the revolution to victory, a political party must depend on the correctness of its own political line and the solidity of its own organization." He said that concerning the basic line and its being carried out, six additions have been made to the constitution.

The first concerned the Cultural Revolution. Wang noted Mao's comment in 1966: "Great disorder across the land leads to great order. And so once again every seven or eight years. Monsters and demons will jump out themselves. Determined by their own class nature, they are bound to jump out." Wang said that "this objective law as revealed by Chairman Mao" has been and will continue to be confirmed by the living reality of class struggle. He said "it is necessary to deepen the socialist revolution in the ideological, political and economic spheres, to transform all those parts of the superstructure that do not conform to the socialist economic base and carry out many great political revolutions such as the Great Proletarian Cultural Revolution."

The second enjoined adherence to Mao's principle: "Practise Marxism, and not revisionism; unite, and don't split; be open and aboveboard, and don't intrigue and conspire." Of these principles the most fundamental was "to practise Marxism and not revisionism," for as Mao had stated, "The rise to power of revisionism means the rise to power of the bourgeoisie." Thus appropriate admonitions were added to the text of the constitution.

Thirdly, Wang declared that "We must have the revolutionary spirit of daring to go against the tide," and he repeated the quote of Mao's already referred to by Chou En-lai: "Going against the tide is a Marxist-Leninist principle." Wang warned that "When confronted with issues that concern the line and the overall situation, a true Communist must act without any selfish considerations and dare to go against the tide, fearing neither removal from his post, expulsion from the Party, imprisonment, divorce nor guillotine." Of course, Wang acknowledged that there is also the question of being able to distinguish an erroneous trend. This is not always easy, but "many comrades have come to realize that according to the dialectic materialist point of view, all objective things are knowable." Mao was quoted: "The naked eye is not enough, we must have the aid of the telescope and the microscope. The Marxist method is our telescope and microscope in political and military matters." Thus study is advocated in order to achieve the ability to make the necessary distinction. Wang also pointed out the need to "study Chairman Mao's theory concerning the struggle between the two lines and learn from his practice." He said, "we must not only be firm in principle, but also carry out correct policies, draw a clear distinction between the two types of contradictions of different nature, make sure to unite with the vast majority and observe Party discipline."

Fourthly, Wang said, "we must train millions of successors for the cause of the proletarian revolution in the course of mass struggles." He quoted Mao, saying, "In order to guarantee that our Party and country do not change their colour, we must not only have a correct line and correct policies but must train and bring up millions of successors who will carry on the cause of proletarian revolution." This need was reflected in the constitution.

Fifthly, Wang spoke of strengthening the Party's centralized leadership and promoting its traditional style of work. He repeated Chou En-lai's point concerning the leading role of the Party. He also reaffirmed that within the Party the lower level is subordinate to the higher level. The Party's centralized leadership was to be strengthened, "and a Party committee's leadership must not be replaced by a 'joint conference' of several sectors." However, "at the same time, it is necessary to give full play to the role of the revolutionary committees, the other sectors and organizations at all levels." Democratic centralism was to be practiced, and "on the basis of Chairman Mao's revolutionary line" Party committees at all levels were to achieve, as Mao expressed it, "unity in thinking, policy, plan, command and action."

Wang said that the style of integrating theory with practice, maintaining close ties with the masses, and practicing criticism and self-criticism were all written into the constitution. Older Communists, he said, were familiar with this "fine tradition of our Party as cultivated by Chairman Mao." However, there remained the question of how to carry it forward under new conditions and for younger members, "the question of learning, inheriting and carrying it forward." Wang said that "Chairman Mao often educates us with accounts of the Party's activities in its years of bitter struggle, asking us to share the same lot, rough or smooth, with the broad masses." He reminded his comrades, as Mao might have done, "We must beware of the inroads of bourgeois ideology and the attacks by sugar-coated bullets; we must be modest and prudent, work hard and lead a plain life, resolutely oppose privilege and earnestly overcome all such unhealthy tendencies as 'going in by the back door.' "

Wang then turned "with special emphasis" to discuss the question of accepting criticism and supervision from the masses. He said that "the working class, the poor and lower-middle peasants and the masses of working people are the masters of our country. They have the right to exercise revolutionary supervision over cadres of all ranks of our Party and state organs." He said that although this was a concept that had taken root in China, thanks to the Cultural Revolution, "there are still a small number of cadres, especially some leading cadres, who will not tolerate differing views of the masses inside or outside the Party." Wang said, "They even suppress criticism and retaliate, and it is quite serious in some cases." Therefore, the exhortation that "it is absolutely impermissible to suppress criticism and to retaliate" has been added to the constitution. Wang held that the Party "must have faith in the masses, rely on them, constantly use the weapons of arousing the masses to air their views freely, write big-character posters and hold great debates and strive [now quoting Mao] 'to create a political situation in which there are both centralism and democracy, both discipline and freedom, both unity of will and personal ease of mind and liveliness, so as to facilitate our socialist revolution and socialist construction, make it easier to overcome difficulties, enable our country to build a modern industry and modern agriculture at a fairly rapid pace, consolidate our Party and state and make them better able to weather storm and stress.' "

Finally, Wang indicated that the phrase "oppose great-power

chauvinism'' was added to the constitution. He echoed Chou's warning to prepare for any war of aggression, but whereas Chou had spoken of guarding against a surprise attack by "social-imperialism" (i.e., the Soviets), Wang also included "imperialism" as such a possible surprise attacker.

Thus Wang's report, somewhat more "radical" than Chou's, mirrored much of what was on Mao's mind in August 1973. The documents altogether of the Tenth Party Congress might be regarded as a fairly tough Maoist text of where the revolution was for the moment and why. They contained most of the essential principles that Party members were to live by. Of course, the previous constitution's reference to Lin Piao as Mao's successor was deleted from the new constitution.

The new Central Committee was enlarged by forty seats. Two hundred and four persons were continued from the Ninth Central Committee; 115 were newly seated. About a hundred seats were assigned to representatives of the masses, i.e., outstanding workers, peasants, soldiers, and leaders of mass organizations that had been recently reconstructed. The Tenth Central Committee included a number of rehabilitated cadres who had served on the Eighth Central Committee but not on the Ninth. As many as nine provincial leaders who were purged during the Cultural Revolution were included among the new Central Committee members. The number of military men was reduced in comparison to the Ninth Central Committee. Officials of the central government, on the other hand, were better represented than they had been on the Ninth. However, their representation still did not reach the levels known before the Cultural Revolution. Included among these officials was the rehabilitated Teng Hsiao-p'ing. Officials involved in foreign affairs made a strong showing. In addition to those continued from the Ninth Central Committee (which included Huang Chen, head of the PRC liaison office in Washington, D.C.) were Foreign Minister Chi P'eng-fei, Deputy Foreign Minister Chiao Kuan-hua, Ambassador to the U.N. Huang Hua, China-Japan Friendship Association head Liao Ch'eng-chih, and rehabilitated former Vice Foreign Minister Wang Chia-hsiang.[24]

The new Politburo retained its former size of twenty-one full and four alternate members. But the Politburo's Standing Committee was enlarged from five to nine members. All of the sixteen surviving members of the previous Politburo held their seats, the three former alternates among them were promoted to full membership. Thus, added to the ranks have been five new full members, and four alternates. All had been on the Ninth Central Committee except for Su Chen-hua, a rehabilitee of the Eighth Central Committee.

Three of the new Politburo members were labor heroes. They are Ch'en Yung-kuei, head of Tachai; Ni Chih-fu, a Peking worker-inventor; and Wu Kuei-hsien, a woman textile worker from Sian. Four of the new members were provincial Party first secretaries.

Of the nine members of the Standing Committee, two were of advanced age—Chu Teh and Tung Pi-wu—and were not very active. K'ang Sheng, one of the five new vice chairmen of the Party, had not appeared to be active in recent months. The others, Mao Tse-tung, Chou En-lai, Wang Hung-wen, Yeh Chien-ying, Li Te-sheng, and Chang Ch'un-ch'iao were all highly active. Chou, Wang, Yeh, and Li were also elected vice chairmen of the Party.

Of course, the Tenth Central Committee and the new Politburo can be analyzed and speculated upon in different ways. It is tempting, especially given Chou En-lai's known ability and his prominence in recent years, to exaggerate his role. This is encouraged by the presence of so many comrades who might be regarded as moderates or as policy sympathizers of Chou's in the new Party leadership. Of course, it is obvious that this is so. But this does not prove that Chou has been victorious in a way that might somehow be considered deleterious to Mao or to what Mao hopes to achieve. In fact, Chou is ascendant because this suits Mao, because Chou is implementing Mao's policies by and large.

In any event, the major characteristic of the Tenth Central Committee and Politburo was that these bodies were representative of different discernible factions, as well as of age groupings. Should an anti-Maoist line evolve soon, it could be quickly countered by the other elements at hand. Should such a line win out, it would undoubtedly be confronted by a vocal rebellion, for such rebellion was actually sanctioned by the Tenth Congress in its advocacy of "going against the tide."

At the end of 1973 Mao dramatically demonstrated his authority and control in a very fundamental way by suddenly shifting a number of the top regional military commands. For a long time there had been speculation that several of the regional commanders had become somewhat autonomous chieftains in their respective regions, and that Peking's political authority over them was sometimes questionable. There were grounds for such speculation inasmuch as some of these commanders had been at their posts for many years.[25] However, in December Mao swiftly and secretly made the shifts which affected eight of China's 11 military regions. The transfers took the form of paired swaps. Thus Canton Regional Military Commander, Ting Sheng, changed places with Hsu Shih-yu in Nanking. Tseng Ssu-yu went from Wuhan to Tsinan, while Yang Te-chih went the reverse direction. Han Hsien-ch'u went from Foochow to Lanchow, changing posts with P'i Ting-chun. The vacant Peking command was filled by Ch'en Hsi-lien, and his Shenyang post went to Li Te-sheng. The three remaining regional military commanders who were not affected had been at their posts only a short time, and none concurrently held a top Party post.[26]

Along with these moves, three civilian Politburo members were made PLA political commissars. Chi Teng-kuei became first political commissar in the Peking Military Region, and Wu Te became second political commissar. Wei Kuo-ch'ing was appointed first political commissar of the Canton Military Region. While seven of the eight transferees also had been provincial first Party secretaries in their erstwhile bailiwicks they do not seem to have been given the same concurrent posts at their new assignments.[27] These moves appear to have signaled a further significant reduction in the PLA's influence in civilian Party affairs, and they reaffirmed Peking (and Mao's) authority over the centrifugal propensities of the outlying military regions.

In late 1973 and going well into 1974 a new campaign began to develop that illustrated one more time Mao's belief that there was need again to educate the public and cadres alike on certain basic points. An anti-Confucius movement became fused with the anti-Lin Piao campaign in which much effort was made to show that Lin had been a supporter of Confucius, however unlikely this actually may have been. Furthermore, Lin was alleged to have aspired for the restoration of the old system, just as Confucius had done so in his day. The campaign seemed to serve the apparent purposes of further denigrating Lin Piao and thus warning his remaining sympathizers. At the same time, it cautioned those on the opposite side of the political spectrum (Lin having been a left extremist as well as a Rightist!) that they must not go too far in accommodations with the West during the current détente phase of Mao's revolutionary diplomacy. This oblique criticism was complemented by more direct attacks on certain examples of Western music.

Just as Confucius was condemned, the first Chinese emperor, Ch'in Shih Huang-ti, was extolled. The "progressivism" of the latter was the principally contrasting point to be made in the comparison with Confucius, but the first emperor's effective handling of feudal lords and unification of China in his day bore pointed resemblance to Mao's similar accomplishments. Perhaps the reference to the first emperor may have had implications with regard to the shifting of the regional military commanders in December. It could be too, that those who might yet have some hankering for regional bases or loyalties since the shifts were made were being indirectly cautioned against sentiments about "returning to the old system"—a la Confucius and Lin Piao.

Mao, in his eightieth year of age, after so many years of revolution and struggle, and after living beyond ten Party congresses, still appears to be in control. Being in control, or as much so as he has ever been, given the natural limitations of his position in a country as large as China and with its particular cultural and subjective restraints and its present stage of development, he continues to insist on the revolution being carried through to the end. He will carry such insistence with him to his deathbed, and in the meanwhile it is unlikely that the revolution will abort. He will see to it that China's scarce resources, however plentifully these may come to be, will be distributed equitably.[28]

The Chinese Revolution has been very largely Mao's revolution. No man has given more to it, as creatively or as persistently. This is something that all Chinese realize. They know too that in making his leadership contributions over the years, he has remained a humble and simple man of the people. He has practiced what he preached, by and large. He has consistently sought to apply theory, and rhetoric, to practice. The ascetic values he enjoins,[29] required in the austerity of development from economic backwardness, are his own. He has preached "serve the people" and his whole life can be seen as such a service. Few other political leaders of the modern world enjoy the credibility among the masses of his own people that Mao does.

Such credibility is the consequence of Mao's insight that revolutionaries cannot, must not, relax on their laurels. Nor is it enough to practice the values of tomorrow today in the awareness that this in itself will help bring about tomorrow's desired society. Mao's essential insight that transcends even this difficult requirement is that men must continually be prodded to keep them progressing toward the desired end-state. A revolution can only be permanent [30] if it is consciously worked at, and unless even its most dependable leaders remain accountable to the people.[31] Verbal admonitions do not suffice to fulfill this purpose. In fact, no single means will so suffice. Mao has discovered that the revolutionary leader must continually devise new techniques for rekindling revolutionary ardor and a commitment to revolutionary objectives. Without such periodic efforts at revolutionary renewal, the revolution must succumb to the weaknesses inherent in man. The Chinese Revolution under Mao's guidance has in fact been a series of revolutionary renewals, whether brought about as a result of the natural development of contradictions that culminated in revolutionary struggle and achievement, or whether induced by means of timely and adroit manipulation.[32]

But it is incorrect and unfair to contend or to imply that Mao advocates struggle and "permanent" revolution exclusively as ends in themselves, or that he provokes or creates artificial antagonisms. Mao is neither irrational nor a fool, nor is he interested merely in power as an end in itself. On the other hand, he is all too human. He makes mistakes, some serious ones. His "infectious laugh" and quick humor do sometimes give way to fits of towering rage. He is willful and arbitrary. His use of history unabashedly as a "weapon of class struggle" when this creates distortions is certainly enough to give critical historians pause. His attitude toward intellectual freedom is unfortunately a circumscribed one, and this seriously limits the creative possibilities of his people and impairs the realization of his own ideal societal vision. Even his heralded emphasis upon persuasion rather than coercion can in the end be seen as merely a subtler but still distasteful form of compulsion. The Mao cult, however downplayed it may now be, seriously discourages even constructive criticism of the country's most important decision-maker. Thus, for example, however harmful cigarette smoking may be, no doctor in China will even discuss the problem publicly. There is, after all, the more immediate problem he must consider—all of those posters and portraits of cigarette-smoking Mao.

And even granted that Mao is accepted as a beneficent despot, there remains the question of the political system of which he is chief exponent. That authoritarian machinery largely in his hands has accomplished much that is positive among a people whom Sun Yat-sen ruefully regarded as being like "a sheet of loose sand." Yet the system possesses the potential for much tyranny if a less nobly motivated and less humane leader succeeds Mao. Yet without the authoritarian system it is doubtful that the Chinese revolution would ever have gotten far, and certainly it is unlikely that millions of poor peasants would be faring as well, or have the "voice" they today possess. The problem of the authoritarian political system and its part in the historical dynamics of modern China and its relationship to the conditions and needs of the country is one of much larger scope than the story of one man, even if he has played so prominent a role.

Whatever the criticisms, one cannot gainsay that Mao has lofty objectives for his country and that he has sincerely tried to realize these. He is, and has been, dedicated more to the objectives than to the means of their attainment. Mao wants a truly communist society peopled by a transformed "new socialist man." He wants this more than he does class struggle or revolution. Whether such a societal goal is humanly possible may be debatable for many. It is less debatable that Mao thinks that it is. Mao is a materialistic idealist, not a cynic. He is a man, who in 1965 during another lonely, uncertain period of adversity, penned this sentiment:

Reach the ninth heaven high to embrace the moon
Or the five oceans deep to capture a turtle: either is possible.

Return to merriment and triumphant songs.
Under this heaven nothing is difficult,
If only there is the will to ascend. [33]

As a Marxist teacher-leader Mao is impelled not only to decipher and explain the direction of events but to make the needful changes come about. Hence his preoccupation with methods and techniques, and the emphasis upon human will. [34] His goals are ambitious and the loftier ones will not be realized in his lifetime which is now well-advanced. Hence he is constrained to continue his concentration on means in his day and hope that others will take up the mission in theirs.

NOTES

PREFACE

1. Edgar Snow, *The Long Revolution* (New York: Random House, 1972), 169.
2. *Ibid.,* 175.

CHAPTER ONE

1. The most important source for Mao's life until 1936 is his own account as told to and recorded by Edgar Snow in *Red Star Over China* (New York: Random House, 1938, which is the edition referred to in this book. A new, enlarged edition was published in 1968, but Mao's own account is unchanged.). The author's own visit to China in 1972 produced yet further information, especially from the Mao Tse-tung Museum in Shao-shan, Hunan, and from other sites where Mao had made a mark during his active career. Of course, other biographies have been most useful for insightful interpretations and important information. The best of these are Stuart R. Schram, *Political Leaders of the Twentieth Century: Mao Tse-tung* (Middlesex, England: Penguin, 1966); Jerome Ch'en, *Mao and the Chinese Revolution* (London: Oxford University Press, 1965); Robert Payne, *Mao Tse-tung* (New York: Weybright and Talley, 1969); and Han Suyin, *The Morning Deluge: Mao Tse-tung and the Chinese Revolution,*

1893–1953 (London: Jonathan Cape, 1972). See also Siao Yu, *Mao Tse-tung and I Were Beggars* (Syracuse, N.Y.: Syracuse University Press, 1959); Siao Emi, *Mao Tse-tung: His Childhood and Youth* (Bombay: People's Publishing House, 1953), and Li Jui, *Mao Tse-tung t'ung-chih ti ch'u-ch'i ke-ming huo-tung* (Comrade Mao Tse-tung's Early Revolutionary Activities) (Peking, 1957).

2. Jerome Ch'en, ed., *Mao: Great Lives Observed* (Englewood Cliffs, New Jersey: Prentice-Hall), 3.

3. Snow, *Red Star,* 123.

4. *Ibid.,* 125.

5. *Ibid.*

6. Visited by the author in March 1972.

7. Snow, *Red Star,* 127.

8. *Ibid.,* 127–128.

9. *Ibid.,* 131.

10. *Ibid.,* 130.

11. *Ibid.*

12. Han Suyin, *The Morning Deluge,* 46.

13. Snow, *Red Star,* 134.

14. *Ibid.,* 135.

15. *Ibid.,* 137; however, this is a disputed point. Schram does not believe a battle for the city was actually fought; see his *Mao Tse-tung,* 32.

16. Snow, *Red Star,* 138.

17. *Ibid.*

18. *Ibid.,* 139.

19. *Ibid.,* 139–140.

20. *Ibid.,* 142.

21. *Ibid.*

22. Visited by the author in March 1972.

23. Snow, *Red Star,* 143.

24. *Ibid.*

25. Han Suyin, *The Morning Deluge,* 58.

26. Snow, *Red Star,* 144.

27. However, the book was not published until 1959 (*Mao Tse-tung and I Were Beggars*).

28. Snow, *Red Star,* 144.

29. Han Suyin, *The Morning Deluge,* 59.

30. See the lengthy extracts translated in Schram, *The Political Thought of Mao Tse-tung* (New York: Praeger, 1963), 152–160.

31. Jerome Ch'en, *Yuan Shih-k'ai 1859–1916* (Stanford: Stanford University Press, 1961), 158–159.

32. Related to author by a teacher at the school in March 1972.
33. *Ibid.*, 145.
34. Han Suyin, *The Morning Deluge*, 64.
35. Schram, *Mao Tse-tung*, 43.
36. Related by Hsiao San or Siao Emi, in Robert Payne, *Mao Tse-tung*, 51.
37. Photographed by the author in March 1972.
38. Snow, *Red Star*, 146.
39. *Ibid.*, 145.
40. *Ibid.*
41. *Ibid.*, 149.
42. Han Suyin, *The Morning Deluge*, 73.
43. Snow, *Red Star*, 149.
44. *Ibid.*, 151.
45. *Ibid.*, 150.
46. *Ibid.*, 151.
47. *Ibid.*, 150.
48. *Ibid.*, 154.
49. See Maurice Meisner, *Li Ta-chao and the Origins of Chinese Marxism* (Cambridge: Harvard University Press, 1967), especially 261–266.
50. Snow, *Red Star*, 157.

CHAPTER TWO

1. The best book on the Movement is Chow Tse-tung, *The May Fourth Movement* (Cambridge: Harvard University Press, 1960).
2. Han Suyin, *The Morning Deluge*, 91.
3. Schram, *The Political Thought*, 239–241; the full translation by Schram is in *CQ*, 49 (January–March 1972), 76–87; see also his introductory essay to the translation, *Ibid.*, 88–105.
4. Schram, *Mao Tse-tung*, 55.
5. *Ibid.*, 56.
6. Snow, *Red Star Over China*, 155–156.
7. *Ibid.*, 157.
8. *Ibid.*, 154.
9. *Ibid.*, 155.
10. *Ibid.*
11. There are a number of books that discuss the First Congress. A good recent work that covers all of the Chinese Communist Party (CCP) congresses through the Ninth in 1969 is James P. Harrison, *The Long March to Power* (New York: Praeger, 1972). See also Schram, *Mao Tse-tung*, 65–66, and Han Suyin, *The Morning Deluge*, 112–116.

12. Han Suyin has been among the first to recognize this neglect and her biography, *The Morning Deluge,* 116–120, begins to correct the record.
13. *Ibid.*
14. Visited by the author in March 1972.
15. Snow, *Red Star Over China,* 159.
16. Schram, *Mao Tse-tung.*
17. Donald W. Klein and Ann Clark, *Biographic Dictionary of Chinese Communism,* II (Cambridge: Harvard University Press, 1971), 678.
18. *Ibid.*
19. See Jean Chesneaux, *The Chinese Labor Movement 1919–1927* (Stanford: Stanford University Press, 1968), 262–289.
20. Snow, *Red Star Over China,* 160.
21. Klein and Clark, II, 678.
22. See Shinkichi Eto, ''Hai-lu-feng-The First Chinese Soviet Government,'' *The China Quarterly* (*CQ*), Part I (October–December, 1961), 160–183; Part II (January–March, 1962), 149–181.
23. Klein and Clark, II, 678.
24. Howard L. Boorman, *Biographical Dictionary of Republican China,* III (New York: Columbia University Press, 1970), 7.
25. See *Selected Works of Mao Tse-tung* (*SW*), Vol. I (Peking: Foreign Languages Press, 1967), 23–59.
26. *Ibid.,* 23.
27. *Ibid.,* 24–25.
28. *Ibid.,* 32–33.
29. *Ibid.,* 24.
30. See Harold R. Isaacs, *The Tragedy of the Chinese Revolution,* Second Revised Edition (New York: Atheneum, 1966).
31. Snow, *Red Star Over China,* 162.
32. Isaacs, 235.
33. John E. Rue, *Mao Tse-tung in Opposition 1927–1935* (Stanford: Stanford University Press, 1966), 64.

CHAPTER THREE

1. See Roy Hofheinz, Jr., ''The Autumn Harvest Insurrection,'' *CQ,* 32 (October–December 1967), 37–87.
2. Isaacs, 282–292; Rue, 85.
3. Jerome Ch'en, *Mao,* 323.
4. *Ibid.,* 142–143.
5. ''The Struggle in the Chingkang Mountains,'' *SW,* I, 73.

6. Jerome Ch'en, *Mao*, 152.
7. *SW*, I, 105–116.
8. *Ibid.*, 107.
9. Snow, *Red Star Over China*, 176.
10. *SW*, I, 117–128.
11. Klein and Clark, 680.
12. Jerome Ch'en, *Mao*, 158.
13. Jui, 231–235.
14. Dick Wilson, *The Long March 1935: The Epic of Chinese Communism's Survival* (New York: Avon Books, 1971), 70.
15. Slightly rephrased from Snow, *Red Star Over China*, 177.
16. Schram, *Mao Tse-tung*, 160–161.
17. *Ibid.*, 161.
18. Klein and Clark, II, 681.
19. Wilson, 74.
20. *Ibid.*, 74–77.
21. See Schram, *Mao Tse-tung*, 166–168.
22. Jui, 258.
23. *Ibid.*, 261.
24. Mao Tse-tung, *Selected Works*, Volume IV (New York: International Publishers, 1956), 206–207. This is a different edition of the *SW* than previously cited; subsequent references will be made to the Peking edition, unless the New York edition is specifically indicated.
25. Jui, 263.
26. Wilson, 79.
27. Edgar Snow, *Random Notes on Red China (1936–1945)* (Cambridge: Harvard University Press, 1957), 60.
28. Wilson, 83.
29. *Ibid.*, 84.
30. *Ibid.*
31. Jui, 266.
32. There is disputation over this point. See Wilson, 105, for an account of this as well as relevant references.
33. Han Suyin, *The Morning Deluge*, 316–317.
34. See Jerome Ch'en, "Resolutions of the Tsunyi Conference," *CQ*, 40 (October–December, 1969), 1–38.
35. Jerome Ch'en, *Mao*, 334.
36. The basic story of the Long March itself is in Snow, *Red Star Over China*, 195–218; the best recent account, much more fully detailed, is Wilson, *op. cit.* Most of our information derives from these sources.

37. Jerome Ch'en, *Mao,* 335.
38. Han Suyin, *The Morning Deluge,* 338–341.
39. Schram, *Mao Tse-tung,* 188.
40. "On Tactics Against Japanese Imperialism," *SW,* I, 160.

CHAPTER FOUR

1. Boyd Compton, *Mao's China: Party Reform Documents, 1942–44* (Seattle: University of Washington Press, 1952), xxviii.
2. *SW,* III, 219.
3. A good account of the war is Chalmers A. Johnson, *Peasant Nationalism and Communist Power: The Emergence of Revolutionary China 1937–1945* (Stanford: Stanford University Press, 1962). Johnson emphasizes the role of nationalism in the CCP's success, but granted the importance of war-bred nationalistic feeling in China, more attention should be given to the appeal of the CCP's social program. See, for example, Donald Gillin, "Peasant Nationalism in the History of Chinese Communism," *Journal of Asian Studies,* XXIII, 2 (February, 1964), 269–289.
4. Lyman P. Van Slyke, *Enemies and Friends: The United Front in Chinese Communist History* (Stanford: Stanford University Press, 1967), 55–59.
5. "On Tactics Against Japanese Materialism," *SW,* I, 153–178.
6. See John Israel, *Student Nationalism in China, 1927–1937* (Stanford: Stanford University Press, 1966), 111–156.
7. Stuart Schram, "Mao Tse-tung and Secret Societies," *CQ,* 27 (July–September 1966), 11–13.
8. Donald Gillin, *Warlord: Yen Hsi-shan in Shansi Province, 1911–1949* (Princeton: Princeton University Press, 1967), 218–228.
9. *SW* (New York edition), I, 332–333.
10. *SW,* I, 295–309.
11. *Ibid.,* 311–347.
12. Harrison, 297.
13. *SW,* II, 79–112.
14. *SW,* II, 113–194.
15. Han Suyin, *The Morning Deluge,* 412–413.
16. *SW,* II, 339–384.
17. Van Slyke, 142–153; and Mark Selden, *The Yenan Way in Revolutionary China* (Cambridge: Harvard University Press, 1971), 161–171. Selden's analysis of the Yenan period in general is the best available and is referred to frequently in this chapter.

18. Selden, 152.
19. Extracts from "On the New Stage," in Schram, *Political Thought,* 172–173.
20. "Rectify the Party's Style of Work," *SW,* III, 35–51; and "Reform in Learning, the Party, and Literature," in Compton, 9–32.
21. Compton, 21–22.
22. *Ibid.,* 21.
23. *Ibid.,* 29–30.
24. *Ibid.,* 31–32.
25. "Oppose Stereotyped Party Writing," *SW,* III, 53–68; and "In Opposition to Party Formalism," Compton, 33–53.
26. Compton, 37.
27. *Ibid.,* xxxvii.
28. *SW,* III, 69–74.
29. *Ibid.,* 74–98.
30. *Ibid.,* 75–79.
31. *Ibid.,* 82.
32. *Ibid.,* 94.
33. *Ibid.,* 96.
34. Selden, 212–224; and "A Most Important Policy," *SW,* III, 99–102.
35. Selden, 224–229.
36. *Ibid.,* 229–237.
37. *Ibid.,* 237–249.
38. *Ibid.,* 249–267.
39. "Get Organized," *SW,* III, 158.
40. "Some Questions Concerning Methods of Leadership," *Ibid.,* 117–122.
41. Selden, 267–274.
42. "The Yenan Revolution in Mass Education," *CQ,* 48 (October–December 1971), 641.
43. *SW* (New York), IV, 171–218.
44. Harrison, 360.
45. *SW,* III, 205–270.
46. See Barbara W. Tuchman, *Stilwell and the American Experience in China 1911–45* (New York: Macmillan, 1971).
47. An excellent account of this period of Sino-U.S. relations is John S. Service, *The Amerasia Papers: Some Problems in the History of US-China Relations* (Berkeley, Calif.: Center for Chinese Studies, 1971).
48. *SW,* III, 271–274.

CHAPTER FIVE

1. Harrison, 367.
2. See John Gittings, *The Role of the Chinese Army* (London: Oxford University Press, 1967), 14.
3. Harrison, 375.
4. *SW*, IV, 20.
5. Harrison, 372.
6. *SW*, IV, 56.
7. Harrison, 387.
8. *Ibid.*, 389.
9. Curiously, there is still no good work on the Chinese civil war of 1946–49. Professor Donald Gillin's volume on the subject is hopefully awaited. See Gittings, 5–6.
10. *Ibid.*, 6–7.
11. *SW*, IV, 157–171.
12. Gittings, 12.
13. *SW*, IV, 162.
14. Harrison, 406–407.
15. See also the views of Dwight Perkins, *Agricultural Development in China, 1368–1968* (Cambridge: Harvard University Press, 1970) and Ramon Myers, *The Chinese Peasant Economy* (Cambridge: Harvard University Press, 1970), among others.
16. Harrison, 409.
17. *SW*, IV, 123–124.
18. Harrison, 413.
19. *SW*, IV, 164.
20. *Ibid.*, 183.
21. *Ibid.*, 193–194.
22. *Ibid.*, 202.
23. *Ibid.*, 254–255.
24. Harrison, 419.
25. *Ibid.*, 420.
26. *Ibid.*, 415.
27. *SW*, IV, 191–192.
28. See "Military Victory," Harrison, 421–431; Gittings, 7–9.
29. *SW*, IV, 374.
30. *Ibid.*
31. *Ibid.*, 411–424.

CHAPTER SIX

1. Schram, *Mao Tse-tung,* 256.
2. K. Fan, ed., *Mao Tse-tung and Lin Piao* (Anchor Books, 1972), 107.
3. Harrison, 435.
4. See Samuel B. Griffith II, *The Chinese People's Liberation Army* (New York: McGraw-Hill, 1967), 138–149.
5. See Gittings, 74–98.
6. Jerome Ch'en, ed., *Mao Papers: Anthology and Bibliography* (London: Oxford University Press, 1970), 78–79.
7. See Robert J. Lifton, *Thought Reform and the Psychology of Totalism* (Penguin Books, 1961) for one of the best studies on the subject.
8. See Edward E. Rice, *Mao's Way* (Berkeley: University of California Press, 1972), 129–131.
9. "On the Question of Agricultural Co-operation (Abridged)," in K. Fan, 117–137.
10. See especially the writings of Jack Gray: "Some Aspects of the Development of Chinese Agrarian Policies," in Ruth Adams, ed., *Contemporary China* (Vintage Books, 1966), 199–219; "The Economics of Maoism," in *China After the Cultural Revolution: A Selection from the Bulletin of the Atomic Scientists* (Vintage Books, 1970), 115–142; and "The Two Roads: Alternative Strategies of Social Change and Economic Growth in China," in Stuart Schram, ed., *Authority Participation and Cultural Change in China* (Cambridge University Press, 1973), 109–157.
11. See, for example, the chapter "Communist China's Red Capitalists," in Barry M. Richman, *Industrial Society in Communist China* (New York: Random House, 1969), 894–912.
12. *People's Daily,* May 13, 25 and June 10, 1955; Jerome Ch'en, *Mao Papers,* 51–54.
13. Harrison, 470.
14. Jerome Ch'en, *Mao,* 65–85.
15. In K. Fan, 151–196.
16. In *ibid.,* 197–209.
17. A good coverage of the movement is Roderick McFarquhar, ed., *The Hundred Flowers Campaign and the Chinese Intellectuals* (New York: Praeger, 1960). The author has done much personal research on this period too.
18. *The New York Times,* June 24, 1957.
19. People's Daily, June 18, 1957, p. 7, in *China News Analysis* (Hong Kong), No. 185, p. 6.

20. K. Fan, 185.
21. *Ibid.,* 185–186.
22. *Ibid.,* 177.
23. "On 'Imperialism and All Reactionaries are Paper Tigers,' " October 27, 1958, in *Ibid.,* 240.
24. *Peking Review,* 36 (September 6, 1963), 10.

CHAPTER SEVEN

1. Harrison, 475–476.
2. Jerome Ch'en, *Mao Papers,* 57–76.
3. Harrison, 476.
4. Schram, *The Political Thought,* 352.
5. Harrison, 476.
6. Harrison, 476–477.
7. See Franz Schurmann, *Ideology and Organization in Communist China,* Second Edition, Enlarged (Berkeley: University of California Press, 1968), 465–467.
8. Harrison, 477.
9. Harrison, 477.
10. Jerome Ch'en, *Mao Papers,* 75.
11. Union Research Institute, *The Case of P'eng Teh-huai,* 1959–68 (Hong Kong: Union Press, 1968), 7–13.
12. Rice, 169.
13. Rice, 171–176.
14. Jack Gray, "Some Aspects . . . ," 218–219.
15. The best over-all coverage of the subject is John Gittings, *Survey of the Sino-Soviet Dispute: A Commentary and Extracts from the Recent Polemics 1963–1967* (London: Oxford University Press, 1968).
16. Byung-Joon Ahn, "Adjustments in the Great Leap Forward and Their Ideological Legacy, 1959–62," in Chalmers Johnson, ed., *Ideology and Politics in Contemporary China* (Seattle: University of Washington Press, 1973), 267–270.
17. *Ibid.,* 271–275.
18. Related to the author by a Chinese spokesman at Anshan, Liaoning, Manchuria in April 1972.
19. Ahn, 279.
20. See Stephen Uhalley, Jr., "The Wu Han Discussion: Act One in a New Rectification Campaign," *The China Mainland Review,* I, No. 4 (March 1966), 24–38.
21. Stephen Uhalley, Jr., "The Cultural Revolution and the Attack on the

'Three Family Village,' " *The China Quarterly,* No. 26 (July–September 1966), 149–161.

22. Rice, 182.
23. Ahn, 287–288.
24. Ahn, 288.
25. Ahn, 289.
26. Ahn, 292–293; Harrison, 486.
27. *Quotations from Chairman Mao Tse-tung* (Peking, 1966), 279.
28. See Richard Baum and Frederick C. Teiwes, *Ssu-Ch'ing: The Socialist Education Movement of 1962–1966* (Berkeley: Center for Chinese Studies, 1968).
29. See especially Merle Goldman, "The Chinese Communist Party's 'Cultural Revolution' of 1962–64," in Chalmers Johnson, ed., *Ideology and Politics,* 219–254.
30. See the author's "The Controversy over Li Hsiu-ch'eng: An Ill-timed Centenary," *The Journal of Asian Studies,* XXV, 2 (February 1966), 305–317.
31. Goldman, 236, quoting translation from the Union Research Service, xxxiv, No. 13 (February 14, 1964), p. 224.
32. Baum and Teiwes, 118–126.
33. Gittings, *Sino-Soviet Dispute,* 174–176.
34. *Ibid.,* 184.
35. *Ibid.,* 229.
36. See Peter Van Ness, *Revolution and Chinese Foreign Policy* (Berkeley: University of California Press, 1971).
37. *Peking Review,* 29 (July 17, 1964), 7–28.

CHAPTER EIGHT

1. K. Fan, 357–412.
2. Rice, 228.
3. Rice, 230.
4. Uhalley, "The Wu Han Discussion."
5. Uhalley, "Attack on the 'Three Family Village.' "
6. *Important Documents on the Great Proletarian Cultural Revolution in China* (Peking, 1970), 107–128.
7. Excerpts in K. Fan, 277–279.
8. *Peking Review,* 35 (August 26, 1966), 6.
9. Robert J. Lifton, *Revolutionary Immortality: Mao Tse-tung and the Chinese Cultural Revolution* (New York: A Vintage Book, 1968), 73.
10. Snow, *The Long Revolution,* 70.
11. *Ibid.,* 66.

12. K. Fan, 279–280.
13. The quoted expressions are from editorial titles in the People's Daily of June 1 and 2, 1966 respectively.
14. For fuller perspective on this intriguing experiment see John Bryan Starr, "Revolution in Retrospect: The Paris Commune through Chinese Eyes," *CQ,* 49 (January–March 1972), 106–125.
15. A graphic account is Stanley Karnow, *Mao and China: From Revolution to Revolution* (New York: The Viking Press, 1972), 367–381.
16. See William Hinton, *Hundred Day War: The Cultural Revolution at Tsinghua University* (New York: Monthly Review Press, 1972) for a detailed account of the turmoil on this campus.
17. Karnow, 441.
18. Hinton, *Hundred Day War,* 226–227.
19. *Important Documents,* 184.
20. Harold C. Hinton, *An Introduction to Chinese Politics* (New York: Praeger, 1973), 71–72.
21. See Thomas W. Robinson, *The Sino-Soviet Border Dispute: Background, Development and the March 1969 Clash* (Santa Monica, Calif.: Rand, 1970).
22. Harrison, 507.
23. *The Ninth National Congress of the Communist Party of China* (*Documents*) (Peking, 1969), 1–108.
24. *Ibid.,* 109–126.
25. James Chieh Hsiung speaks of a philosophy of selfless struggle that Mao wants to establish. See Hsiung, *Ideology and Practice: The Evolution of Chinese Communism* (New York: Praeger, 1970), 236–239.
26. See pamphlets *Taching: Red Banner on China's Industrial Front* and *Tachai: Standard Bearer in China's Agriculture,* both (Peking: Foreign Languages Press, 1972).
27. The author visited the "East is Red" May Seventh cadre school near Peking in April 1972; see also John N. Hawkins, "Mao Tse-tung and Bureaucracy: The May 7th Cadre Schools," *Journal of Continuing Education and Training,* Vol. I (May 1972), 259–266.
28. For a good analysis of Maoist views on bureaucracy see Martin King Whyte, "Bureaucracy and Modernization in China: The Maoist Critique," *American Sociological Review,* Vol. 38, No. 2 (April 1973), 149–163.
29. Good recent articles on education are: John Gardner and Wilt Idems, "China's Educational Revolution," in Schram, ed., *Authority Participation,* 257–289; S. Garrett McDowell, "Educational Reform in China As a Readjusting Country," *Asian Survey,* XI (March 1971), 256–270; and Don-

ald Munro, "Egalitarian Ideal and Educational Fact in Communist China," in John M. H. Lindbeck, ed., *China: Management of a Revolutionary Society* (Seattle: University of Washington Press, 1971), 256–301.

30. For a good discussion of Maoist techniques in industry see Stephen Andors, "Revolution and Modernization: Man and Machine in Industrializing Societies, the Chinese Case," in Edward Friedman and Mark Selden, eds., *America's Asia: Dissenting Essays on Asian-American Relations* (New York: Vintage Books, 1971), 393–444.

31. See, for example, Victor W. Sidel, "Medicine and Public Health," in Michel Oksenberg, ed., *China's Developmental Experience* (New York: Praeger, 1973), 110–120.

32. See the intriguing essay by John G. Gurley, "Capitalist and Maoist Economic Development," in Friedman and Selden, eds., *America's Asia,* 324–356.

33. See Leo Goodstadt, *China's Search for Plenty: The Economics of Mao Tse-tung* (New York and Tokyo: Weatherhill, 1973), especially pp. 201–232.

34. See Jon Sigurdson, "Rural Economic Planning," in Oksenberg, ed., *China's Developmental Experience,* 68–79.

35. Jack Gray, "The Two Roads," 145.

CHAPTER NINE

1. Early book-length accounts were *The New York Times*'s, *Report from Red China* (New York: Avon Books, 1971); and the Committee of Concerned Asian Scholars, *China! Inside the People's Republic* (New York: Bantam Books, 1972). A continuing bibliography of articles by travelers to China is listed semiannually in the *China Exchange Newsletter,* published by the Committee on Scholarly Communications with the People's Republic of China.

2. Hinton, *An Introduction to Chinese Politics,* 75.

3. Mao Tse-tung, *People of the World, Unite and Defeat the U.S. Aggressors and All Their Running Dogs* (Pamphlet) (Peking, 1970), 1.

4. As seen in Mao's Letter of July 8, 1966 to Chiang Ch'ing, *Central Daily News* (Chung-yang jih-pao), Taipei, November 4, 1972.

5. "Central Circular No. 12," in the *Sing Tao Daily,* Hong Kong, August 11 and 12, 1972.

6. *The New York Times,* July 23, 1972.

7. *Ibid.*

8. Wilfred Burchett, "Lin Piao's Plot: The Full Story," *Far Eastern Economic Review* (August 20, 1973), 23.

9. *Ibid.,* 24.

10. See *The President's Trip to China* (New York: Bantam Books, 1972).
11. *Peking Review,* 9 (March 3, 1972), 4.
12. *Ibid.,* 4–5.
13. *SW,* IV, 55–63.
14. Conversation with Mr. Jack Ch'en, former editor of the *Peking Review* in Honolulu, September 18, 1973.
15. Based on personal interviews during the author's visit to China in March–April 1972.
16. William Beecher, *The New York Times,* July 24, 1972.
17. See, for example, Serge Romensky's Agence France-Presse report from Peking, *Honolulu Advertiser,* July 10, 1973.
18. *Peking Review,* 35 & 36 combined issue (September 7, 1973), 5.
19. Conversation with Mr. Jack Ch'en, September 18, 1973.
20. *Peking Review,* 35 & 36, 7.
21. *Ibid.,* 17–25.
22. *Ibid.,* 29–33.
23. See the yet rare, brief biography of Wang in *Current Scene,* Vol. X, No. 12 (December 1972), 20–21.
24. See "Profile of New Party Leadership," *Current Scene,* Vol. XI, No. 10 (October 1973), 22–26.
25. For example, see William Whitson, *The Chinese High Command: A History of Communist Military Politics* (New York: Praeger, 1973).
26. *Current Scene,* Vol. XII, No. 2 (February 1974), 19–23.
27. *Ibid.,* 20.
28. Michel C. Oksenberg, "Policymaking Under Mao, 1949–68: An Overview," in John M. H. Lindbeck, ed., *China: Management of a Revolutionary Society* (Seattle: University of Washington Press, 1971), 114.
29. See Maurice Meisner, "Utopian Goals and Ascetic Values in Chinese Communist Ideology," *The Journal of Asian Studies,* Vol. XXVIII, No. 1 (November 1968), 101–110.
30. An interesting discussion of "permanent revolution" is Stuart R. Schram, "Mao Tse-tung and the Theory of Permanent Revolution, 1958–59," *CQ,* 46 (April–June 1971), 221–244.
31. Accountability and responsiveness on the part of the vanguard (the Party) which is brought about in no small part by means of the politics of mass participation is a key thesis in Richard M. Pfeffer, "Serving the People and Continuing the Revolution," *CQ,* No. 52 (October–December 1972), 620–653.
32. A thorough analysis of such manipulation seen as the mobilization of "sentiments of aggression" in the Chinese population in order to change

established authority and custom that are "rooted in personal anxieties" is Richard H. Solomon's *Mao's Revolution and the Chinese Political Culture* (Berkeley: University of California Press, 1971).

33. From his poem "Chingkangshan Revisited," translated in Jerome Ch'en, ed., *Mao,* 113.

34. For an intensive intellectual exploration of the role of will in Mao's schema see Frederic Wakeman, Jr., *History and Will: Philosophical Perspectives of Mao Tse-tung's Thought* (Berkeley: University of California Press, 1973).

BIBLIOGRAPHY

Archer, Jules. *Mao Tse-tung: A Biography.* New York: Pocket Books, 1972.

Barnstone, Willis. *The Poems of Mao Tse-tung.* New York: Bantam Books, 1972.

Boorman, Howard L. *Biographical Dictionary of Republican China.* 4 vols. New York: Columbia Univ. Press, 1967–70; "Mao Tse-tung," Vol. III, pp. 2–22.

———. "Mao Tse-tung as Historian," *The China Quarterly,* No. 28 (October–December, 1966), pp. 82–105.

———. "Mao Tse-tung: The Lacquered Image," *The China Quarterly,* No. 16 (October–December, 1963), pp. 1–55.

Boorman, Scott A. *The Protracted Game: A Wei-ch'i Interpretation of Maoist Revolutionary Strategy.* London: Oxford University Press, 1969.

Ch'en, Jerome, ed. *Great Lives Observed: Mao.* Englewood Cliffs, N.J.: A Spectrum Book. Prentice-Hall, 1969.

———. *Mao and the Chinese Revolution.* Oxford University Press, 1965.

———. *Mao Papers.* London: Oxford University Press, 1970.

Chen Chang-feng. *On the Long March with Chairman Mao.* Peking: Foreign Languages Press, 1972.

Chen Po-ta. *Mao Tse-tung on the Chinese Revolution: Written in Commemoration of the 30th Anniversary of the Communist Party of China.* Peking: Foreign Languages Press, 1953.

Cohen, Arthur A. *The Communism of Mao Tse-tung.* Chicago: University of Chicago Press, 1964.

Devillers, Philippe. *What Mao Really Said.* New York: Schocken Books, 1969.

Doolin, Dennis J., and Golas, Peter J. "On Contradiction in the Light of Mao Tse-tung's Essay on 'Dialectical Materialism'," *The China Quarterly,* No. 19 (July–September, 1964), pp. 38–46.

Dorrill, William F. "Transfer of Legitimacy in the Chinese Communist Party: Origins of the Maoist Myth," *The China Quarterly,* No. 36 (October–December, 1968), pp. 45–60.

Eunson, Roby. *Mao Tse-tung: The Man Who Conquered China.* New York: Franklin Watts, 1973.

Fan, K., ed. *Mao Tse-tung and Lin Piao: Post Revolutionary Writings.* Anchor, 1972.

Fremantle, Anne, ed. *Mao Tse-tung: An Anthology of His Writings.* A Mentor Book. New York, 1962.

Goodstadt, Leo. *China's Search for Plenty: The Economics of Mao Tse-tung.* New York: Weatherhill, 1973.

Gray, Jack. "The Economics of Maoism," in *China After the Cultural Revolution: A Selection from the Bulletin of the Atomic Scientists,* pp. 115–142. New York: Vintage Books, 1970.

Griffith, Samuel B. *Mao Tse-tung on Guerrilla Warfare.* New York: Praeger, 1961.

Gurley, John G. "Maoist Economic Development: The New Man in the New China," *The Center Magazine,* III, 3 (May 1970), pp. 25–33.

Han Suyin. *The Morning Deluge: Mao Tse-tung and the Chinese Revolution.* London: Jonathan Cape, 1972.

Harding, Harry, Jr. "Maoist Theories of Policy-Making and Organization," in Thomas W. Robinson, ed., *The Cultural Revolution in China,* pp. 113–164. Berkeley: University of California Press, 1971.

Hawkins, John N. *Mao Tse-tung and Education: His Thought and Teachings.* Hamden, Connecticut: Linnet Books, 1974.

Holubnychy, Vsevolod. "Mao Tse-tung's Materialistic Dialectics," *The China Quarterly,* No. 19 (July–September, 1964), pp. 3–37.

Hsueh, Chun-tu, ed. *Revolutionary Leaders of Modern China*. New York: Oxford University Press, 1971; "The Early Life of Mao Tse-tung," pp. 395–421.

————. "A Review Article: The Years of Triumph," *The China Quarterly*, No. 11 (July–September, 1962), pp. 225–235. *Selected Works*, Vol. IV. Mao Tse-tung. Peking: Foreign Languages Press, 1961.

Kagan, Richard, and Diamond, Norma. "Father, Son, and Holy Ghost: Pye, Solomon, and the 'Spirit of Chinese Politics,' " *Bulletin of Concerned Asian Scholars*, Vol. 5, No. 1 (July 1973), pp. 62–68.

Karnow, Stanley. *Mao and China: From Revolution to Revolution*. New York: The Viking Press, 1972.

Klein, Donald W., and Clark, Anne B. *Biographic Dictionary of Chinese Communism*. Two Volumes. Cambridge: Harvard University Press, 1971; "Mao Tse-tung," Vol. II, pp. 676–688.

Lifton, Robert Jay. *Revolutionary Immortality*. New York: Vintage Books, 1968.

Mao Tse-tung. "The Great Union of the Popular Masses," *The China Quarterly*, 49 (January–March1972), 76–87.

————. Translation, introduction and notes by Hua-ling Nieh Engle and Paul Engle. New York: A Delta Book, 1972.

————. *Quotations from Chairman Mao Tse-tung*. Peking: Foreign Languages Press, 1966.

————. *Selected Military Writings of Mao Tse-tung*. Peking: Foreign Languages Press, 1968.

————. *The Selected Works of Mao Tse-tung*. 4 volumes. Peking: Foreign Languages Press, 1961–65.

Meisner, Maurice. "Leninism and Maoism: Some Populist Perspectives in Marxism-Leninism in China," *The China Quarterly*, 45 (January–March 1971), 2–36.

————. "Utopian Goals and Ascetic Values in Chinese Communist Ideology," *The Journal of Asian Studies*, Vol. XXVIII, No. 1 (November 1968) pp. 101–110.

Munro, Donald J. "The Malleability of Man in Chinese Marxism," *The China Quarterly*, 48 (October–December 1971), 609–640.

Oksenberg, Michel. "Policy Making Under Mao, 1949–68: An Overview," in John Lindbeck, ed., *China: Management of a Revolutionary Society*, pp. 79–115. Seattle: University of Washington Press, 1971.

Paloczi-Horvath, George. *Mao Tse-tung: Emperor of the Blue Ants.* Garden City, New York: Doubleday & Company, 1963.

Payne, Robert. *Mao Tse-tung, Ruler of Red China.* New York: Schuman, 1950; New edition: published as *Mao Tse-tung.* New York: Weybright and Talley, 1969.

Pfeffer, Richard M. "Revolting: An Essay on 'Mao's Revolution,' by Richard Solomon," *Bulletin of Concerned Asian Scholars,* Vol. 5, No. 4 (December 1973), pp. 46–55.

Rejai, Mostafa, ed. *Mao Tse-tung on Revolution and War.* New York: Doubleday, 1970.

Rice, Edward E. *Mao's Way.* Berkeley: University of California Press, 1972.

Rue, John E. "Is Mao Tse-tung's 'Dialectical Materialism' a Forgery?" *The Journal of Asian Studies,* Vol. XXVI, No. 3 (May 1967), pp. 464–468.

————. *Mao Tse-tung in Opposition 1927–1935.* Stanford: Stanford University Press, 1966.

Schapiro, Leonard, and Lewis, John W. "The Roles of the Monolithic Party Under the Totalitarian Leader," *The China Quarterly,* No. 40 (October–December, 1969), pp. 39–64.

Schram, Stuart R., ed. *Chairman Mao Talks to the People: Talks and Letters, 1956–1971.* New York: Pantheon, 1974.

————. "Chinese and Leninist Components in the Personality of Mao Tse-tung," *Asian Survey,* III, 6 (June 1963), pp. 259–273.

————. "From the 'Great Union of the Popular Masses' to the 'Great Alliance,' " *The China Quarterly,* 49 (January–March 1972), pp. 88–105.

————. "Mao Tse-tung and Secret Societies," *The China Quarterly,* No. 27 (July–September 1966), pp. 1–13.

————. "Mao Tse-tung and the Theory of Permanent Revolution, 1958–69," *The China Quarterly,* 46 (April–June 1971), pp. 221–244.

————. "On the Nature of Mao Tse-tung's 'Deviation' in 1927," *The China Quarterly,* No. 18 (April–June, 1964), pp. 55–66.

————. *Political Leaders of the Twentieth Century: Mao Tse-tung.* London: Penguin Books, 1966.

————. *The Political Thought of Mao Tse-tung.* New York: Praeger, 1963. Revised and Enlarged Edition, 1969.

————. "A Review Article: Mao Tse-tung: A Self-Portrait," *The China Quarterly,* 57 (January–March 1974), 156–165.

———. "A Review Article: Mao Tse-tung as Marxist Dialectician," *The China Quarterly,* No. 29 (January –March, 1967), pp. 155–165.

———. "What Makes Mao a Maoist," *The New York Times Magazine* (March 8, 1970), pp. 36–82.

Schwartz, Benjamin I. *Chinese Communism and the Rise of Mao.* Cambridge: Harvard University Press, 1958.

———, Wittfogel, Karl A., and Sjaardema, Henryk. "Comments on the Maoism Legend Controversy," *The China Quarterly,* No. 4 (October–December, 1960), pp. 88–101.

———. "The Legend of the 'Legend of "Maoism," ' " *The China Quarterly,* No. 2 (April–June, 1960), pp. 35–42.

———. "Modernisation and the Maoist Vision—Some Reflections on Chinese Communist Goals," *The China Quarterly,* No. 21 (January–March, 1965), pp. 3–19.

———. "The Reign of Virtue; Some Broad Perspectives on Leader and Party in the Cultural Revolution," *The China Quarterly,* No. 35 (July–September, 1968), pp. 1–17.

Siao Emi. *Mao Tse-tung: His Childhood and Youth.* Bombay: People's Publishing House, 1953.

Siao-yu. *Mao Tse-tung and I Were Beggars.* New York: Collier Books, 1973.

Snow, Edgar. *The Long Revolution.* New York: Random House, 1971.

———. *The Other Side of the River: Red China Today.* London: Victor Gollancz Ltd., 1963.

———. *Red Star Over China.* New York: Random House, 1944; 1st Revised and Enlarged Edition. New York: Grove Press, 1968.

Solomon, Richard H. *Mao's Revolution and the Chinese Political Culture.* Berkeley: University of California Press, 1971.

Starr, John Bryan. "Conceptual Foundations of Mao Tse-tung's Theory of Continuous Revolution," *Asian Survey,* Vol. XI, No. 6 (June 1971), 610–628.

———, and Dyer, Nancy Anne. *Post-Liberation Works of Mao Tse-tung: A Bibliography and Index.* Berkeley: University of California Press, 1974.

Teiwes, Frederick C. "Chinese Politics 1949–1965: A Changing Mao," Parts I & II, *Current Scene,* Vol. XII, No. 1 (January 1974), pp. 1–15, Vol. XII, No. 2 (February 1974), pp. 1–19.

Wakeman, Frederic, Jr. *History and Will: Philosophical Perspectives of Mao Tse-tung's Thought.* Berkeley: University of California Press, 1973.

Whyte, Martin King. "Bureaucracy and Modernization in China: The Maoist Critique," *American Sociological Review,* Vol. 38, No. 2 (April 1973), pp. 149–163.

Witke, Roxane. "Mao Tse-tung, Women and Suicide in the May Fourth Era," *The China Quarterly,* No. 31 (July–September, 1967), pp. 128–147.

————. "More Deluge in Mao's Way," *Journal of Asian Studies,* XXXIII, No. 1 (November 1973), pp. 99–103.

Wittfogel, Karl A. "Part I: The Legend of 'Maoism,' " *The China Quarterly,* No. 1 (January –March 1960), pp. 72–86. "The Legend of 'Maoism' (concluded)," *The China Quarterly,* No. 2 (April–June, 1960), pp. 16–31.

Yen Chang-lin. *In His Mind a Million Bold Warriors: Reminiscences of the Life of Chairman Mao Tse-tung during the Northern Shensi Campaign.* Peking: Foreign Languages Press, 1972.

INDEX

Bloc-within technique, 26
"Bolshevik forward and offensive line" (1931), 45, 46
Bolshevik Revolution (1917), 16, 23, 26
"Bombard the Headquarters" (wall poster), 152
Borodin, Mikhail, 33
Boxer rebellion (1900), 18
Braun, Otto. *See* Li Teh
Buck, Pearl, 3
Bureaucracy, 66, 67; and Cultural Revolution, 163–64; and democratic-centralism, 136, 187; Mao on (1956), 116; May Seventh cadre schools and, 150, 163–64, 171; "simple administration" campaign (1941–42), 74–75; and Tenth Party Congress (1973), 187

Cambodia, 183; U.S. invasion of, 172
Canton Commune (1927), 35
Capitalism: absence of, 44; and communes, 130, 135, 158; and "democratic dictatorship" (1949), 104–105; Mao and, 82–83, 113, 118; and Ninth Party Congress (1969), 159–60
Chang Ching-yao, 21, 22
Chang Ch'un-ch'iao, 185, 190
Chang Hsueh-liang, 59, 60
Chang Kuo-t'ao, 15, 39–40, 43; and Long March, 50, 53, 54
Changsha Bookstore, 24
Chang Tso-lin, 174
Chao Heng-t'i, 22–23, 25, 28
Chengchow massacre (1923), 25
Cheng feng campaigns. *See* Rectification campaigns
Cheng Kuan-ying, 4

Cheng Tse-hua, 47
Ch'en Hsi-lien, 191
Chen Kung-po, 15, 24
Ch'en Po-ta, 150; removal of (1970), 172–73; and Tenth Party Congress (1973), 181, 182
Ch'en Shao-yu. *See* Wang Ming
Ch'en Tsai-tao, 155
Ch'en Tu-hsiu, 15, 18, 22, 24, 29, 30; deposition of, 34; and Tenth Party Congress (1973), 182
Ch'en Yi, 64, 100
Ch'en Yun, 71
Ch'en Yung-kuei, 190
Chiang Ch'ing (Lan P'ing; wife), 74; and Cultural Revolution, 149, 150, 156
Chiang K'ai-shek, 81; and Civil War (1945–49), 86–105 *passim;* coup of 1926, 29; and Long March, 50, 51, 52, 55; vs. Red Army (1930s), 40, 42; supporters of, 15; and United Front, 30–33, 46, 58, 59–60, 63, 64; and U.S. (1945), 85. *See also* Kuomintang (KMT); Taiwan
Chiao Kuan-hua, 189
China-Japan Friendship Association, 189
Ch'in dynasty, 5
Chinese Communist Party (CCP): Army of (*see* People's Liberation Army; Red Army); beginnings of, 9, 11, 13, 20, 23; "Bolshevik reconstruction" of, 46 (*see also* Twenty-eight Bolsheviks); bureaucracy of (*see* Bureaucracy); and Civil War (1945–49), 87–105 *passim;* and communes, 130–31, 134–35; Congresses of (*see* Party Congresses); Constitutions of (*see* Constitu-

France: and PRC, 178; Society for Work and Study in, 13–14
Fukien Revolt (1933), 46–47
Fu Tso-yi, General, 101

Grain harvests, 131, 134
Great Britain, and Cultural Revolution, 156
"Great Empty Talk" (newspaper column), 139
Great Hall of the People (Peking), 127–28, 180
Great Heroes of the World (book), 5
Great Leap Forward: failures of, 128, 130, 132, 136, 139–40, 158, 170, 172; themes of, 136–37
Great Wall, 184
Group of Five, 149, 150
Guerrilla warfare, 39, 41, 45, 133; vs. Japan, 62–64; during Long March, 64

Haig, General Alexander, 175
Hai Jui Dismissed from Office (Wu Han), 138–39, 148–49
Hai-kuo t'u-chih (Wei Yuan), 2
Han dynasty, 5
Han Hsien-ch'u, 191
Han Wu-ti, 5
Han Yü, 9
Harrison, James, 98
Hero(es): labor, 78, 190; Mao as (*see* Mao Tse-tung—cult of). *See also* Models
History of Socialism (Kirkupp), 22
History of the Communist Party of the Soviet Union, 71
Ho Ch'ang-ling, 1–2
Ho Lung, 39–40, 49

Hong Kong: Chinese cession of (1842), 18; seamen's strike (1922), 28
Ho Tung, 47
Ho Tzu-chen (wife), 74
How to Be a Good Communist (Liu), 140
Hsia-fang campaigns, 122; and communes, 133
Hsia-hsiang ("to-the-village") campaign (1941), 75
Hsiang River Review (magazine), 20, 21
Hsiang Ying, 43, 64
Hsiao Hsü-tung (Siao-yu), 9–10
Hsifan nomads, 54
Hsin-min Hsueh-hui (New People's Study Society), 13
Hsu Shih-yu, 191
Hsü Te-li, 9, 12, 13
Huai-Hai Campaign (1948–49), 100–101
Huang Chen, 189
Huang Hsing, 2, 4, 6
Huang Hua, 189
Huang Yung-sheng, 156
Hu Feng, 115
Hu Han-min, 27
Hunan Provincial Peasant Association, 33
Hunan United Association of All Circles, 20
Hundred Flowers campaign, 116, 117, 118–22, 126; revisionist modification of (1961–62), 138–39
Hundred Regiments Offensive (1940), 63–64
Hungary, 1956 rebellion in, 117, 118
Hurley, General Patrick, 85, 90, 91

ABOUT THE AUTHOR

STEPHEN UHALLEY, JR., is Professor of History and Chairman of the History Department at the University of Hawaii, Honolulu. He was educated at the University of California at Riverside, the Claremont Graduate School, and the University of California at Berkeley (Ph.D., 1967). Dr. Uhalley, who served in the Korean War, has taught at Cornell, Berkeley, the National Taiwan University, the University of Arizona, and Duke University. He has made several visits to mainland China.